Job Talk

Other works by the author:

Living Communication (Englewood Cliffs, N.J.:
Prentice-Hall, 1975)

Understanding Communication in Business and the Professions
(New York: Macmillan, 1978)

CO-AUTHOR:

With Joseph A. Ilardo. *Argument: An Alternative to Violence*
(Englewood Cliffs, N.J.: Prentice-Hall, 1972).

With Ralph Smith. *Nonverbal Communication* (New York:
Bobbs-Merrill, 1971)

Job Talk

Communicating Effectively on the Job

Abné M. Eisenberg

Macmillan Publishing Co., Inc.
New York

Collier Macmillan Publishers
London

Macmillan Publishing Co., Inc.
866 Third Avenue, New York, N.Y. 10022
Collier Macmillan Canada, Ltd.

Library of Congress Cataloging in Publication Data
Eisenberg, Abné M
  Job talk.
   1. Success. 2. Industrial sociology.
3. Communication in management. I. Title.
HF5386.E34   1979   650'.1   79-19237
ISBN 0-02-535120-6

First Printing 1979

Designed by Jack Meserole

Printed in the United States of America

To my brother Donald

CONTENTS

BRIEFING

The purpose of this briefing is to give you some idea of what you are getting into by reading this book, the direction it will take, and to supply you with a sense of what you can expect to find in the chapters ahead.

To begin, it is essential for you to realize that this is *not* a business book but, rather, a book about how people in business communicate with one another. An attempt will be made to convince you that there is no such thing as "a business"—only people working together who have similar interests and goals.

Whatever line of work you are in, or hope to be in at some future time, you will always find people above, below, and at the same level as you traveling the ladder of success. Being able to communicate with them effectively is a must! The poorer your ability to communicate, the less likely you are to achieve your expectations on the job.

If traced back to their psychological roots, commonplace terms such as *self-esteem, self-worth, assertiveness,* and *self-image,* frequently associated with successful people, all lead to the door of a single art—*communication.* To help develop this art in you, *Job Talk* will provide a wide variety of insights and guidelines concerning getting, holding, and growing in a job.

Before going ahead, you might like to take a little quiz to determine how good a communicator you are.

ACKNOWLEDGMENTS

I should like to extend my sincerest appreciation to the many business and professional people who gave so liberally of their time, knowledge, and expertise concerning the problems of communication on the job in a wide variety of work situations.

I owe a special debt of gratitude to Marianna Ciraulo, whose sensitive editorial and typing skills were indispensable to the evolution of *Job Talk*; to my editor, Toni Lopopolo, whose keen eye and ear for style and substance piloted the manuscript through its gestation period to a viable birth, to Lorraine Alexander Veach for her distinctive copyediting, and to my dear friend, Jonathan Abramowitz, for his critical reading of the book and his perceptive suggestions.

QUIZ

HOW GOOD A COMMUNICATOR ARE YOU?

	TRUE	FALSE
1. You monopolize most conversations.	____	____
2. You remain silent in most conversations because others won't let you get a word in edgewise.	____	____
3. People repeatedly ask, "What do you mean?"	____	____
4. You quickly lose interest in what people are saying, if what is being said doesn't interest you.	____	____
5. You are accused of looking angry or bored when, actually, you are not.	____	____
6. You are often asked to repeat what you have said.	____	____
7. The right words don't come easily in conversation.	____	____
8. The tone of your voice is often misleading.	____	____
9. You are impatient with people who do not speak as rapidly or as slowly as you.	____	____
10. You are inclined to be a poor listener.	____	____
11. Your language has a tendency to offend others.	____	____
12. People frequently reword or rephrase what you have said.	____	____

If you answered *False* to all of the questions, either you are lying to yourself, you are unaware of how you actually communicate with others, or you are a perfect communicator. Either way, you stand to gain a great deal by reading this book. If, indeed, you are a perfect communicator, you might want to read this book to discover how communication operates from the other person's point of view.

Each of the statements used in this quiz represents a potential source of interference with the communicative process. To their misfortune, a large number of people have problems communicating but flatly refuse to acknowledge them. As a result, they have varying degrees of difficulty translating their thoughts and feelings into readily negotiable units of shared meaning. Perhaps they are unwilling or unable to take full responsibility for their verbal and nonverbal language. This is a luxury they cannot afford in the majority of job situations.

Job Talk

1
Taking Stock
of Yourself

You may think you know yourself, but do you? Chances
are excellent that you have hidden resources, human
potential that you never dreamed you possessed. It's
like an estate; you are convinced that you have
none until a lawyer sits down with you and points
out what you really own. It will be the objective of
this chapter to turn your thoughts inward, aim them
at some of your natural or acquired assets, and, at
the same time, draw attention to some of your liabilities that require mending.

WHAT TAKING STOCK OF YOURSELF MEANS

The expressed purpose of this chapter is to hold an imaginary mirror
in front of you so that you may see as many angles of yourself as possible.
People spend an enormous amount of money at the psychiatrist's or
psychoanalyst's office for an opportunity to talk about themselves. For
the price of admission, you and you alone are the star. Every interview
you will ever have in your lifetime will be about *you*. Interviewers have a
favorite question: "Tell me about yourself." Haven't you gotten the impression by now that you are the most important person in your life?
Well, it is about time that you find out a little more about yourself.

ARE YOU A "WHO" OR A "WHAT"?

If someone were suddenly to ask, "Who are you?" how would you
answer? Now, consider how you would answer being asked, "What are
you?" How would you answer that question? Most people, when asked who

they are, answer with their names—I am Jimmy Brown or Fran Underhill. To the "What" question, they usually state their occupation—lawyer, plumber, teacher, etc. Answers to Who and What questions are not always that straightforward. Stop a police officer on the street and ask, "Who are you?" You might easily get a What answer—"I am a police officer." In a restaurant, asking someone serving customers at a counter who she is might be met with, "I'm a waitress." Instead of being given a name (an appropriate response to a Who question), you are given a What answer.

If you are wondering about the significance of all this fuss about *who* or *what* you are, let me explain.

Job talk, in any field, consists of making references to people, things, and concepts. If you are an accountant, much of your communication consists of references to arithmetic entries, mathematical formulas, or various tables. If you are a farmer, your language is filled with references to things one finds around a farm, e.g., barns, fields, fences, animals. Should you be a philosopher or a logician, concepts are your stock in trade. And finally, if you are a physician (aside from the usual doctor talk about drugs, surgical procedures, and hospital facilities), you talk about your patients—who happen to be people. In all these cases, human beings are involved, either directly or indirectly. As such, one would hope that when people and things are referred to, a distinction would be made between them. Unfortunately, this doesn't always happen.

Since the Industrial Revolution, people have been placed in competition with things. Have you ever had a job in which you were made to feel like a thing, a non-person, a piece of merchandise, a cog in a wheel? The tendency to treat people as things is growing steadily. Consequently, communication on the job is changing.

As part of an effort to take stock of yourself, try the following exercise. List your answer to the question "Who am I?" ten times. Next to each entry, write your immediate response:

Who am I? _____
Who am I? _____
Who am I? _____
Who am I? _____
Who am I? _____
Who am I? _____
Who am I? _____
Who am I? _____
Who am I? _____
Who am I? _____

From your answers, you will be getting your first set of insights into the person you *think* you are. For example, did you refer to yourself as a man or boy, woman or girl, male or female? Also notice whether you were past-, present-, or future-oriented. Observe if your responses were positive or negative. Did you speak of yourself as an independent person or someone belonging to another, such as, "I am the son/daughter of Florence and Henry Miller?"

YOU AT THREE STAGES OF LIFE

Another interesting clue to your inner world can be gotten from this exercise: Draw three pictures of yourself: (1) at age six, (2) as you are today, and (3) at seventy-five. Completely ignore the fact that you cannot draw a straight line. Do the best you can.

(1) You at age six

(2) You as you are today

(3) You at seventy-five

Look at each drawing and see what you can say about yourself. Ask a parent, spouse, lover, business acquaintance, or friend to look at them and tell you what they see, think, or feel. Compare what they say about you to what you think and feel about yourself. Offer opinions about your dress (or lack of it), physical appearance, surroundings (if any), props, (baseball bat, doll, pets), temperament (smiling, scowling, frowning, smirking), or disabilities. Try to infer, from what is or is not present in your drawing, information about yourself. Then, infer further whether those characteristics are apparent in your present communication at work.

WHAT YOU BELIEVE DICTATES YOUR BEHAVIOR

If you believe the Earth is flat, you will stay away from the edge. If you are a playboy or a playgirl and believe the world is going to end tomorrow morning, you are going to have a wild time tonight. If you believe you are a loser, you will speak in negative terms like a loser. If you believe you are a winner, you will speak in positive terms like a winner. Whatever you think and feel usually will determine what you say and do.

At work, your job talk is a constant source of advertising. Through your verbal and nonverbal language, you are telling others what is going on inside your head and heart. While there are things you can conceal, you would be surprised at how much information about yourself you do reveal. By taking stock of yourself, you rob others of an advantage. You deny them the opportunity of discovering things about yourself of which you are not aware. Thus, by getting to know yourself and, in the process, using such information as a means of self-defense, you are developing both an inner and an outer strength, a strength that will help you succeed.

Throughout your present and future working life, your self-image (a mixture of your assets and liabilities) will be challenged—if not by you, by others. For some, keeping a self-image in a steady and intact state presents little or no problem. For others, it represents a continuous source of difficulty. Whether you realize it or not, your self-image is a starting point or baseline from which you must adjust. To communicate at all, you must take stock of yourself and, with the information you gather, weave an acceptable—or at least tolerable—self-image. How you see yourself could play a crucial role in your private as well as your public life.

ROUTES TO YOUR SELF-IMAGE

There is more than one way of arriving at your self-image. First, from infancy, your parents leveled a stream of compliments and criticisms at you. In addition to their being based on your behavior and appearance, they also reflected your parents' perception of what should have been,

4

rather than what actually existed. Coming at you from another direction were comments and criticisms from your brothers and sisters, friends and neighbors, and even perfect strangers.

The second route to the molding of your self-image came from the making of comparisons. What child or teen-ager has not heard the charge, "Why can't you be like——?" Teachers, likewise, have a tendency to make comparisons by dividing a class according to student performance levels.

A third route is arrived at through a series of self-evaluations consisting of labeling, judging, and criticizing oneself. For a variety of psychological reasons, people manipulate the information they receive from their environment and assign it personal meaning that insures their ability to survive. As a result, many of these concepts are not only illogical but frequently inconsistent. Such psychological tampering with information frequently leads to illogical speech and inconsistent behavior.

Regardless of what led up to your present self-image, you must make one concession. Since you cannot go backward, you must go forward. This means that you dare not rehearse or recall how you used to be. What counts most is how you are now. After learning what the past has to teach, move on to and through the present.

ASSERTIVENESS

If one aspect of management psychology were to get a gold star, it would be *assertiveness*. Rarely can success, at any level, be reached without the quality of assertiveness. Simply put, assertiveness consists of a positively issued statement or action. For example, if you ordered a well-done steak and it was brought to you rare, what would you say to the waiter? If you said, "Waiter, I asked for my steak to be well done. This one is rare. Please, bring me another," that would be an assertive act. However, to be assertive, you must have self-confidence, and to have self-confidence, you must develop your self-esteem.

It is possible that you are already an assertive type, or perhaps you are an assertive type and don't know it. Whatever the case, take the following quiz and find out just how assertive you are.

HOW ASSERTIVE ARE YOU?

Instructions: Place the number 1, 2, 3, or 4 in front of each of the following items, depending upon whether your answer is: (1) Always, (2) Often, (3) Sometimes, or (4) Never.

5

_____ 1. Do you find it hard to reprimand a subordinate?
_____ 2. Do people tend to take advantage of you?
_____ 3. Can you compliment people with ease?
_____ 4. Do you tend to alienate people in conversation?
_____ 5. If someone were talking loudly during a concert or a movie, would you feel inclined to tell him to be quiet?
_____ 6. Are you satisfied with the way you behave at work?
_____ 7. Can you accept compliments graciously?
_____ 8. Are you able to refuse an unfair request made by a friend?
_____ 9. Would you rather make a scene or keep your feelings to yourself?
_____ 10. If you found a defect in a pair of slacks you had just bought, would you return them immediately to the store?

Although you may be confident that the answers you gave in this quiz are accurate, it would be interesting to see whether one of your friends agrees with you. Cover your answers and have your friend answer each question pertaining to your assertiveness. Then, compare both sets of answers.

Thus far in this chapter, taking stock of yourself has turned your attention to (1) the difference between _who_ and _what_ you are, (2) projecting yourself backward and forward in time with self-portraits, (3) exploring how what you believe influences how you behave, (4) plotting how your self-image was arrived at, and (5) how assertive an individual you are. Let us now proceed to examine your orientation to business and professional life.

YOUR WORKING PHILOSOPHY

People approach work differently. Some are uni-valued, others are two-valued, and still others, multi-valued. This is how each philosophy tends to operate. Uni-valued people have tunnel vision. No matter what you discuss with them, they consistently hold to a single and unshakable viewpoint. They are closed-minded to any opinion that dares to differ from their own. In plain language, they are "one-way" in their thinking on all matters.

6

Two-valued types have an either/or philosophy. For them, there is no middle ground. They say things like "Look, you are either a manufacturer or a distributor—either a Communist or an American." Two-valued people seem incapable of believing that anything exists between the extremes. They divide their world psychologically into neat little packages of twos.

The most desirable philosophy, from the standpoint of communication, is the multi-valued approach. The people adhering to it are usually more open-minded and flexible. Take the case of a hypothetical sales manager who is extremely concerned about the rapidly failing morale of his company. Rather than singling out a specific cause and declaring it responsible for the problem, or seizing upon two likely causes and vying between them, he will attack the problem on a number of different fronts. Because the multi-valued philosophy sees the larger picture, it supports the belief that every problem can have more than one cause or cure.

Still another possibility exists. Instead of subscribing to one of these working philosophies exclusively, you may endorse a mixture of them. Granting that each situation may dictate a somewhat different approach, human behavior has been observed to display itself in patterns. In the majority of cases, allowing for an occasional exception, most people who are uni-valued act one way. By way of contrast, you will seldom find a multi-valued type behaving only one way. People have a strong tendency to behave consistently. As a result, they tend to be remarkably predictable.

Aside from your philosophy being uni-valued, two-valued, or multi-valued, you can pick up another clue about yourself by finding out what you think other people think. Ironically, what you say about others actually tells more about you than it does about the people to whom you are referring. Have you noticed how certain employees of one company talk about their competitors? Suspicion seems to follow those who knock their competitors. If it is their nature to criticize people or products, they will do it regardless of which company employs them. Job talk is common currency, freely exchanged by all members of any organization. And, since many individuals do not remain in one position or with one firm for their entire lives, their job talk travels with them. Hence, if you listen to them carefully, you can get a pretty clear picture of their working philosophy.

LET'S ASSUME

To what extent do you make assumptions? An assumption is a point of view, a guess, or a theory, the truth of which remains to be determined.

Whether something is true or not can only be determined after a sufficient amount of evidence can be brought to bear upon it. You would not believe how much mental luggage you carry around in your head that is based on *assumption*. To unlock some of these assumptions, try the following exercise.

LET'S ASSUME

Instructions: Complete the following statements as spontaneously as you can. The less time you take to think, the better.

1. When a position is said to pay top salary, I assume_____.
2. If I work on a job a week and find it unpleasant, I assume _____.
3. When I call about a position three times and each time the secretary tells me that the boss is not in, I assume _____.
4. If, after the interview, I am told to call back in about a week, I assume _____.
5. When I see a sign reading No Refunds, I assume

   _____.

   _____.
6. If someone works for the same firm for twenty-five years, I assume _____.
7. When I see the same job advertised in the newspaper for three weeks straight, I assume _____

   _____.
8. If a person is said to be successful, I assume

   _____.
9. If a doctor, lawyer, or accountant is licensed, I assume _____.
10. If an article comes with a lifetime guarantee, I assume _____.

Did you notice anything special about the way you answered these questions? Did they follow a pattern? Were your answers mainly negative or positive? The way you assumed things is a fairly good indication of how you think. When you see a crowd, do you tend to think something good or bad has happened? If you see the man next door at home in the middle of the day, would you assume that he was fired, taking the day off, or home to tell his wife that he was made vice-president of his firm? Of all the ways

8

we gather information, making assumptions without the proper foundations clearly surpasses all other methods.

LET'S STEREOTYPE

If you are not prone to making assumptions, perhaps you stereotype. This consists of singling out one characteristic (usually a bad one) of a class of people and attributing that characteristic to them all. In the vernacular, "seen one, seen 'em all" says it best. Not only is stereotyping unfair to the individual, it is also a very dangerous practice in the business world. A classic illustration of this is the stereotype: If it breaks five minutes after you bought it, it was probably made in _____. For a time, the most common insert was Japan. Now, it is Hong Kong, Taiwan, Korea, or India.

In the event that you wholly reject the allegation that you make assumptions or stereotype, perhaps this quiz will add further dimension to taking stock of yourself.

LET'S STEREOTYPE

Instructions: Complete the following statements as spontaneously as you can. If you catch yourself hesitating, move on to the next statement and come back to it later.

1. If he is a doctor, he probably drives a _____.
2. Anyone on an expense account _____.
3. If an item comes with a guarantee, it means _____.
4. Sexy-looking secretaries generally _____.
5. If you can buy it wholesale, it _____.
6. Most politicians are _____.
7. A college degree _____.
8. Good salespeople are usually _____.
9. If something was stolen, it was probably taken by _____.
10. A successful businesswoman is usually one who _____.
11. Anyone who has more than three drinks with a meal _____.

Whereas most business people frown upon making unwarranted assumptions and stereotyping, the reality is that many of them do it. While they

9

may not do it openly or directly, they do it covertly and indirectly. Take any average retail store and observe the nonverbal behavior of its sales-people as a customer approaches. More specifically, think of an elegant Fifth Avenue shop into which a poorly dressed couple wander. Notice the way the salespeople look at them, the time they take getting to them, and the enthusiasm with which they attempt to make a sale. Compare such body language with that displayed when an extremely well-dressed couple enter the shop. There can be little doubt that a difference in customer attitude does exist.

If what you believe does dictate how you think, feel, and behave, it is essential that you become aware of the extent to which you make assumptions and stereotype. More than ever before, today's job market is being saturated with people from different cultures and sub-cultures. As Marshall McLuhan put it, we are living in a "global village." We must, therefore, learn not only to live together but to work together as well. To do this effectively, we must learn not only all we can about the other fellow but as much as we can about ourselves. The more we know about ourselves as human beings, the more we are inclined to know about every other human being on this planet. *Reason*: we share a common humanity.

MOTIVATION

In fancy language, the term *motivation* refers to forces—innate or acquired, internal or environmental, conscious or unconscious—that serve to stimulate, sustain, and direct human behavior. In plain language, it refers to behavior brought on by needs and directed toward goals. You cannot see, hear, taste, touch, or smell a motive. It is an abstraction that can only be inferred from a person's behavior. Other names for motive are want, wish, need, desire, and drive.

In your present and past work experiences, have people ever referred to you as a go-getter, dynamo, fireball, hustler, mover, or hotshot? These are common labels often assigned to people with high energy levels who demonstrate an exceptional degree of motivation in a particular direction.

Basically, there are three types of people: those who think a great deal about what they are going to do but never talk about it, those who talk a great deal about what they are going to do but never do it, and those who just pick themselves up and do it! Actions, then, would appear to be the most reliable way of judging someone's level of motivation.

Think back for a moment of the people you've known who were "doers." Did their daily communication include a lot of talk about what they were going to do? Doers generally do more and say less. The opposite is often true of non-doers: they talk more and do less. What is your tendency? How does your own motivation manifest itself?

According to psychologist Abraham Maslow, there are five things that motivate people: (1) physiological needs (survival, hunger, thirst, sex); (2) safety needs (clothing, shelter, protection from physical harm, security); (3) social need (friendship, belonging, love, affection, acceptance); (4) self-esteem needs (respecting oneself, getting respect from others); and (5) self-actualization needs (to become, to grow from within, to fulfill one's potential at an optimal level).

On close inspection, you will find that none of us is motivated by a single motive. While one may seem to be motivated exclusively by love, money, power, competition, fear, responsibility, or hate, motivation is usually a mixture of emotions and drives. And, depending upon an individual's personal character, mood, and circumstances, a particular motive will surface and not another.

Most of the things about which you feel strongly motivate you. Perhaps you have had people tell you, "Aw, all you ever think about is ———." This should be taken as an indicator of some need that makes you tick. With additional introspection, you will discover still other clues to your motivational makeup.

Management is constantly searching for ways to motivate people. The list of things they have tried is both long and impressive. People have been offered salary incentives, better working hours and conditions, job security, fringe benefits, promotions, profit sharing, elaborate health plans, stock options, bonus plans, vacations, and retirement plans. Yet, in spite of these incentives, reports of low morale, shutdowns, low productivity, excessive absenteeism, inefficiency, and a general lack of interest continue to plague management. What kind of an incentive would motivate you to work harder? To help you gain a better grasp of your own drive system, try the following exercise.

IF IT WERE ME, I WOULD . . .

Instructions: Here are five true-to-life situations in which average people occasionally find themselves. Read them carefully and, according to your own way of thinking, complete the sentence or paragraph beginning with: If I were _____, I would . . .

1. John saw an ad in the newspaper advertising a particular typewriter he had been looking for at

an unusually low sales price. Later that day, the store manager said that they were all sold out of that particular model. If I were John, I would

_____
_____.

2. Mary had a very successful conversation with a potential employer on the telephone. He suggested that she come downtown for a personal interview and gave his address as Room 512 on the forty-second floor of the Empire State Building. Upon her arrival, Mary was met with a sign reading: Elevators Not Running. If I were Mary, I would ___

_____
_____.

3. Frank had just been discharged from the army and, on his way back to his hometown, he was robbed and left in a strange city without a penny in his pocket. If I were Frank, I would _____

_____
_____.

4. Mark has been employed by the same company for the past eighteen years. It is an excellent position with unusual benefits. The president of the company has just died of a heart attack and his son has taken over the company. Mark has just received his dismissal notice. If I were Mark, I would _____

_____
_____.

5. Alice has had a pain in her chest for the past two weeks and, after some prodding from her family, went to see her doctor. She was given some medication and sent home. A week passed and she felt no improvement in her condition. She went to another doctor, was given another prescription, and again was sent home. Another week passed and she felt the pain in her chest. If I were Alice, I would _____

_____
_____.

Obviously, there are no right or wrong answers to these situations. Whatever you would choose to do would depend upon the attitudes, values, and beliefs you bring to the situation Your health, for example, might represent a higher priority than your job, and in a situation where your health was at stake, you would behave differently. Then again, you might be highly motivated by principle, as suggested in situation 1. You might go to any lengths if you were John and found that the sale typewriter advertised in the newspaper was not available when you arrived at the store. The unfairness of it all might exasperate you considerably more than most people.

People are stirred into varying degrees of action by everyday occurrences on the job And, depending upon what stirs them, their line of communication is similarly affected. There are individuals who are so preoccupied with the question of honesty and fair play that, should they be overcharged in a restaurant, they would talk about the incident for weeks, sometimes months—and, in rare cases, years.

A final word about motivation. While there may be a mysterious and magical force out there that generates the energy within you to do things, it often masquerades as Lady Luck, a lucky break, good fortune, or your big chance .You would be wise not to rely too heavily upon luck's favoring you. By placing fate out of your reach, you relinquish control over it. Frederich Herzberg, a motivational researcher, argues, "There must be a 'generator' within a person before that person can be motivated, and that [sic] such a person will need no outside stimulation." The source of motivation, therefore, is to be found within, not without. Hence, the purpose of this chapter remains clear—that you take stock of yourself and, by so doing, grow through improved communication with yourself.

YOUR SENSE OF HUMOR

A good yardstick of an individual's character can be determined by what he/she finds laughable.

It wasn't too long ago that many educators believed the myth that learning and laughing did not mix. This same attitude also existed in the business world; when people laughed, they didn't work. For some vague reason, the reputation of humor in the classroom and the office was not good. Bosses and school principals alike, upon hearing their employees or students laughing, were often convinced that they were neither working nor learning.

It is only recently that management has begun to take humor more seriously. In a number of instances, it has been incorporated into the screening and hiring of personnel. Among other things, panels of cartoons are shown to prospective employees to determine whether or not they have a sense of humor.

Have you ever worked with someone who lacked a sense of humor? What was it like? How would you rate your own sense of humor—great, average, or poor? Have you ever been in a movie theater, laughing your fool head off, and not another soul in the theater was laughing? How did you feel about those who weren't laughing? Or perhaps it was the other way around; you were sitting in complete silence and the rest of the audience was rolling in the aisles with laughter.

The things people laugh at cover a wide range of human experience: surprise, ridicule, absurdity, exaggeration, distortion, exploitation. Each of these human experiences is a commonplace occurrence in the business and professional community. You will rarely find an organization lacking its share of inside jokes. In some fields, a sense of humor is essential. One day, in conversation with the administrator of an organization for the education of retarded children, I was surprised to discover that she would not hire anyone who lacked a sense of humor. She explained that without an ability to see the humorous side of misfortune, dealing with it on a daily basis soon overwhelms the nervous system.

While there are some people who deny that they have a sense of humor, most of them will insist that if there is something funny out there, they will pick up on it. This claim is misleading. Just as there are people who lack the ability to carry a tune, differentiate one color from another, or perform simple arithmetic, there are those who have no sense of humor. The problem, in many of these cases, is not that they lack a sense of humor but that they honestly think they have one and in reality they don't.

The importance of a sense of humor on the job should not be underestimated. In many businesses it is not uncommon for an executive of a large corporation to place a coast-to-coast or trans-Atlantic call to share a good joke. Las Vegas hotels and nightclubs think enough of humor to pay comics staggeringly high salaries to make people laugh. Perhaps it is time that you took stock of your own sense of humor.

Two things seem to offend people acutely: attacks upon the way they speak and upon their sense of humor. Rumor has it that habitual joke-tellers take themselves very seriously. When they tell a joke and no one laughs, they frequently take it as a personal rejection. Instead of realizing that it is the joke that is being rejected, they think they are being rejected personally.

Basically, your sense of humor may fall into two categories. It may be auditory or visual. Stated another way, it may be based upon the things you hear or the things you see. Naturally, it is not always a matter of one or the other. There are times when a combination of what you see and hear may strike you as funny. Most of us, it seems, are inclined to favor one or the other in the majority of laugh-producing situations. Think for a moment whether those things in your life that caused you to roar with laughter were seen or heard.

To better understand your sense of humor, reflect upon exactly what makes you laugh. To help you, here are some jokes. Each is based on one of the laugh-producing dimensions mentioned earlier. Be reminded before you begin reading them that their funniness is not at issue here. More important is figuring out why you think a particular joke is or is not funny. This will provide you with still another dimension of yourself as a communicator.

JOKE 1 [*Based on the element of "surprise"*]

A couple had been married for twenty-six years. One morning, the wife got up and snapped at her husband, "Phil, I've had it with that brother of yours. Either he leaves this house or I do." The husband, with eyes wide and mouth open, replied, "My brother? I thought he was *your* brother."

JOKE 2 [*Based on "ridicule"*]

A woman was walking down Main Street carrying a duck under her arm. Suddenly, the town drunk reeled out of a neighborhood bar and almost knocked her over. With his nose scarcely an inch away from her face, the drunk said, "Where did you get the pig?" To which the woman replied, "That's not a pig, it's a duck." The drunk, with a smirk on his face then said, "Madam, I was talking to the duck."

JOKE 3 [*Based on "absurdity"*]

On the death of her beloved husband, Morris, Mrs. Cohen gave this instruction to the funeral director: "I want my husband buried in his blue suit." The next day, as fate would have it, Morris was laid out in his brown suit at the chapel. His wife was furious. She stormed into the funeral director's office and demanded to know why her instructions were not obeyed. A master of diplomacy, the director suggested that she remain calm and that he would take care of everything. In a matter of minutes, her husband was wheeled out of the chapel and returned wearing his blue suit. Mrs. Cohen was dumbfounded at the speed with which the change was made from the brown to the blue suit. Unable to contain herself, she asked the director how he did it. He replied, "It was easy, Mrs. Cohen. We just switched heads."

JOKE 4 [*Based on "exaggeration"*]

A young man was extremely troubled because he was so short. Finally, he decided to seek out a psychiatrist for help. After several sessions in which the psychiatrist allayed his fears and frustrations over being so short, the man felt greatly relieved. He thanked the doctor profusely for his help, left the office, walked two blocks—and was eaten by a cat.

Joke 5 [*Based on "exploitation"*]

Three men died and went to heaven: a Jew, an Italian, and a Negro. At the gates of heaven, St. Peter proceeded to ask each of them why they thought they should be admitted. The Jew explained that since the beginning of time, Jews were oppressed and persecuted all over the world, and that he had suffered enough. St. Peter seemed sympathetic and said, "All right, my son, because you have suffered, I shall let you enter heaven, if you can answer this simple question: How do you spell the word *rose?*" The Jew spelled it, "*r-o-s-e,*" and was admitted.

It was then the Italian's turn. He was asked the same question concerning being admitted to heaven. He claimed that he had been a good man, frequently helped others, and went to church regularly. St. Peter then asked him to spell the word *rose.* He did, and was admitted.

St. Peter then asked the black man why he thought he should be allowed into heaven. He argued that all his life he was a victim of racism—forced to sit at the back of the bus, forced to use a separate washroom, and kept from getting a good job. St. Peter then reassured him that there was no racism in heaven, no prejudice. All he had to do was to spell the word *chrysanthemum.*

JOKE 6 [*Based on "distortion"*]

A woman was unable to conceive a child. She went to her family doctor and had a thorough examination. On her return home, her husband asked her what the doctor said. She answered, "I have a fish in my canal and if I have a baby, it will be a mackerel." The husband could not believe that he had heard her correctly. Confused, he decided to call the doctor himself. "Hello, doctor, this is Mr. Schmuckler. My wife, Esther, just came home and told me that you said she had a fish in her canal and that if she had a baby, it would be a mackerel. Is that what you said?" "No, not exactly, Mr. Schmuckler. What I said was, 'You have a deficiency in your canal, and, if you have a baby, it would be a miracle.' "

16

It is not important whether or not you consider these jokes funny. More significant is the basis for your reaction to them. The reason for this is that your sense of humor is richly integrated with your value system. Consequently, taking stock of yourself without making a careful analysis of what you find laughable must, of necessity, be considered incomplete.

In this chapter, your attention was directed inward. In the next two, it will be directed outward in an effort to determine the impact you have on others through your words and actions.

2
Advertising Yourself with Body Language

This chapter will concentrate on how others perceive
the silent messages you send through your body
language. Since the people you will encounter in the
business world are not mind readers, their only means
of getting to know you is by how you look, act, and
speak. Information coming to them on job applica-
tions, résumés, and transcripts must be considered
secondhand. Nothing less than a face-to-face meeting
with you should be considered firsthand. While
documents serve useful purposes, they tend to reduce
people to ink marks on pieces of paper. This, to say
the least, is a rather impersonal means of communicating.

Holding a look at your speaking self in abeyance
for the next chapter, this one will serve to put you
in closer touch with such things as your physique,
eye contact, gestures, smile, handshake, touch,
posture, smell, dress, and attitude toward time and
place. All of these characteristics transmit silent
messages (which usually precede spoken ones) about
you on the job and, by so doing, more clearly define
who and what you are.

While you may already be aware of how a number of
the messages you dispatch are interpreted by others,
there may be some of which you have absolutely no
knowledge or which you have completely misunderstood.
In short, by carefully noticing how your looks and

actions are synthesized into what this book calls job talk, you will gain a richer appreciation of their relevance to such organizational activities as interviewing, negotiating, meetings, and customer relations.

YOUR SILENT SELF

Without saying a word, how much do you reveal about yourself? Probably more than you think. For instance, do you have a distinctive way of walking, standing, smiling, gesturing, shaking hands, or dressing? If a couple of your friends were asked to describe your body language, how similar would their descriptions be? Better still, could you describe your own body language? Perhaps because we live in a predominantly speech-oriented society, most people possess a somewhat anemic sense of their own nonverbal behavior. One possible explanation has its roots in the field of psychology. It has been suggested that most of us could not handle a clear and undistorted view of ourselves as we really are. Consequently, we often tend to adjust our self-image so that we can live with it more comfortably. But it doesn't end there. Others adjust their perception of us to conform with their own survival needs. For example, good talkers frequently perceive poor talkers as being dull and uninteresting. Poor talkers do just the opposite. They perceive good talkers as being pushy and overbearing. Whatever differences exist among members of our society, they tend to be rationalized at almost every turn. This is particularly true when it comes to our body language. A possible explanation of this phenomenon is that *our minds and bodies don't speak the same language.*

In the marketplace, more information about people is exchanged without words than with them. Psychologist Albert Mehrabian performed a study that supports this view. His findings suggest that only 7 percent of the impact of everyday (non-technical) communication results from *what people say,* 38 percent from *how they say it,* and 55 percent from *how they look while saying it.* From your personal experience, do you agree? In previous conversations, did the way people looked when they said things have a greater impact on you than what they said or how they said them?

Originally, body language (*kinesics*—the technical word for it) focused exclusively on body movements, gestures, and facial expressions. Today, due to increased public interest, researchers have extended it to include a wider range of human activity. Outstanding among these are the ways people use time (temporality) and space (spatiality).

19

Before we begin to explore each aspect of your silent self separately, you must become familiar with something called *pseudoaffective behavior*. It is a term used to describe a situation in which an individual's words and appearance contradict each other. To illustrate this, imagine meeting a friend on the street. From his appearance, you would think he was ready for the grave; with bags under his eyes, hair uncombed, face unshaven, clothing soiled, and his hands trembling, he looks positively horrible. You say, "Hi, Larry. How are you feeling these days?" He, without a moment's hesitation, answers, "Fine! I feel terrific!" This is a classic example of pseudoaffective communication—where Larry's words and appearance disagree. In similar situations, which message would you be apt to believe, what people say or how they look? How people look seems to be the more popular basis for belief.

While pseudoaffective communication might be harmless off the job, it could have serious consequences during business hours. Surely you have walked into a restaurant and found yourself being waited on by someone who looked angry at the world. While they might say all of the appropriate things a waiter or waitress should say, that angry look cannot be ignored. Although such an individual might actually be angry, there are many people who are not, but simply "look angry."

Does the way you look ever confuse people? Have you ever been accused of looking sad, angry, annoyed, bored, or insincere? If you were, and felt none of these emotions, how would you go about convincing someone, with words, that you were not sad, angry, annoyed, bored, or insincere? One of two things may have happened. Either they were reading things in your face that did exist or you were unaware of the messages your face was sending. This is a good example of your mind and body not speaking the same language. To help resolve this breakdown in communication, let us now consider those aspects of your body language that could breed misunderstanding on the job.

YOUR PHYSIQUE

Just as there are employers who are preoccupied with such things as cleanliness, punctuality, politeness, mode of dress, respectfulness, or thoroughness in an employee, there are also those who harbor a similar preoccupation with body types. Their preferences generally divide people into those who are fat (endomorphic), muscular (mesomorphic), skinny (ectomorphic), tall (leptosomatic), and short (pyknic).

For some time, researchers have attempted to establish a relationship

20

between body types and personality. Thus far, they have only been partially successful. Listed under each category are those personality traits upon which the greatest agreement has been reached.

ENDOMORPHS	MESOMORPHS	ECTOMORPHS
sluggish	dominant	detached
tolerant	cheerful	introspective
affable	reckless	serious
warm	argumentative	cautious
affectionate	hot-tempered	meticulous
generous	optimistic	thoughtful
complacent	enthusiastic	sensitive
kind	confident	tactful
less needful of sex	efficient	shy
dependent	competitive	suspicious
relaxed	non-conformist	conscientious
even-tempered	independent	anxious

While these personality traits are not always associated with the body types under which they are listed, they are sufficiently commonplace to be given serious consideration.

When you were growing up, do you recall how kids used to make fun of one another on the basis of their physical appearance? Nicknames such as Fatso, Tubby, Scarecrow, String Bean, Shorty, Runt, Peewee, Small Change, Ox, and The Body frequently identified a boy or girl who was unusually short, tall, fat, skinny, or well built. Now that we are adults, one would think that insulting practices like these would have been left behind. Unfortunately, they haven't. Supposedly mature people lash out at one another from time to time by using body-oriented put-downs. This is particularly common when they are under great stress.

Body Bigots

These people are a breed unto themselves in that they reject others on the basis of a particular physical characteristic. When you don't like someone, you rarely dislike the entire person. More often, you dislike certain parts of him. Surely you've heard people say, "If there is anything I can't stand, it's a _____." "It" could refer to big ears, long noses, thick lips, pudgy little hands, bowed legs, broad hips, beady little eyes, heavy thighs, or flaky skin. While many of these individuals are "closet body bigots"—

that is, they are hostile or prejudiced against these body parts and don't realize it—they nevertheless practice their bigotry unknowingly.

Have you noticed that certain companies (airlines, restaurant chains, etc.) hire particular types of people? Some prefer young, fresh-faced women who look like "the girl next door," while others favor tall, slender, slightly older women who present a more sophisticated appearance. Obviously, those doing the hiring have some rather definite ideas about the physiques they consider acceptable.

If you owned a weight-watchers' restaurant, would you hire waitresses who were fat, skinny, or well built? Do you think their physiques would have an effect upon your customers? Furthermore, do you think an individual's body image affects her communication with others? Although people are not always conscious of their bodies, their body image does exert an extremely strong influence upon their behavior. If they perceive their body image as frail, they will be more protective of it and deal with the outside world differently than if they saw it as husky and strong. If they saw it as ugly, they would probably dress differently, walk differently, and sit differently than if they saw it as attractive.

Another thing about people and the way they communicate about their bodies is that they tend to accept and reject various parts according to how they feel about them. For instance, a man went to a doctor with a serious leg problem. In taking the case history, the physician noticed that the patient repeatedly referred to his leg as "that leg." Instead of saying, "My leg hurts me," he would say, "The damn leg hurts me." His manner of speaking suggested that he had disowned his leg. However, after the leg was completely healed, he began to refer to it as "my leg" again. He repossessed it!

By no means should you get the impression that, unless you have a specific body type or physique, you will not be able to get a particular job. What is being suggested, however, is that you recognize the existence of such prejudice and the need to confront it when necessary. There are people who, because of how they perceive their bodies, flatly refuse to go after certain positions. This is wrong, and if you require proof, try this personal experiment. During the coming week, observe about a dozen people in the following fields: librarians, college teachers, police officers, salespersons, barbers, beauticians, and bankers. Carefully notice how each of them is built. Observe whether their physiques are more different than alike, and in what ways. All things being equal, you should discover that there are more variations than you thought there would be. While the physique itself communicates a nonverbal message, it constitutes only a partial statement of who and what a person is, and the extent to which that person can "become."

EYE CONTACT

Successful business people all agree on the importance of good eye contact. Of the body language being studied, eye contact has received the greatest amount of attention. Consider the number of different messages your eyes can deliver. There are mean eyes, suspicious eyes, jealous eyes, honest eyes, evil eyes, intelligent eyes, shifty eyes, sexy eyes, hypnotic eyes, sad eyes, wise eyes, and angry eyes. More than any single form of human communication, the eyes seem to be able to establish the most immediate basis for a relationship. Whether it be a party, board meeting, interview, or convention, the first thing most people do is "eye one another." Faster than our most modern computers, the mind seems to set a psychological foundation for a relationship solely on the look in a person's eyes. Allowing for an occasional error in judgment, the eyes appear to be an extremely reliable source of information about the person behind them.

As previously stated, the words people use to communicate their thoughts and feelings convey only a part of their intended meaning. All too often, it is only the smaller part. It is left for us to glean from other sources the remaining meaning. Here, the eyes have it. Those situations at work in which you could use an additional source of insight into people's personalities are numerous. Eye-contact research has turned up the following helpmates.

There are situations where a person of higher status maintains greater eye contact. *Application*: When talking with someone whom you wish to impress with your self-confidence and assertiveness, maintain more eye contact than you would ordinarily. Without staring, put the person to whom you are speaking on notice (with your eyes) that you are speaking to him and to him alone.

People tend to use more eye contact with people from whom they seek approval or recognition. *Application*: When applying for a position, use concentrated eye contact with whomever you meet, from the secretary to the person who will decide whether or not you will get the job. Do not allow yourself to aimlessly look away at walls, desk objects, or passersby when someone is speaking to you. With your eyes, tell him that he has your undivided attention.

Speakers feel more powerful when the people they are addressing give them more eye contact. *Application*: The more eye contact you maintain with people, the more important they feel. Looking away frequently detracts from this sense of importance and, in the process, detracts from you.

Speakers rate people who look at them as being more instrumental to their goals. They also tend to value them more than those individuals who look away. *Application*: Employers, managers, and supervisors rate highly a spirit of cooperation among their subordinates. Good eye contact reinforces this spirit of cooperation. They seek out employees with superior eye contact.

Good eye contact generates better listening. *Application*: People listen more often and with greater intensity to those who furnish them with a direct gaze—look them squarely in the eyes. Regardless of your interest in the subject or the people speaking, if you want to communicate the illusion of interest, look at them while they speak.

How would you rate your own eye contact? In most cases, do you look at people when they speak? Granting that your degree of eye contact often depends upon the other person, your mood at the time, where you are, and what you have to gain or lose by looking at that person, chances are that you follow a pattern. Most people are either "lookers" or "non-lookers." Prying even further, how do you feel having a conversation with someone whose eyes wander all over the place while you are talking? Do you get the feeling that the person isn't really listening, has something else on his mind, has little respect for you, or has some kind of a hang-up about looking people in the eyes?

If you are unclear about your own eye contact, give it some special attention. Experiment. The next person you meet, alter your usual eye-contact behavior and see what happens. Tomorrow morning, greet someone whom you consider important with a crisp "good morning" and look that person squarely in the eyes. Observe his reaction and your own. Not only will it make a noticeable improvement in the general quality of your communication, it will make people listen to you more attentively and lend more credibility to what you say.

Superior eye contact will give you a conversational advantage. According to Jean-Paul Sartre, "When it comes to eye contact, to look at another encroaches upon a person's autonomy, and when two glances meet, a wordless struggle ensues until one or the other succeeds in establishing dominance." Eyeball encounters like these are widespread at every level of the business and professional community. Hence, any future discussion of job talk would be remiss if it failed to include the subject of eye contact.

GESTURE

There are basically two types of gestures: purposeful and purposeless. Most of them, regrettably, are purposeless. Instead of contributing to whatever meaning is being shared or exchanged, they detract. Pretend that you are being interviewed for a position and, while the interviewer is speak-

24

ing, you consciously or unconsciously pick your fingernails or at the arm of the chair. These purposeless gestures would definitely reduce your chances of getting the position. On the other hand, if you were to smile and nod appropriately when the interviewer seemed to be making a point, such gestures would be taken to be purposeful.

Conversely, an interviewer who shuffles papers, straightens items on the desk, looks out of a window, sharpens pencils, or engages in finger drumming on the desk is clearly displaying another series of purposeless gestures. Whether a particular gesture is purposeful or purposeless is always open to argument. There are people who delight in reading all kinds of psychological meaning into the raising of an eyebrow or the straightening of a tie. Each situation must be judged on its own merits. However, as a rule of thumb, any gesture that contributes to the meaning intended by either party should be considered purposeful; if it detracts from that meaning, it should be considered purposeless.

To discover the extent to which you display gestures that are purposeless, scan the following list and answer yes or no.

DO YOU:

	Yes	No
1. fool with your keys?		
2. play with the change in your pocket?		
3. fiddle with your hair?		
4. tear paper into tiny pieces?		
5. continuously jiggle a part of your body?		
6. bite your nails or cuticles?		
7. crack your knuckles?		
8. suck air through your teeth?		
9. repeatedly adjust your clothing?		
10. peel off fingernail polish?		
11. chain-smoke?		
12. put pens, pencils, or paper clips in your mouth?		
13. frequently look at your watch or the clock on the wall?		
14. crack or pop chewing gum?		
15. rub a part of your body?		

Some of these purposeless gestures are so deeply ingrained in your body language that you are completely unaware of making them. People say, "Will you stop that!" And you snap back with, "Stop what?" If you are interested in correcting these negative gestures, the first step toward

25

getting rid of them is to become consciously aware of the fact that you perform them, and to what extent.

A friend of mine was making a presentation at a book publishers' convention some years ago. He had a peculiar purposeless gesture consisting of running his index finger back and forth under his nose. I decided to count how many times he did it during his twenty-minute speech. Would you believe 163 times? Some gestures consisted of five or six passes, others as many as eighteen. When I confronted him with my account after his presentation, he was shocked and accused me of gross exaggeration. While this gesture had been brought to his attention in the past, he had absolutely no idea of how severe it had become.

As with bad breath, even your best friends won't tell you. This same tendency often applies to purposeless gestures. People are reluctant to tell you that you make them. It therefore becomes your responsibility to monitor your gestural behavior more closely. Beg close friends to tell you what they see you do when you speak. If possible, have a motion picture film or videotape run of yourself delivering a public speech or in conversation.

SMILE

While traveling throughout the United States, I got the distinct impression that the act of smiling was rapidly becoming extinct. This was particularly noticeable in big cities. In restaurants, retail stores, and sources of public transportation, waitresses, waiters, sales help, and attendants exercised their responsibilities with straight faces and expressionless voices. Transactions were executed not only with a minimum of dialogue but with a minimum of facial expression. Are people beginning to take on the stoic character of the machines that threaten their jobs? Why are people smiling less?

In my opinion, your most valuable form of body language is your smile. In every business or profession, it is conceivable that millions of dollars probably could be traced back to someone who smiled at the right time, in the right place, and at the right person. Although this may be somewhat of an exaggeration, the notion has a great deal of merit from the standpoint of communication.

A smile on a physician's face can speed a patient's recovery; the absence of one can inhibit it. In banks, the teller with the most ready smile often has the longest line waiting to be served. Because smiles are an endangered species, people, like moths to a flame, are drawn to those who display them.

26

But smiles are not all alike. There are people who insist they are smiling and, for the life of them, cannot convince others of it. Perhaps it is because the muscles surrounding their mouths are not the same. This fact can be validated by glancing at any textbook in anatomy. The muscles, from mouth to mouth, are not necessarily the same. Occasionally, the muscles on one side are underdeveloped or absent. In other cases, muscles have been known to be doubled. The result is that smiles differ from face to face. For example, it has been found that people not only smile differently throughout the country but for different reasons. Southerners seem to think they are friendlier because they smile; New Englanders think they are more reserved because they don't.

Work in the field of body language suggests that fundamental expressions are the same in all cultures. But, in terms of that basic response, there are those inherent variations just mentioned. Whereas most smiles are fairly reliable indicators of a person's mood or temperament, there are exceptions. Most frustrating among these is the smile on a policeman's face while he is issuing you a speeding ticket or the smile on an employer's face as you are informed that you are fired. Some justification for such frustration can be attributed to the fact that most of us associate a smile with friendliness and sincerity. Counterfeit smiles sometimes masquerade as leers, smirks, or sneers. It would be a good idea for you to check out your smile and see exactly what it communicates to others. Compare your smile with that of someone you consider to be genuine. It will be worth your while to cultivate the habit of smiling. A good way to begin is to casually observe how others smile.

HANDSHAKE

Handshaking is an ancient custom, varying only in style, circumstance, and intensity. One of its original purposes was to demonstrate that no weapon was being carried. In our society, we shake hands on arrivals and departures, at social functions, to seal a deal, and as an expression of congratulations.

Aside from classifying handshakes as strong, medium, and weak, they can be categorized according to whether they are self-determined or other-determined. Self-determined handshakes include those that are significantly influenced by a person's physical and mental health. People whose vital energies are down, or who are suffering from an inferiority complex, will reflect such a state in their handshake. On the other hand (a bad pun), when people feel good or have a superiority complex, it, too, will be reflected in their handshake. In many ways, our manner of shaking hands provides additional clues to who and what we are.

Other-determined handshakes are influenced by the person's hand being shaken. Dashing young men, for example, have been known to shake the hand of a beautiful young lady differently from the way they shake the hand of another dashing young man.

The most interesting aspect of a handshake is its style. You have probably exeprienced them all. There are the *pumpers*, who, once they have your hand in theirs, begin to move your arm up and down as if they were pumping water or churning butter. Then there are the *crushers*, who look you straight in the eye and summarily attempt to break every bone in your hand. Another handshaking style is the *massager*, who, depending on your age and sex, holds your hand and gently gives it either a romantic or a medical massage. The *trapper*, having taken your hand, immediately imprisons it so that it cannot escape. Least appealing is the *limpy*, whose hand remains motionless in yours, like a dead fish, until you release it. Finally, and most distinctive, is the handshake delivered by the *shocker*, who, without warning, gives your arm one violent shake, which delivers a bolt of lightning to your brain, leaving you temporarily paralyzed. Needless to say, each of these handshakes is capable of leaving a rather definite impression on the shakee.

Fortunately, in most business situations, we do not encounter these extreme forms of handshaking. Instead, we experience a reasonably mild blend of these styles, which we loosely call the "normal" handshake. But do not be misled. Those minor variations that do exist communicate more than we realize.

Handshaking trends have also undergone some change since the women's liberation movement. With a spirit of equal rights in the air, many women no longer abide by the customs of a bygone era. Having left the curtsy far behind, those subscribing to the cause of women's liberation freely extend their hands to men in the marketplace. Men, in turn, sensing this desire for parity, do likewise.

Wherever handshaking is done, it should be done with directness, firmness, and conviction. To accomplish this, the web of each person's hand must meet the other's. And, lastly, the handshake should be brief and accompanied by direct eye contact.

TOUCH

As I mentioned in connection with body bigots, some individuals reject others on the basis of one objectionable part—big nose, crossed eyes, big ears, etc. This same form of body prejudice occurs with the language of touch. Assume that you are meeting someone for the first time and, during the course of the conversation, the person repeatedly touches you on the arm, hand, or shoulder while speaking. Further, assume that you are the kind of person who dislikes being handled. In spite of the fact that such an individual may be intelligent, warm, and interesting, it is quite possible that you may reject him entirely on the basis of his touching habits.

People who are compulsive touchers while talking could be called "touchophiliacs." Of those who fall into this category, you will find some who do it lightly and others who do it with annoying vigor. And, because they usually have been doing it for many years, they are often unaware of the extent to which they do it. In fact, some, when confronted with the charge, "Hey, would you mind not doing that!" are taken aback and seem unclear as to what you mean. I once had a friend who was a touchophiliac and I became curious to learn what would happen if I returned his touches with the same frequency and intensity as he touched me. I did it and, believe it or not, he became terribly upset. He didn't seem able to figure out what I was doing and why I was doing it. Not unlike the practical joker who plays jokes on others but cannot take them himself, the touchophiliac touches but does not seem to appreciate being touched back to the same extent.

The counterpart of a touchophiliac is the "untouchable." This is a person who does not like to be touched. In addition to a dislike of conversational touching, he has an added aversion—to being touched on public transportation, i.e., buses, trains, elevators, and escalators. This preference for not being touched in public should not, however, be taken to include touching in private. Such individuals might tolerate, if not thoroughly enjoy, private touching that they personally authorize.

One of the things that determines how touchable people are is the integrity of their nervous system. Some are so sensitive that being touched without warning can cause them to jump out of their shoes. Others possess nervous systems so rugged that it would take something short of a mini-mugging to make them respond. Another factor is the culture in which people are reared. In his book *Hidden Dimension*, anthropologist Edward Hall tells us that people of the Arab world have a different set of attitudes when it comes to being touched than do westerners. For the Arab, the "person" exists somewhere deep inside the body and, consequently, Arabs do not consider being touched an invasion of privacy. In America, the outer surface of a person's body is synonymous with the inside. To touch someone's clothes or skin requires permission, if you are a stranger.

Still other culture-related attitudes toward touching exist. By comparison, the French touch one another somewhat less than do the Puerto

Ricans, and the English less than both of them. The Germans touch frequently in the form of the handshake. They shake hands at every meeting with strangers, acquaintances, friends, and family (male or female). In social settings, men nudge and pat each other often during the course of a lively conversation.

With the world getting smaller and smaller, it is essential that you become familiar with what N. M. Henley calls *The Politics of Touch*. It raises serious questions within and across cultural boundaries. For instance, it is important for you to realize that status can be dictated by touching accessibility; the individual of higher status is generally granted the privilege of touching someone of lower status. While your superior could conceivably place his arm around your shoulder while giving advice, you could not do that to him. In effect, the higher the status, the greater the touching rights. You may also be interested in knowing that touching research has indicated that when people like one another, or when they are basically more affiliative, there is apt to be more touching. Therefore, the more someone of higher status touches you, the more favorably that person may regard you.

Without being aware of it, your touching politics may require some serious attention. If your touching offends people and you don't know it, you had better find out—and fast. Likewise, if you are an untouchable, find out just *how* untouchable you are. In either case, whether you are guilty of having too great or too little an appetite for touching, investigate this aspect of your silent self as soon as possible.

POSTURE

Most of us can tell whether people are happy or sad by the way they sit or stand. While our observation might lack the scientific accuracy of an electron microscope, it is often an amazingly reliable sign of an individual's mood. One writer put it more poetically when he said, "Flexion is sadness, extension is happiness." Flexion is when the head is pitched forward and downward, shoulders are rounded and drooped, and the arms or hands are folded inward.

Whatever posture a person assumes, there is always a certain amount of tension. Whereas a well-trained athlete's erect posture often suggests a calm and collected appearance, postures of the Nazi soldiers depicted in World War II films caused the men to look extremely tense. Studies of posture have revealed that the amount of relaxation associated with a given posture can be taken as a clue to a person's status. Picture an officer of a bank talking with a teller. Which of the two do you think would display the more relaxed posture? If you think it would be the bank officer, you are right. The person of higher status usually manifests the more relaxed posture; the person of lower status, the more tense posture.

A popular misconception about posture is that it is always a still or motionless state. Posture in motion is seldom considered. While you may sit or stand perfectly straight, your walking posture might be exceptionally irregular or jerky. Your posture therefore dispatches messages about you when it is at rest as well as in motion.

What does your posture say about you? Does it advertise that you are self-confident, arrogant, shy, friendly, or insecure? Could you alter your posture so that it says something else about you? How would you do it? On the basis of a series of experiments in which he photographed a human mannequin in different positions, William James concluded that postures can provide clues to people's attitudes. Males, for instance, assume more relaxed postures than females in this culture. It is interesting to speculate whether this difference in postural tone will undergo any change because of the recent feminist movement. Perhaps, as more women are elevated to positions of higher status, their postures will become more relaxed and those of the men obliged to work under them, more tense.

As with so many other aspects of the silent self, many people are oblivious to how they walk or stand. If someone who walked exactly as you do were to come toward you on the street, it is unlikely that you would say, "Hey, look at that girl, she walks just like me." The same goes for standing postures. While it may be hard to believe, many people don't realize how their posture looks to others. They may think they are standing up straight but in reality they aren't. Others cock their heads to one side when they talk and haven't the faintest idea that their heads are not on straight. Then there is the question of how they hold their arms. Are they fully extended or slightly bent at the elbows; are their elbows near to or held away from the body; do the palms of the hands face the thighs or are they directed backward? And their feet—do they toe inward or outward? How each of these body parts is held could make a significant difference in someone's posture and the messages it conveys.

Whether it is a lawyer pleading a case, a prizefighter approaching ringside, or a baseball player stepping up to bat, their postures communicate. A closed posture (where flexion predominates) communicates a negative attitude. An open posture (where extension predominates) communicates a positive attitude. However, regardless of the posture an individual displays, whether it be stationary or moving, it cannot *not* communicate.

31

An assertive posture, one that will tell others that you are important, someone worth knowing and being associated with, can be developed in two ways. One method is to picture your posture the way you would like it to be. The other way is to stand with your back against a wall every day (morning and night) for one minute with your eyes closed. Be sure that your head, shoulders, buttocks, and heels are firmly touching the wall. This will help supply you with a mental blueprint of good posture.

SMELL

What greater insurance of survival is there than tasting and smelling bad? Dr. Louis Leakey, who discovered the earliest bones of *homo sapiens* in Africa, which are estimated to be 400 million years old, has this to say about smell: "Man survived because nature endowed him with an unpleasant taste and unpleasant smell." Whether this is true or not, it raises an interesting, but perhaps embarrassing, question: "How do you smell?"

It is rumored that two days before arriving home, Napoleon sent his mistress a note saying, "Don't wash. I'm on my way home." Apparently, an individual's smell has played different roles throughout history—at least it did with Napoleon. Would you believe that Queen Isabella of Castile boasted that she had only two baths in her entire life? Or that, when Queen Victoria ascended to the throne, there wasn't a single bathtub in Buckingham Palace? Except for brief periods in history, the use of soap or even water for washing was considered unnecessary or undesirable. Because the Puritans of early America regarded bathing as injurious to health and morals, they went around unwashed and unperfumed. Laws banning bathing entirely, or limiting the number of baths a person was permitted each year, were passed in such states as Virginia, Pennsylvania, and Ohio.

Big business thinks enough about how you smell these days to spend over a billion dollars a year reminding you of it. "Smelling clean" is a twentieth-century phenomenon.

Do you monitor your own body odors or do you rely on others to do it for you? If you went to a dentist who happened to have bad breath, would you tell him? Probably not. If you needed the dental work, and he was a really good dentist, you might continue to grin and bear his bad breath. Should his nurse tell him? Whose responsibility is it to alert people whose breath offends?

Unfortunately, there is no clear line of distinction between a person's private and occupational life. Personal habits involving offensive odors carry over into the job. Cigar and cigarette smokers, along with garlic and onion eaters, lead the pack. A close second are people who douse themselves with perfumes, colognes, toilet water, and a variety of hair sprays. In third place, there are those whose laundering activities leave a great deal to be desired. Too often they smell as if they just stepped out of a hamper.

Either you have had the misfortune of working with someone sporting bad breath or body odor or, without realizing it, you were the offending party. Has anyone ever told you that you offend? If so, what was your reaction? People who offend, instead of appreciating being told, sometimes resent it. While they might thank you for telling them, their non-verbal communication frequently suggests resentment and annoyance.

Be aware that a completely successful interview for a good position could be totally canceled out by the way you smell. Although this is only one of the many situations in which smell might play an important role, its importance could be decisive. So do yourself a favor and find out (ask a friend) what kinds of odor messages you give off and, if they offend, correct them.

DRESS

What makes you dress the way you do? Is it based upon how you feel, where you are going, with whom you are going, the people you want to impress, the limitations of your wardrobe, or the weather outside? Does how you dress affect your behavior, or does your behavior affect how you dress? Since we are the only creatures on this planet who wear clothes, it might be rewarding to explore some of the reasons why we dress the way we do.

Picture this scene. Five men are sitting in a steam bath, naked. They are all strangers. To pass the time of day, while their bodies sweat out impurities, they chat about such things as politics, baseball, and business trends. Soon, one of them says, "Well, that's it for me today. I've had enough," and leaves. After a while, another one leaves, and so on. In the locker room, each of them dresses differently. One puts on an army uniform having three stars on each shoulder. The second puts on a business suit. The third, a pair of Levis and a T-shirt. The fourth, a parcel post driver's uniform. And the last, a pair of very flashy slacks, a matching shirt and sports jacket, and suede shoes. On the street, the general gets into a staff car; the man in the business suit, into a chauffeur-driven limousine; the parcel post driver, into his truck; the man in the T-shirt and Levis, onto a bus; and the snappy dresser, into a cab.

Assuming that none of them had revealed the nature of his occupation or profession while in the steam bath, do you think any of them could have guessed what the others did for a living? How much information about each man was available in the naked state as compared to when they were fully dressed? Presumably, this same dilemma would apply to women in a steam bath—or would it?

If, as psychiatrist Jean Rosenbaum suggests, "When you're selecting clothes, you're choosing a kind of substitute body," perhaps the way you dress for work communicates more than you think. Take something as traditional as the use of clothing to indicate the sex of the wearer. With the advent of uni-sex clothes, it is sometimes difficult to tell the males from the females. Then, there is the expensiveness of clothes, which reflects status; their condition, suggesting a concern over appearance; style to indicate fashion consciousness; and type to signify age. Rest assured, if your clothes could talk, they would have something rather definite to say about you.

In a sense, you wear a uniform that prompts people to relate to you in a particular way. An excellent example of this involved the police force at a large midwestern university. Possibly as an experiment, they were taken out of uniform and deprived of their weapons. Instead, they were dressed in blue blazers with a crest on the coat pocket. Robbed of their self-image, morale on the force took an immediate dive and many men simply quit. Arguments favoring having the men back in uniform were many: (1) uniforms acted as symbols of authority; (2) police were easier to find when needed; (3) uniforms acted as a deterrent to lawbreakers; (4) fights could be stopped more easily; and (5) uniforms kept the police officers from blending in with the crowd. In general, the way the men were dressed made a great deal of difference in terms of the job they were being paid to do.

To further support the view that clothes and grooming can affect attitude and behavior, here is what happened at the detention center of the Massachusetts Department of Youth Services. The Clairol company, operating on the premise that, if you "look good," chances are that you will feel good and perceive your environment more favorably, decided to try an experiment. Nine teen-age girls were used as subjects. Their offenses included prostitution, drug abuse, attempted suicide, and truancy. When asked if they felt beautiful, they all shouted, "*No!*" The girls were then started on a four-week grooming junket. The question raised by those conducting the experiment was: Will such external changes affect their internal state? The results were excellent. Their behavior was noticeably changed for the better.

34

Another consideration involves the colors you wear. Millions of people every day, consciously or unconsciously, wear colors that relate to their attitudes and moods. For centuries, certain colors have been associated with passion, courage, cruelty, justice, and health. Green, because it is the color of nature, has been considered the easiest with which to live. Blue, the color of the sky and the sea, has been said to have a calming effect.

One airline took color seriously and painted the interior of their aircraft earth colors instead of blue. It seems that blue, being so near the color of the sky, made people apprehensive. Colors in the brown family made them feel less apprehensive.

There seem to be heated arguments these days over what a person should wear to work. Broadly, they can be divided into two camps: (1) suits and dresses and (2) jeans. Naturally, in each of these camps you will find a number of variations. For example, along with the traditional look there are sport jackets and slacks, blouses and skirts. In the jeans family you will find dungarees, Levis, overalls, khaki shirts, pants, caftans, and dashikis. The borderline dividing these clothes preferences is by no means distinct. You will find bank tellers and psychologists wearing jeans and soda jerks wearing shirts and ties. One possible explanation for these clothes preferences on the job is a desire for physical comfort over that of personal appearance.

Drs. Jane Anton and Michael Russell conducted a study on how more than 100 personnel recruiters from seventeen different industry groups felt about clothes and hiring. Among their findings, they discovered that: (1) it is best for a job applicant to dress neatly; (2) a young man may create a mildly positive impression if he wears a sport coat, shirt, tie, and slacks, but makes a stronger impression if he wears a suit; and (3) the wearing of jeans, shorts, sandals, or lack of bras (in the case of women applicants) creates mildly to strongly negative impressions.

While clothes may not make the man or woman, they certainly can communicate some very definite information about the man or woman living in them. Granting that what is inside clothes is more important than clothes themselves, one has to get past them before the person within can become known.

TIME

Every job involves time. Your attitude toward it and its management could make the difference between success and failure. The more time someone gives you, the more important you are. The longer someone keeps

35

you waiting, the less important you are. In our society, we are preoccupied with time. Alarm clocks wake us in the morning, church bells chime every quarter of an hour, radio announcers provide us with the time on a regular basis, neon lights throughout the city tell us what time it is, and we wear timepieces on our wrists. Some people become extremely nervous and upset when they discover that they have lost track of the time. Too many of them have become helplessly addicted to time in such forms as deadlines, agendas, schedules, calendars, time clocks, and timetables. Time moves them the way a puppeteer moves puppets on their strings.

Time communicates—and it communicates in many languages. In the Western world, we are locked into a linear-spatial concept of time that divides it into a past, present, and future. The present is some sort of midpoint between the past and the future. We fancy ourselves moving "through time." Other cultures, in contrast, are concerned with the immediate present, with "felt time." There is no concept of past or future. The Greeks, for example, see themselves as stationary, with time coming up from behind, overtaking them, and becoming the past. There is no past or future, only the present. Something even more curious occurs in the language of the Sioux Indians. There are no words for *time, late,* or *waiting.* Among the Pueblo Indians, things take place "when the time is right," whenever that may be. Our government lost thousands of dollars in construction because the Hopi Indians didn't have a concept of a "fixed date" by which a house or a road would be completed. Punctuality does not seem to be prized in all cultures. Mañana may not be tomorrow but some indefinite time in the future. American businessmen tell angry tales of having to wait a half hour or longer to see a Latin American associate. A similar delay is said to occur in dealings with the Arab businessman. In this country, being kept waiting that long would be considered an insult, whereas in other countries it seems to be appropriate. Here are four common forms of punctuality in the United States:

Lateness: Whatever your excuse, your absence or tardiness communicates that some party or occasion was more important. When you keep people waiting, you make them wonder how important they are to you. Lateness also communicates unreliability.

Earliness: Arriving a few minutes early tells the other people that you are considerate of their time. If you arrive very early, it may give them the impression that you have nothing to do and are not very dynamic.

Fashionable lateness: When you are invited to a private party of a business associate and arrive a little late, you are indirectly telling your host that you realize there are a great many things that need to be done in preparation for a party.

Promptness: If you arrive on time for your appointments, people will take you to be both sociable and composed. This is a quality to be developed in anyone who seeks to communicate his responsibility to those with whom he plans to work.

Structuring Time

Organizations of every description, from governments to your neighborhood grocery, structure time formally and informally. Formal time, in an industrial society, is measured in seconds, minutes, hours, days, weeks, months, and years—by calendars and clocks. Informal time is represented by such terms as *in a while* and *when you get a chance*. It is vague and subject to a wide variety of interpretations. Formal time is precise and subject to common agreement by all involved. Whereas the vocabulary of informal time is generally the same as formal time, meaning is more inclined to be missed because it depends on the situation rather than on a clear-cut definition.

People who work together use both formal and informal time and, occasionally, communication breaks down because the wrong one is employed. While an executive might tell one of his managers to "take a late lunch" (informal time), he should not say, "See that that shipment goes out later," when referring to a shipment that *has* to go out. The order requires the use of formal time, i.e., "See that that shipment goes out at 3:30 P.M." Entirely too many people are victims of misunderstandings because they used the wrong kind of time.

Larks and Owls

Do you feel bright-eyed and bushy-tailed when you get up in the morning? Can you think clearly the moment you wake up? If you answered yes to both of these questions, you may be a *lark*. Larks are day people. They get up early and go to sleep early; their energies peak at midday and wane as the sun goes down. Owls are night people. They get up late and go to sleep late. Their energies peak toward evening. When the lark is ready for bed, the owl is ready to go out on the town. In a work situation, serious problems could arise when an employer is a lark and an employee is an owl. Each structures time differently and the result is often confusion. Unless, of course, one of them is willing to accommodate the other's biological clock—the mechanism within us all that dictates how we structure time.

No discussion of *chronemics* (how people use time) would be complete if mention was not made of monochronic types and polychronic types of

37

individuals. The monochronic type is a person who can do only one thing at a time. The polychronic type can do many things at one time. The majority of people seem to be monochronic, with only a small percentage of the population being polychronic. Production is certain to suffer when an individual who is monochronic is assigned to a job requiring someone who is polychronic, and vice versa. A short-order cook who cannot do several things at once is doomed. A receptionist who can do several things at once, working on a job that does not require such talent, will be bored to tears.

The management of time is a very personal matter. You can waste it, kill it, use it, stretch it, consolidate it, spend it, or save it. Whatever you do, bear in mind that time makes a strong statement—non-verbally.

PLACE

A man came home unexpectedly from a business trip to find his wife had been carrying on an affair with one of his associates. As he inserted his key into the front door, his wife and her suitor heard the latch turn. Quickly, rather than be discovered, the wife's suitor hid in a nearby closet. The husband made his way to her bedroom and confronted her with accusing words and a condemning look. "Where is he?" the husband shouted. The wife replied, "Where is who, dear?" The husband snapped, "You know damn well who—your lover." He then began to seach the room, and in a matter of moments, he stood at the door of the closet containing the suitor. He angrily jerked the door open, and there before his eyes was his associate, standing in his underwear. "What in the hell are you doing here, Steve?" asked the husband. To which the associate answered, "Everyone has to be somewhere."

Surely you have heard the expression "you have to be in the right place at the right time." In every field, employed personnel have a place. It can range from a private office to a shared office to an area. A guard, for example, might regard his place as the front or back door to an office building; a cashier, the register; or a stock boy, the stock room. Everyone must have a place and that place must be known to the organization for which he works. If it is changed, that change must be reported and noted.

The study of *proxemics* deals with how spatial relationships between people serve to communicate. To illustrate this concept, imagine that you have an invisible bubble surrounding you. Call it your "personal bubble." It will vary in diameter not only from person to person but also according to the situation. Have you noticed that whenever a stranger walks up to you and gets too close, you begin to back off? This will happen not only with strangers but with anyone who invades your bubble without your permission. If you are anxious to learn how big your bubble is, here's what you should do. Find someone whom you know casually and ask him to stand about ten feet away facing you. At a signal from you, ask him to slowly inch his way toward you. As he gets nearer and nearer, have him *stop* when his closeness makes you feel uncomfortable and you want to pull away or lean backward. At that moment, that person has invaded your bubble.

Edward Hall, a pioneer in the field of proxemics, has suggested that there are various zones that regulate interpersonal distances. The *intimate zone* represents a distance from physical contact to approximately eighteen inches. Telling secrets, whispering, lovemaking, and wrestling operate in the intimate zone. The *personal zone* ranges from one-half foot to four feet and is the distance at which normal people have conversations. The *social zone*, from four to twelve feet, is maintained by people at a social gathering or business transaction. And finally, the *public zone*, twelve feet and beyond, operates during a lecture or some other form of speaker–audience situation.

What has been described until now are two forms of spatial communication: personal space and territoriality. Personal space is not fixed. It varies from person to person and from culture to culture. Territoriality, however, remains fixed. Your office at work is a specific area; it does not change according to your whim or mood. At home, you find other examples of territoriality, i.e., your study, the kitchen, and the bedroom. In crowded urban areas, various gangs or youth groups often proclaim certain territory as "their own" and will fight to protect it.

How close people sit to one another and the angles at which they sit suggest the kind of communication that will occur between them. Studies have indicated that while sitting face to face is a more competitive arrangement, sitting kitty-corner inclines to be more cooperative. Then, there is the question of sex. Two females will often sit or stand closer to each other than they will to males. Males, in turn, will sit or stand closer to the opposite sex than they will to each other. With regard to race, blacks and whites tend to maintain greater distance from each other than from people of their own race.

According to professors Jeffrey Fisher and Don Byrne, it is also important to know which is someone's "good side." They suggest that "getting on someone's good side" is more than a figure of speech. In two different studies, they found that women feel more comfortable when approached face to face by strangers. Men prefer strangers to approach them from the side. With friends, however, women like them to come from the side and men prefer a frontal approach. These researchers were unable to give **any** sound reason why these preferences exist, only that they do.

Our lives are filled with proxemic incidents. Arguments over a parking space, a theater seat, a place in line at the local bank, supermarket, or **car** wash are common to us all. Each is an exercise in the manipulation of personal space and territoriality—silent forms of human communication.

3
Advertising Yourself with What You Say and How You Say It

"Funny, you don't talk like a doctor."

"I'll be damned if I'm going to talk to a machine."

"Don't you dare use that tone of voice with me!"

"Just watch your language, young man."

"You sounded different on the phone."

We have all heard these remarks. Each involves what people say, how they say it, and to whom. The meanings they convey will be the target of this chapter. It shall be divided into two parts. Part One will deal with the words and sounds people make to each other at close range. Part Two will explore the use of these words and sounds across distances through the use of telephones and telephone-answering machines (TAMs), i.e., telecommunication.

There are few things that make a more personal statement about you than the way you speak. Is there anything special about your speech, voice, or style of speaking that makes it easy to identify? Do people immediately recognize your voice on the telephone? What, exactly, is there about the way you speak that causes you to be remembered? Is it your diction, politeness, slight accent, or that you remember names?

Information about your age, education, intelligence, emotional state, attitudes, values, and beliefs can

be determined by what you say and how you say it.
This alone is more than enough to recommend a serious
reading of this chapter.

Not only will it make you more conscious of how your
speech advertises who and what you are, it will also
elevate your appreciation of any need for improvement.

PART ONE: WORDS AND SOUNDS AT CLOSE RANGE

Stereotyping Speakers

In our society, perhaps due to the influence of radio, television, films, and theater, we have developed various ideas about how certain people should speak and sound. Meeting a man at a party with a deep and resonant voice might prompt you to think he is an announcer or an actor. Or, meeting a woman whose speaking style has that clinical tone might cause you to think she is a psychotherapist or a psychiatrist. While some people sound more like what they are, others do not. For example, a truck driver with a high-pitched, squeaky voice and a pronounced lisp somehow doesn't conform to the public image. At the other extreme, a shipping clerk with a rich, resounding voice and an unbelievably large vocabulary is equally difficult to accept.

Verbal and vocal messages, like the non-verbal messages described in the previous chapter, are both susceptible to stereotyping. People almost routinely put those different from themselves into categories, which makes them easier to talk about. The cliché "he/she sounds like   " is a phrase that breeds a multitude of sins. For some reason or other, treating people as individuals, separate and distinct from other members of a given class, is a rarely practiced art. People with accents know only too well what it feels like to be placed in a separate category with others who speak English the way they do. This compulsive form of stereotyping people according to how they speak, however, goes beyond accents. It takes in those who speak loudly or softly, grammatically or ungrammatically, fast or slowly, with good or bad diction, large or small vocabularies, high- or low-pitched voices, and those who do or do not use obscene language.

Whether or not you believe that such stereotyping actually exists is not at issue here. The reality is that it does. The only question left to be answered is how people do it, and to what extent. While some of the following examples of stereotyping might be a little more outrageous than others, see how many you accept and how many you reject:

1. Loud talkers are usually rude, vulgar, insensitive, pushy, not terribly bright, and rather egocentric.
2. Soft talkers are usually sensitive, even-tempered, gentle, sympathetic, intelligent, and tolerant.
3. People who use correct grammar are frequently educated and knowledgeable, more cultured, respectful of the language they use, and somewhat intolerant of those who abuse or misuse the English language.
4. People who speak ungrammatically, unless the job they have or the one for which they are applying requires little or no written or oral communication, generally do not advance.
5. Fast talkers are inclined to be unpolished and rather common types of people. Because others have difficulty grasping what they say, they are rarely believed. They are often thought to be either con men or crafty salesmen.
6. Slow talkers are usually slow thinkers. They often suffer from insecurity, non-assertiveness, low self-esteem, a lack of self-confidence, and a socially timid personality.
7. People who speak with good diction are apt to be considered phony, supercilious, and overly affected. Since the way they speak makes them stand out like sore thumbs, they often enjoy only a limited credibility.
8. People with poor diction tend to come from a low socioeconomic class, have little formal education, and lack an awareness of the more aesthetic things in life such as poetry, ballet, opera, classical music, and literature.
9. People with large vocabularies are thought to be well educated, possess social graces, and be intelligent, knowledgeable, and highly credible.
10. People with small vocabularies are perceived to have a limited education, experience difficulty expressing themselves, and have lower-paying jobs.
11. Males with high-pitched voices are apt to have their masculinity challenged; females with low voices, their femininity challenged. Big men with high-pitched voices are often thought to be laughable; little men with very deep voices, the same thing.
12. People who use obscene language usually have filthy minds and an anemic source of word power. They are vulgar, crass, impolite, and unpleasant company.

Some or parts of these twelve stereotyped statements sound familiar, others do not. Notice that each of them contains just enough truth to hold your attention for a couple of seconds. After some thought, however, you should realize that they cannot apply to everyone, and should be treated

43

as irresponsible generalizations. The danger they pose is a result of that "little bit of truth" they all possess being distorted by those who use them. Thus, stereotyping in any of its forms should be strongly discouraged as a means of communication.

Words by Mouth

Do people listen to you when you speak? Perhaps they fidget, look at their watches, and seem to be thinking of other things. Before you begin searching for a remedy to the situation, you should become aware of four things that can happen as a result of having a poor speaking technique. First of all, the person to whom you are speaking might pay little or no attention, and if you are trying to sell him something, it will probably squelch the deal. Second, it might serve as a source of irritation to the listener, which could sour him on both the existing transaction and any future ones. Third, your poor speaking technique could cause your message to be misunderstood. And finally, your meaning could be missed entirely. While, to some degree, all of these things happen normally, your inability to speak effectively could make matters substantially worse. If at all possible, you should not allow this to happen. Bear in mind that communication, at its best, is a weak means of adequately expressing what you think and feel. Thus, you cannot afford to sell short any of the methods by which information exchanged on the job can be improved.

Meaning Is in People—Not Words

One of the most serious communication problems people have in business and the professions is that they reify. The word *reify* comes from *reification* (to treat something that doesn't materially exist as though it did exist). Even more simply, to reify is to "thingify." When an employer or a manager accuses an employee of lacking motivation, one gets the impression that motivation is something inside a person, like a liver, spleen, or gallbladder. And, to lack motivation is to actually suffer a material deficiency in the body.

Words themselves do not exist in nature like birds, trees, fish, and flowers. Words are man-made, like plastics, automobiles, rowboats, and beach balls. As symbols, words stand for things that materially exist. For instance, you do not write with the word *pencil*, but with an object to which the label "pencil" has been arbitrarily assigned. It might just as well be called elbow or pickle relish. It is also incorrect to speak of the "real word" for something as opposed to a word that is not real. For example, the word we use to describe the stuff we pay to a cashier is *money*. To suggest that it is the "real word" for that stuff would be nonsense. In German, it would be *Geld*; in Italian, *denaro*; and in French, *argent*. They are all words in the language being used at the time.

Words from your mouth can also be regarded as abstract or concrete. Abstract words, as already suggested by the term *reification*, lack materiality. Such words as *enthusiasm, dedication, honesty, integrity, dependability, assertiveness, confidence, and ethics* are all abstract. Seldom do the people using them mean exactly the same thing. Again, the meaning is not in the word but in the person using the word.

Finally, there are two remaining categories into which words fall: denotative and connotative. When you look up a word in the dictionary, you will find its denotation—that is, the dictionary meaning of it. If you ask a friend what a word means, and she gives you her meaning of it, you will be getting her connotation—that is, her personal interpretation of what it means. As you can see, denotations and connotations frequently clash when people attempt to pass off their connotations as denotations.

Becoming a Wordsmith

Saying what you mean is not easy. Notice how many people in daily conversation use the phrases *what I really mean* or *what I am really trying to say is.* . . . While knowing precisely what you mean to say is one thing, being able to accurately convey that meaning is quite another. Knowing how to weave your words into meaningful units of thought is essential. To do this, as the watchmaker and silversmith manipulate the tools of their crafts, the wordsmith must choose, assemble, and deliver his words so that they convey the exact message for which they were intended. Peter Farb, in his book *Word Play: What Happens When People Talk,* describes America's present-day language trends this way:

An entire generation has grown up that distrusts language's ability to express a true picture of reality and that relies upon the empty intercalations of like, you know, I mean. The world has grown inarticulate at the very time that an unprecedented number of words flood the media. The output has burgeoned, but speakers have retreated into worn paths and stock phrases.

The need for you to become a wordsmith is greater now than ever before. The emphasis upon body language is probably a result of our failure to communicate effectively with words. Where vocabularies should be growing, they are dwindling; where people should be taking more pride in the language of the land, they are taking less. Ironically, instead of being admired and imitated, people who speak well are often singled out as unorthodox or deviant by those who do not speak well. Exceptions are made, however, if such individuals are members of a profession where clear and articulate speech is part of their stock in trade (teachers, actors, announcers, etc.). Such tolerance, unfortunately, is rarely extended to the average working man or woman.

The wordsmith must be mindful of something else. People don't think in words but in pictures. When someone says *horse*, you do not mentally picture the letters *h-o-r-s-e* but rather an animal with four legs, a head, mane, and tail. We carry around images of those things that exist in our environment having size, shape, color, and position that can be experienced by our senses. Not only are these images based on our sense of sight, they are also based on hearing such aspects of sound as its tone, rhythm, and melody. Sounds do things: they clink, clatter, clang, crackle, and crash. Hence, when we speak, we must generate images of these sights and sounds that listeners can easily conjure up in their minds. Odors, tastes, and felt sensations are not to be excluded from this imagery. Whatever pictures the mind of the wordsmith can generate, each will help make its communication that much clearer.

Whatever field you happen to be in, you will probably have to describe something to someone. Salespeople describe their merchandise, physicians their patient's illness, bank officers their customer's loan agreement or checkbook balance. In each case, using words without corresponding pictures or mental images often leads to confusion or misunderstanding.

Cliché-itis

"On the other hand," "all things being equal," "with human nature being what it is," "as luck would have it," "you are what you eat," and "in the long run, life is a bowl of cherries. . . ." Thousands of clichés like these clog the wordways by obscuring meaning and boring readers. While they cannot be entirely avoided, they should be guarded against and substituted for wherever possible with straightforward language. Being original is difficult because bad language habits are formed early in life. Discovering what they are and what to do about them takes both time and effort. We become attached to pet phrases that, like other bad habits, become part of our mind-body system of behavior. Sometimes these clichés become such a deeply rooted part of us that we are unaware they exist until someone brings them to our attention.

To rid yourself of cliché-itis, you must do two things: First, you must become sensitive to the fact that you have it, and second, search out simple and precise words to substitute for the clichés. Leave clichés out entirely if you can satisfy yourself that they make no significant contribution to what you are saying. Using clichés will identify you as a rubber-stamp kind of speaker, one who borrows worn-out phrases from others instead of inventing new ones of your own. In any business or profession where creativity is essential, you dare not allow your language to become afflicted with cliché-itis.

Slang

While most people know and understand a number of slang expressions, only a small percentage uses them openly and freely. Actually, slang words are words in transition. Although they are currently used by certain members of our society, they have not yet been fully accepted as part of our standard language. In a special way, the type of slang you use and the extent to which you use it serves to verbally advertise your level of sophistication. Imagine a wealthy, well-dressed woman being shown a diamond pendant in an elegant Fifth Avenue jewelry shop. During the course of the sale, the salesperson happens to say, "Actually, madam, this is the snazziest pendant we have in stock." Clearly, the word *snazziest* is inappropriate to the situation. Next, imagine a young surgeon coming out of of an operating room to tell a family that their grandfather has died. He says, "Your grandfather has just croaked!"

In both instances, the words *snazziest* and *croaked* were out of order. Substitute terms such as *vibrant, chic, unique, striking,* or *incomparable* should have been used by the salesperson. Instead of the word used by the physician, he could have said the man *has passed on, is with God now,* or simply—*has died.*

The use of slang not only cheapens the individual, it also suggests a lack of sensitivity to one's listeners. Bank customers are not apt to appreciate having their deposits referred to as *loot,* or the barber's customers terribly pleased to be called *heads.*

Think of slang in this way. The more common the situation, job, or individual, the more inclined you are to hear slang. Only in select situations where there is common consent by both parties is slang tolerated. Or, when a word or an expression is elevated to legitimate status in our language, it can be used without fear or reservation.

Obscenity

If words are not the things for which they stand, why all the fuss? Is it that some people are offended by certain letters of the alphabet, the way they are strung together, the sounds they make, or the images they bring to mind? But why certain words offend and not others is not the main issue here. The main issue is that specific words in our language have been classified as obscene. Usually, they are of a religious, sexual, or excretory nature. Religious obscenity has been banned from Judeo-Christian cultures since the Third Commandment: "Thou shalt not take the name of the Lord thy God in vain." Sexual obscenity in America grew out of the Puritan belief that such words were designed to incite lust and depravity.

We have come a long way in this country since the 1930s. Then, such words as *whore, harlot, tart, eunuch, wench,* and *sex* were banned from American movies. Today, one is hard pressed to think of any words that aren't being used in American films and plays. Even television scripts are beginning to use words that were formerly considered obscene. Though the objects or acts they symbolize remain the same, attitudes toward them have relaxed—at least outwardly.

While we have come a long way since the thirties, people continue to be offended by certain words. When asked why, they are often unable to present sound arguments in defense of their feelings. They often say, "I don't know, I just don't like such lauguage used in my presence." People with such language preferences must be extended the same courtesy as those who advocate obscenity. A fair analogy would be your dislike of Wagnerian music. You may not be able to explain why you do not like it in musical terms; all you know is how it makes you feel when you hear it. This same kind of fractured logic applies to hearing obscene language. It makes certain people feel uncomfortable. As an expression of common courtesy, a wise course of action would be to refrain from using it in their company. With those who are comfortable using obscene language, feel free to join in and do likewise. Let the people with whom you work and the situation at hand dictate the appropriate level of communication.

Pronunciation

How often are you accused of mispronouncing words? When it happens, do you yield and stand corrected, ignore the accusation, or retaliate in kind? When you hear people mispronounce a word, do you correct them or let it pass? How important do you think pronunciation is in any business or profession? For example, if you brought your car to a mechanic because it wouldn't start, and he said it was due to your "ca-*boor*-i-tor," would you leave it to be fixed? How about a doctor who said you had "gold stones" rather than gallstones—would you let him operate? Should the personnel in any given field know how to pronounce correctly the terminology they use? Could the mispronunciation of a trade word destroy someone's credibility? Well, it happened at a midwestern university. Its library staff was to be visited by a speaker from a special agency. After the usual introduction, the guest speaker began his address. Ten minutes into his speech, he happened to mention the study of library science. He pronounced the word *library* as though it were *l-i-b-e-r-r-y*. The audience could not understand how someone with his background and status could mispronounce a word so fundamental to his profession. And yet it happened! As the word left his mouth and struck the ears of his audience, a silence came over the room. How would you have reacted?

There are five ways you can mispronounce words. First, you can do it by omitting certain sounds. Examples, saying lib*err*y instead of lib*rar*y, gov'ment for gov*ern*ment, and prob'ly for prob*ab*ly. Second, you can add certain sounds to a word that don't belong there. Examples: ath*a*lete rather than athlete, el*u*m instead of elm, acros*t* instead of across, wa*r*sh for wash, and hyd*e*rant for hydrant. Third, you can invert sounds. Examples: a*ks* instead of a*sk*, in*tr*egal for in*teg*ral, and reve*l*ant for re*lev*ant. Fourth, you may substitute one vowel for another. Examples: t*i*n for t*e*n, *ae*g for *e*gg, extr*i* for extr*a*, and k*a*tchup for k*e*tchup. The fifth and final difficulty results from misplaced stress. Examples: mu*nic*ipal rather than mu*nic*ipal, *a*dult instead of a*dult*, *in*famous instead of in*fam*ous, *ci*gar for ci*gar*.

Deciding upon the correct pronunciation of a word is not always easy. In the long run, your ears are your best guide. Pay close attention to what educated, cultivated, prominent leaders are saying, for it is they who generally set the styles for acceptable usage. They are a good gauge of what pronunciations you should use. For an even more reliable source, look up the word you are questioning in *A Pronouncing Dictionary of American English*, by John S. Kenyon and Thomas A. Knott.

Before leaving the subject of pronunciation, here is a fitting anecdote. Jake was due for his annual physical; so, off he went to his doctor. After a thorough examination, his physician sent him on his way. Frightened by the bad news he was given, he barely made his way home to tell his wife, Becky. As Jake opened the front door, Becky could tell by his face that something was wrong. "What is it, Jake? What did the doctor say?" In a weak and trembling voice, Jake said, "The doctor told me that I had a 'flucky.'" Before Jake could say another word, Becky had Jake in bed and had notified the whole family of her husband's serious condition. His son, Jerry, who was away at college, was also called and told to come home immediately. Everyone but Jerry was satisfied that Jake's days were numbered. Having never heard of a "flucky," he decided to call his father's physician and ask. "Hello, Dr. Siegel? This is Jake Goldfarb's son, Jerry. Last week you examined my father and told him he had a 'flucky.' Exactly what is a 'flucky'?" "What flucky?" answered the doctor. "I told him he got off lucky."

Vocabulary

Without words, we are immediately reduced to the grunting and groaning stage of the cave dweller. Everything we have discussed thus far becomes meaningless without words. By stringing words together, we have a language with which to examine our inner and outer worlds. Think of words as stepping-stones by which we move nearer or further apart. In any line of work, words can act as either walls or bridges.

Actually, you have two vocabularies. One is thrown into gear when you speak; the other, when you read or write. It is entirely possible that you may recognize and understand the meaning of a written word and never use it when you speak. Perhaps you know someone who can comfortably read the most pornographic novel but who becomes unnerved at having to say certain obscene words out loud.

Making the distinction between your written and spoken vocabularies could be important when you have to decide the best way to communicate with a patient, client, or customer. You may decide to telephone, write a letter, or see the person face to face. Whatever your decision, you will need words, and the more of them you know, the better. Your vocabulary should grow as you grow. Unfortunately, this seldom happens. Most people use the same worn-out words year after year. New words have a way of frightening them. Or, if they do learn a new word, they are reluctant to use it for fear that others will not know its meaning. The fear of being called a show-off also enters into the picture.

Learning and using new words requires courage, a new courage with every new word. A failure to muster such courage can stifle the growth and development of your language, which, in turn, can lessen your ability to communicate. Think of the endless number of job situations where someone asks, "What do you mean?" Clear explanations are crucial to understanding; understanding is the payload of effective communication.

Aside from something known as "commercial speech," which is lean, useful, and deals with objects rather than people, there is another assortment of words serving to unite all human beings. They include words like *love, security, friendship, patience, dignity, consideration, prestige, loyalty, kindness, faith, trust, appreciation, respect, devotion,* and *honor.* Used appropriately on any job, these words provide the glue necessary for the personal and collective growth of any organization. It is the stuff that makes togetherness possible. The tragedy is that not only are these words underused but also their meanings have likewise been robbed of their original impact. Words such as *expedience, opportunity, relevance, assertiveness, perseverance,* and *availability* have pushed them off to the side roads of our contemporary wordways. Not only are we seeing a new vocabulary growing up in the marketplace, we are also seeing a shift in the meanings of old and familiar words. This shift can best be seen by carefully listening to the vocabulary of the older versus the newer members

50

of the current labor force. Their words often paint two different pictures of existing work conditions.

Your vocabulary was not very specialized while you were growing up. It was not designed to meet a specific technological demand. Like that of millions of boys and girls, it was probably dominated by words related to play and study. Only when your thoughts turned toward a career and how you would spend the rest of your life did your vocabulary begin to change. If your interest drew you in the direction of psychology, words such as *ego, id, superego,* and *libido* began to creep into your everyday language. If business administration beckoned, words like *merchandising, production costs, discounts, cost/benefit analysis,* and *inventory* became more familiar. Each field seems to possess terminology that differentiates it from the others.

In time, what you should have discovered is that, in addition to learning field-related terminology, you have to maintain, expand, and continuously use words that will enable you to communicate with people in all fields. Your vocabulary, like a muscle, will waste away if you don't exercise it. Word power has proven itself to be an extremely valuable ally and therefore should be taken full advantage of whenever and wherever possible.

Style

When casting a film or play, directors and producers are very interested in a performer's style. The word *style* is not easily defined. One authority defines it this way: "Style signifies the manner in which a man (or woman) expresses himself, regardless of what he expresses, and is held to reveal his nature, quite apart from his actual thought—for thought has no style." Thus defined, it continues to require further clarification. Lord Chesterfield tried his hand at defining style when he referred to it as "the dress of thoughts."

Just as a good physician should dress the wound while searching for its cause, the same should be done with that human quality we refer to as style. Without understanding it, we are able to recognize some of its characteristics. Mario Pei described five styles of speaking. See which of them most closely resembles your own:

"Those individuals do not possess
any. . . ."   (stiff-pedantic-supererudite style)
"Those men haven't any. . . ."   (literary-prose-cultured style)
"Those men haven't got any. . . ."   (spoken-standard style)
"Those guys haven't got any. . . ."   (colloquial–lower-class style)
"Dem guys ain't got no. . . ."   (vulgar and slang style)

51

No expression of your inner self emerges more clearly than your "style." In this case, we are referring to your speech style. Wilson and Arnold in their *Public Speaking as a Liberal Art* sketch three styles of speech. Try to guess what kinds of people would use them:

1. The posterior portion of the mansion embraced a rude pergola under which a saucy damsel attired in a bathing costume retired.
2. The rear of the house supported a rickety arbor beneath which sat a beautiful girl in a bathing suit.
3. The back of the club propped a shaggy shade below which a hot bikinied babe laid.

There can be little doubt that people speak differently, and that the difference has an effect upon how we perceive them. Some people who are not bosses sound like bosses; some people who are bosses don't sound like bosses. Have you noticed how certain speaking styles render a person more believable than others? One study in particular had a very practical application with regard to the credibility of witnesses and jurors in a courtroom. It seems that the subtle differences in the way lawyers and witnesses speak can have a profound effect on the outcome of a criminal trial, according to William O'Barr, professor of anthropology at Duke University. He discovered that witnesses tend to be *more* believable to juries if they use a narrative style of speaking. Also, the speech characteristics of women tend to make heard testimony *less* believable to jurors.

To develop a speaking style that will cause people to react the way you want them to, you must first get a very clear picture of your present style. Many young actors and actresses, when they begin their professional careers, have an uneven and extremely awkward style of speaking. After a great deal of hard work and deep concentration, they often develop a new and exciting style. Your speaking style, unlike your fingerprints, can change. Unchanged, it can lock you into an employment slot from which you can never escape.

Voice

Although it's true that the voice coming from your mouth is "you," there are other factors to be considered. From an environmental standpoint, you tend to sound like those people around you. Your family, your teachers, the part of the country in which you were reared, and your neighbors all helped shape the way you speak. Voice experts Robert King and Eleanor DiMichael contend, "Speech is caught rather than taught; we learn to speak by interpersonal contact and imitation." Aside from our genetic makeup, we are influenced by the voices around us. Does your voice sound like anyone's at home? Are you mistaken for your mother, father, brother, or sister on the telephone? Most voices, it seems, are composites drawn from many external sources.

Your voice reflects your moods, thoughts, and behavior. It is continuously influenced by your physical and mental states. If you are "up," your voice is up; if you are "down," your voice is down. It is probably one of the most reliable indicators of your inner self.

Several things can affect the sound of your voice and, by so doing, influence the people with whom you speak. For example, there is the range of your pitch. Ordinarily, standard speech consists of raising and lowering the voice. A failure to do this may result in a monotone, which is both uninteresting and boring to most listeners. Then, there is the intensity of your voice, that is, its loudness or softness. Few things drive soft-spoken people up a wall more quickly than having to listen to a loudmouth. The reverse is also true. Loudmouths are annoyed by people who don't speak up. One is constantly saying, "Please, would you mind keeping your voice down?" and the other, "What's that you're saying? Speak up! Don't mumble."

A final consideration deals with the way you emphasize certain words and not others. Take the sentence "What do you mean?" Say it five times, and each time place the emphasis on a different word. See whether you can alter its meaning.

What do you mean?

What *do* you mean?

What do *you* mean?

What do you *mean*?

On a more personal level, try this:

I want a raise!

I *want* a raise!

I want *a* raise!

I want a *raise*!

However you may use your voice to send and shape a message, you are engaging in something called *metacommunication*. *Meta* (from the Greek, meaning "next to" or "along with") imples that there is a message being communicated in addition to the main message. Metacommunication is effected through varying your emphasis on certain words. When writing, it is done through punctuation. A teacher drove this point home when she wrote this unpunctuated sentence on the blackboard.

Woman without her man is nothing.

The men in her class punctuated it this way:

Woman, without her man, is nothing.

The women punctuated it differently:

Woman! Without her, man is nothing.

Obviously, by varying the emphasis placed on certain spoken words, or by altering the way they are punctuated, their meaning can be significantly changed.

PART TWO: WORDS AND SOUNDS ACROSS DISTANCES

Telecommunication

In the business world, thousands of people have jobs that depend almost entirely upon how they speak. In Part One, an emphasis was placed on how you speak at close range. Here, it will be on how you speak across distances through the use of telephones and telephone-answering machines.

Millions of dollars are spent and earned each year by people who have never seen one another. Their entire relationship is over the telephone and, on the basis of it, they form some rather definite impressions of the other party. These impressions have been further complicated by the telephone-answering machine, which, in a mechanical sense, has enabled them to clone themselves—that is, leave a mechanical representation of themselves at their home or office.

Humans are linked to one another in public and private endeavors through networks of communication. The evolution of the power of speech communication corresponds with the beginning of human history (approximately 500,000 B.C.). At that time, all information was stored in the human memory.

Information was transported by man on foot. Later, drum talk and smoke signals came into use. These inventions are the fundamental forms of telecommunication, i.e., communicating over distances.

From 500,000 B.C. up to the middle of the eighteenth century, change was rather slow. The period from A.D. 1750 to about A.D. 1900 introduced the telegraph, the wireless radio, and the telephone. At the beginning of the Space Age in 1970, telecommunication technologies took shape as full-service world communication networks. The result: we are now members of a world community in which telephones and their peripherals play a vital role.

54

The Telephone The telephone could easily be held responsible for the success or failure of any business. The cause, however, does not usually lie in the instrument but in the people using it.

Whereas business people throughout the world are quick to agree on the assets of the telephone, there are some serious drawbacks associated with its use. Answer the following questions truthfully and you may see the basis for the existence of these drawbacks:

1. Do you speak at a normal speed on the telephone?
2. Are the people with whom you speak repeatedly saying, "What? I'm sorry, I didn't catch what you said."
3. Do you have an accent?
4. Is the volume of your voice usually loud, medium, or soft?
5. Are you prone to use a great deal of field-related jargon?
6. Do you speak differently to members of the opposite sex?
7. How far from your mouth do you generally hold the receiver?
8. Do you gesture while speaking?
9. Are you polite?
10. Do you chew gum or food while speaking on the telephone?
11. Do you identify the person with whom you are speaking by name?
12. Does your voice convey any of your personality traits?

Based upon your answers, a trained communicologist (an expert in human communication) could accurately judge your telephone technique.

SPEECH SPEED The average speech speed is approximately 125 to 150 words per minute (WPM) and the average thought speed, about 500 to 600 WPM. This means that during an average face-to-face conversation, people have a great deal of time to take mental side trips while listening. Realizing this tendency, the experienced face-to-face conversationalist must pay a great deal of attention to facial expressions, body movements, and hand gestures. Such nonverbal feedback is, however, unavailable while talking on the telephone. Thus, telephone speech must rely almost entirely upon the quality and use of the voice.

DICTION Clear speech is essential to good telephone technique. Most people respond not to what they heard but rather to what they think they heard. Fuzzy speech on the telephone is definitely out. A misunderstood order to a nurse or a pharmacist over the phone could result in the loss of a life. Less dramatically, on the business front, a misunderstanding could result in the loss of a big order or an important client.

ACCENT Not all people with accents will admit that they have accents. "Who me? I have an accent?"

Because we are rapidly becoming a world community, global telecom-

55

munication is now an everyday occurrence. People from all nations *must* communicate with one another. Thus, in dealing with accents on the telephone, one must discover which words and/or phrases are causing the greatest difficulty and correct them.

VOICE VOLUME   Certain individuals always shout when they speak on the telephone. This is especially true when they talk over long distance. They seem to think either that the party on the other end is hard of hearing or that they must raise their voice in order for the sound to carry. Such people frequently deny that they speak in a loud voice.

Because the telephone normally amplifies the human voice, excessive volume becomes doubly objectionable. Those on the other end are forced to hold the receivers away from their ears and, as a result, are inclined to care less about what is being said.

Whereas excessively low voices can also be a source of annoyance, they are less likely to offend because of the telephone's sensitive electronic equipment.

JARGON   Field-specific speech or, as it is sometimes called, jargonese, must be used with discretion. In every business or profession there are people with varying degrees of experience. Unless you know the experience and expertise of those with whom you are speaking, jargon should be kept to a minimum. A newcomer to the theatrical field, for example, might not be familiar with such jargon as a *run-through* or *blocking*. The same would apply to someone new to the publishing field if terms like *galleys*, *page proofs*, and *folios* were bandied about.

Jargon is usually well tolerated within its field. When it is used outside of it, problems can arise. Take those who have spent some time in psychotherapy and, as a result, have incorporated such psychotherapeutic terms as *hostility, aggression, repression, projection, alienation,* and *sublimation* into their vocabulary. Too often, they use this jargon with people who are not in therapy and who fail to appreciate having their ignorance exploited.

Many people, while talking on the telephone, assume that anyone holding down a particular job should be familiar with the associated jargon. Such an assumption can be risky. An employee may pretend to understand the jargon and miss the point entirely. As a rule of thumb, when in doubt, leave the jargon out. If, however, the other person uses certain jargon with which you are familiar, feel free to do likewise if you think such language is appropriate to the situation.

In certain circles, men speak differently to women on the telephone from the way they do to other men. If a woman has a sexy voice, they may venture beyond the business nature of the call and make a man-to-woman solicitation. On the other hand, some women, upon hearing a man with a sexy voice, immediately turn on their feminine charm.

56

From a strictly business perspective, telephone communication should be non-sexist. Central to every conversation should be the best interest of the organization, not the individual.

MOUTH TO MOUTHPIECE Aside from speaking, some people do other things while on the phone (eat sandwiches, clean their fingernails, open mail, straighten their desks, etc.). As a result, the receiver strays from their mouths. Naturally, this makes their voices sound distant.

When they finally recapture the mouthpiece, their voices suddenly become very loud and jar a listener's eardrum. This can be extremely annoying to the other party and prompts a comment like, "Hey, what the heck are you doing there? It sounds like you're opening a can of sardines."

Good telephone technique demands that you maintain a two- to three-inch distance from the mouthpiece at all times. This will insure a consistent volume at the other end.

GESTURING Gesturing while you speak on the telephone helps turn a dull, dreary voice into a brighter, more vital one. Your timbre and inflection will reflect the interest you're expressing in your gesturing. Pretend that you're speaking to the other party in the flesh, not to a piece of plastic in your hand.

POLITENESS The art of telephone communication should include mentioning certain magical phrases. These include "thank you," "glad I could be of assistance," "if I can ever be of further help," "I like that idea," or "I just called to say 'congratulations.' " They show an interest in others and build goodwill.

People listen more attentively when you refer to them by name. Avoid trite and possibly offensive substitutes (e.g., sweetie, honey, darling, babe, ole buddy). People need to be recognized as separate and distinct individuals, not nameless members of a fictitious society made up of sweeties, honeys, and ole buddies. They have names—use them! Refrain from using a first name unless the person to whom you are speaking invites you to do it. Even if they use your first name, resist the temptation of using theirs unless they say, "Please call me Larry."

PERSONALITY Have people ever judged you on the basis of how you sound on the telephone? How accurate are they? Do you think you sound cheerful, cordial, interested, pleasant, and warmhearted? It might be worthwhile asking some of the people with whom you talk on the phone how you come across.

Developing what is referred to as a "personal tone" requires time, patience, and application. However, before you begin, you must find out how you sound to others on the phone at present. Buy yourself a tape recorder and begin practicing. You must get the sound and character of your voice clearly established in your head.

Telephone-Answering Machine Whereas the step from the telephone to the telephone-answering machine is a small one, its impact on business communication has been substantial. Telephone-answering machines have increased in number enormously since 1975. At that time, there were more than 1,850,000 in use. Current esimates put the figure at over six million in the United States. And, by the time you read this, there will be a great many more.

While machines have no difficulty talking to each other, many people do have difficulty talking to machines. There are some very mixed emotions when it comes to machines that talk (TAMs). Here are some of the more common reasons why people in business are either for or against the telephone-answering machine.

ARGUMENTS IN FAVOR OF THE TAM

1. It is more personal than a telephone-answering service; that is, the voice on the TAM is that of a principal member of the business being contacted.
2. There is no third party to confuse the message.
3. The caller is never kept on hold, as sometimes happens with live answering services.
4. Whereas many live answering services pick up on the fourth or fifth ring, the TAM can be pre-set to pick up on any desired number of rings.
5. It serves as a record of when and how often a client, customer, or patient called.
6. By giving the callee the exact message left by the caller, it is more efficient.
7. It is better than no answer at all.
8. It is more confidential than leaving a message with a secretary or an operator at an answering service.
9. Consistent politeness can be programmed into each message.
10. It can be used to screen incoming calls, enabling the callee to be selective with regard to callers.

ARGUMENTS IN OPPOSITION TO THE TAM

1. Immediate needs of the caller are not met. For example, specific questions cannot be answered.
2. A caller wishes to speak to a particular person and nobody else will do.
3. It is too impersonal.
4. The caller doesn't want a permanent record of his or her call kept by the receiver.

5. There is no way of knowing when the call will be returned.
6. The incidence of prank callers, wrong numbers, and sales pitches often proves an annoyance.
7. The caller cannot recheck the message that was left on the TAM.
8. The person making the call may be caught off guard by a TAM rather than a human receiver.
9. Technical difficulties render them valueless.
10. Callers are occasionally confused by unnecessarily complicated messages recorded on the TAM.

In present-day America, communication consciousness has become one of the top awarenesses of business management. One of the most valuable skills a young man or woman can bring into the business world is the ability to communicate well with others. Why, then, if communication is so important, are more businesses cutting down on it by using telephone-answering machines?

Have you ever tried to call a large corporation or a public service office after five o'clock in the afternoon? Chances are slim that you will reach anything but a recording telling you to call back during business hours. Most of them do, however, give emergency numbers in case you should have a gas leak in your stove or your telephone is out of service. The last stronghold for what used to be called "business hours" seems to exist almost exclusively among large corporations and public service offices.

Smaller businesses and people in business for themselves seem to be doing just the opposite. They are doing everything in their power to make themselves reachable twenty-four hours a day. All-night numbers are rapidly becoming more and more popular. Television commercials, at 3:00 A.M., urge people to run to their phones and place an order—operators are waiting.

Reachability has become a watchword in a great many businesses. Have you noticed how many people are wearing signaling devices on their belts and carrying beepers? Their purpose is to maintain a continuous and uninterrupted line of communication with their home office. Either they beep in or their office beeps them. The remark "I can't be reached" will soon be a thing of the past. The business working day will no longer end at the conventional 5:00 P.M. It will follow workers and executives into their homes and social lives.

This preoccupation with reachability is not without contradiction. According to a recent telephone company report, the percentage of people requesting that their home numbers be unlisted has grown markedly. The contradiction is clear. In matters of business, people want to be reachable (public telecommunication); in personal matters, they want to be unreachable (private telecommunication). If there is a deeper meaning associated with this contradiction, and this writer feels there is, it seems worthy of the social psychologist's attention.

MECHANIZATION   The TAM is but one example of a dehumanizing process. Look around you and notice how many people have jobs forcing them to behave like machines. Since many of them will be replaced by machines in the near future, it is a fair assumption that they are currently behaving like machines.

Surely you have heard someone from personnel pull an employee's card and say, "Here she is—here is Joan Smith." Rather than the person's saying, "Here it is; here is Joan Smith's card" or "a card with Joan Smith's name on it," the card is treated as though it were one and the same with the person of Joan Smith. Although the person pulling the card certainly knows that there is a difference between a card and a person, this distinction is not communicated in the language being spoken.

Millions of us exist as index and computer cards in current records held by local, state, and federal agencies. To the file clerk with the Internal Revenue Service (IRS), we are all computer cards, identifiable only by variously arranged holes. Just as all the world is a tooth to the person with a toothache, all the world is a computer card to the clerk with the IRS.

The telephone-answering machine, like the computer card, stands for something and that something is *you*. If you own a TAM, before leaving your office you must turn it on so that it can receive your calls. In a telecommunicational sense, you are leaving yourself behind to answer your phone. Once you are on the outside, you must call yourself to find out if you received any calls.

OPTIONS   A sober look at our highly industrialized society indicates that the by-products of the Space Age are already suffocating us. Telecommunication is one of these by-products, i.e., our ability to communicate across distances. We have two options: to accept or reject it. Each course of action has its price. If, in the interest of financial gain and increased productivity, we accept and fully implement those technological advances, we stand to forfeit a large measure of our humanity. If we reject them and in the process preserve our humanity, our standard of living, life-style, and potential for growth may suffer considerably.

The implications are staggering when one considers that there are currently 398 million telephones in the world and 155 million of them are in the United States. Consider the effect upon world commerce should each of these telephones be equipped with a telephone-answering device. Consider the effect upon global communication.

4
Figuring Out What to Do for a Living

There is no such thing as being in the wrong business or profession; there are only side roads and detours leading to the right one. How did you decide to go into the field for which you are now studying or the one in which you are currently employed? Can you pinpoint the individual or set of circumstances that launched you in that direction? Was it a well-thought-out decision, a whim, or an emotionally charged consequence of some outside influence (family, friend, teacher, etc.)?

Scores of people have jobs they can't stand. When you ask how they got into them or why they don't quit, they often shrug their shoulders and say, "What am I going to do? It's a living." If the mental and physical pressure of their jobs ended each day at quitting time, they would be more tolerable. The tragedy is that such pressures frequently spill over into their private lives. This is compounded by the hobby myth: if you are unhappy at work, you get yourself a hobby to compensate for it. According to clinical psychologist Scott Baum of New York City, this is not altogether true. He suggests that individuals who are happy with their jobs are more psychologically able to pursue hobbies than those who are not. He reasons that individuals who are unhappy with their jobs invest so much mental and physical energy coping with them that little energy remains with which to actively pursue a hobby. While there are some people who compensate for an unrewarding job by taking up a rewarding hobby, they do not represent the bulk of the working population.

A report to the secretary of the Department of Health, Education and Welfare has turned up an interesting set of findings. The subjects studied were asked, "What type of work would you try to get into if you could start all over again?" Seventy-five percent of the blue-collar workers said they would not voluntarily choose the same work they were doing, and 57 percent of the white-collar workers said they would not make the same choice again.

The bottom line seems to be that too many people end up working at jobs they don't like. This chapter will attempt to convince you that by engaging yourself in the pursuit of a sound career strategy, you can find a job that will enable you to communicate your way to success.

WHAT DO YOU WANT?

Most of the things people say they want out of life are symptoms of deeper desires. Simply saying you want a job in which you will be happy is not enough. That elusive state we call "happiness" comes in different forms and quantities. For you to find happiness in a career, you must be very clear on exactly what it is that will make such happiness possible. Thus, to answer the question "What do you want?" you must conduct a serious search of your own needs in the order of their importance. Then, compare each of these needs with the following elements.

Financial

"I don't particularly like the job, but the money is good." Have you ever found yourself saying this? It is important that you honestly admit where money stands on your list of priorities. Why? Because if financial growth is essential to your being happy, you had better not waste your time with jobs that cannot deliver what you need most—*money*! It is also necessary for you to understand that if this is your primary goal, compromises in other need areas will often be required.

People whose expressed purpose in life is to make money seem to communicate differently from those who value other things. In monitoring their waking hours, these money-oriented people spend the majority of their time talking about ways and means of making and managing money. Listen to yourself. Are you preoccupied with money? If you say yes, steer clear of jobs where you work with your hands. They rarely lead to a great deal of money. Investigate and pursue only those careers in which large amounts of money can be made.

Power

How necessary is it for you to exert an influence over others? Does your personality require that you be in a position of authority? If so, you must ask yourself, "What kinds of jobs will allow me to exert power over others? Do I feel more comfortable giving or taking orders?" Such careers as politics, medicine, education, theater, journalism, and advertising all permit a wide sphere of influence.

Job talk involves upward and downward communication. If your ego need is to influence others, the power in the marketplace operates from above downward, not from below upward. If the idea turns you off and you feel more comfortable in a structured situation where others make decisions and you carry them out, avoid jobs in which you will be expected to assume responsibility for others.

Independence

No matter what career you pursue, you will be expected to work either alone or as a member of a team. To some individuals, personal freedom on the job is essential. They cannot work comfortably and productively with others. Their personalities reject concepts that entail a group effort, team spirit, or committee life. They are "loners." Have you noticed how some physicians prefer working on a hospital staff, while others elect to go into private practice? This preference for independence also applies to lawyers, engineers, therapists, accountants, etc. Some like working with others, some like working alone.

If you are a loner, investigate jobs that feature independence, self-reliance, self-motivation, and personal judgment. If you are not a loner, shy away from jobs demanding such a personality trait. In each case, the communication is different. The element of risk alone is greater when working with others. Each time you express yourself verbally or non-verbally, you leave yourself open to criticism. While working alone is not without risk, it is considerably less risky than working with others.

Acceptance

The importance of being liked by the people with whom you work varies with both the job and the individual. A person's acceptance is fre-

63

quently based upon emotional rather than intellectual grounds. Employees have been known to like or dislike one another for reasons other than their credentials, experience, reputation, or special knowledge. Other human factors often enter into their judgment.

Few things are as frustrating and depressing as working with people who do not accept you. Rejection or acceptance could go beyond race, color, and creed. It could be based on a person's sense of humor, willingness to work, punctuality, politeness, dress, table manners in the cafeteria, or trustworthiness. Any one of these behaviors could determine whether a person will be accepted or rejected on a job.

To insure your being accepted and to guard against your being rejected, you must do some investigating. Let's say you want to become a buyer in the garment industry. If you do your homework, you will soon discover that most buyers dress well and reflect their sensitivity to trends in fashion. If you are not a good dresser or feel that clothes are unimportant, don't become a buyer and expect to be accepted by other buyers. By your attitude toward dress, you will stand out like a sore thumb.

Be aware that people in every field are linked to one another by a number of visible and invisible traits that they hold in common. And, should someone enter their ranks who does not share those traits, their acceptance will be highly unlikely. To find out what these field-related traits are, ask some people in the business. Then, ask yourself, "How well would I fit into this field? Would they accept me?"

Physical

For whatever psychological reasons, most of us fail to perceive our physical selves accurately. We either underplay our shortcomings or exaggerate our strengths. Every career makes its own physical demands. Characteristics such as size, strength, appearance, manual dexterity, endurance, speed of movement, ability to go without sleep for long periods, and keenness of the senses must each be carefully considered in relation to the career of your choice.

If you have poor manual dexterity, why would you strive to be a brain surgeon, draftsperson, or electrician? If you have an underdeveloped body and limited strength, why would you strive to be an astronaut, stonemason, or professional wrestler? Connected with every job, there are physical attributes that help or hinder its performance. During the tax season, accountants work long and hard hours, often pushing their endurance beyond that to which they are accustomed during the rest of the year. Salespersons selling on the road must have good digestive systems because of the need to eat in different restaurants all the time. Examples like these are plentiful, and because they could make the difference between succeeding or not succeeding on a job, overlooking them would be unwise. The odds favor your success as being in direct proportion to the extent to which your physical state is compatible with the career you choose.

Creativity

There is no such thing as a creative job or profession. Creativity exists in people who bring it with them to whatever they happen to be doing. A truly creative person can usually take the most boring and meaningless job and make it come to life. If you are a creative person, you must seek out a job in which your creativity will flourish, not be stifled. A word of caution. Beware of careers that, on the surface, give the illusion of being creative when in reality they are dreadfully bland and thoroughly unrewarding. The publishing philosophy of a newspaper or magazine, for instance, could easily thwart the creative efforts of an individual the moment he or she goes beyond what the company considers to be appropriate behavior.

Creative people experience and express things differently. As a result, they need to invest additional care and planning in their career strategy. In reverse, those who fancy themselves as creative, and who actually are not, will find themselves on dangerous ground when they worm their way into jobs requiring the creativity that they cannot deliver.

Security

The compulsive desire for security among the working class is now greater than ever before. Increasing numbers of young men and women are opting for careers in civil and federal service because they offer more security than jobs in the private sector. Large corporations, recognizing this felt need for security, are now offering security as one of their major means of attracting new blood into their ranks. Hence, if you cannot cope with uncertainty—the thought of having one job in May and another in June—it is crucial that you seek a career that provides you with security.

Status

Perhaps your need is to become someone important, of distinction, someone who will be looked to with respect. If you are mentally nodding yes to this statement, you had best pursue a job in which you can grow and develop, not be frozen into a position from which you cannot escape. If you are open-minded enough to admit that you want status and without it your chances of being happy are poor, you must immediately rule out those careers least capable of affording you an opportunity to acquire it. Instead, consider only those that can offer you a chance to acquire the kind of status you need.

Benefits

Unlike during the first half of this century, job benefits have now become big business. In an age of soaring inflation, the work force in this country has become educated to want more than job security. Regular salary increments, guaranteed paid vacations, profit sharing, extended medical coverage, shorter work week, stock options, and bonuses are considerations that monopolize union negotiations. If you think in these terms, selecting a career might be easier simply because you can quickly push to one side those occupations or professions that fail to offer such benefits.

Location

Would being away from home six months out of the year bother you? Or, is coming home every night and having supper with your family something you refuse to do without? Depending upon how you answer these questions, certain jobs should be approached with caution. Occasionally, the inexperienced or naïve individual will take a job thinking that it will involve no traveling, only to find later on that it does. Then there are those who anticipate that a job will include a great deal of traveling only to discover that it doesn't. In fields such as filmmaking, acting, national and international sales, certain branches of government service, advertising, and journalism, the probability of being away from home frequently is high. Jobs in which one works in a factory, store, or home office generally provide little or no traveling.

If your temperament dictates that you be with your family and friends all year around, that you have roots, avoid careers in which you will be obliged to move around a great deal. If staying put is one of your primary career needs, respect it and direct your vital energies toward an occupation that is location-stable.

While there is no guarantee that a career strategy that considers the needs you have just read will bring happiness, it should enable you to have a clearer understanding of what you want and what you don't want in a job.

ENVIRONMENTAL FACTORS

There is serious doubt whether any of us were born with job genes, genes that pre-destined us to become doctors, computer programmers, or

United States senators. While there are certain mental and physical traits that make some people more suitable to a job than others, the ultimate determination is more apt to be environmental rather than genetic. None of us came into this world with the ideas we now have about what to do with our lives. We must have gotten them from our families, friends, societal norms, and the things we read about in books. As adults, we must sort out the impressions these ideas made on us and come up with a responsible answer to the question: What am I going to do with my life? Unfortunately, there is no guarantee that we will make the "right" choice. If the study mentioned earlier has any validity, the majority of us will not make the right choice. Ideally, armed with the courage of our convictions, we will change jobs a couple of times on our way to the right choice.

Family Influence

In the past, it was customary for young men to follow in their father's footsteps when it came to a career. Today, many a father must turn to a stranger because his son refuses to take over a business or practice he has built. With the advent of women's liberation, many young women are now finding the prospect of keeping house and rearing children less rewarding than their grandmothers did. Fewer and fewer jobs are being labeled "for men only" or "for women only." There was a time, not very long ago, when only women went into the nursing profession and only men into medicine. Today, this is no longer true. Dividing lines based upon sex are rapidly being erased in many fields. Consequently, parents have had to revise their thinking in counseling their children about a career.

Despite changing times, parents continue to exercise a strong influence upon the job direction their children take. Using bed and board as instruments of persuasion, they insist that their sons and daughters pursue a particular course of study, or enter a particular line of work, until they are able to support themselves. Too often, such parents are self-serving. Whereas many of them are convinced that they are doing the right thing for their children, this may not be so. Sons and daughters, in opposition, argue that what they think and feel is best for them is usually ignored or treated as immature.

Then there are those parents who take their children's futures very seriously. They do their homework. They listen to what their children have to say, read between the lines whenever possible, and make every conceivable effort to help them discover whatever career will make them happy. These parents willingly share with their children the lessons life has taught them. And, unlike those parents described in the preceding paragraph, they maintain open rather than closed lines of communication with their children at all times.

Friends

Has your mother or father ever said, "Why can't you be like ——?"
Though this may sound like a question put to a teen-ager, it is often leveled
at grown men and women by their friends. Whether they mean it or not
isn't the issue. The point is that entirely too many people are unfairly being
compared with others. And it doesn't stop in school, where certain teachers
are notorious for comparing one student with another. It continues well into
adult life. Human nature often prompts us to take more than a casual
interest in what our friends are doing with their lives. They likewise take
a similar interest in ours. With a "grass always looks greener" philosophy
at our backs, friends often wonder whether they should have gone into each
other's line of work.

The degree to which your thoughts about a career are influenced by
friends will depend upon several factors: (1) how independent a person
you are; (2) the persuasiveness of your friends; (3) whether you have
already made up your mind about a specific career; and (4) the extent to
which you are committeed to pleasing others.

Peers can exert an enormous amount of pressure. Frequently, they
can easily overpower that of one's own family. Because of this, career
decisions based entirely upon the recommendations of friends must be
weighed carefully. Although two friends might imagine themselves having
the same attitudes, values, and beliefs, they are usually separate and distinct people who must be treated separately and distinctly when it comes
to deciding upon a career strategy. The hidden danger is that good friends
are prone to experience a sense of oneness, which, if not kept in perspective,
can fog up their individuality. A sound career decision must be kept an
entirely personal matter.

Society

None of us lives in a vacuum. In addition to family and friends, that
concoction of influence we call society does a great deal to shape our
lives. Founded on a mixture of race, color, and creed, it touches us in a
number of ways. Books, magazines, radio, television, records, films, and
newspapers continuously tell us what to think, who is good and who is bad,
where to live. how to spend our money, and what to study to become
successful. The impact upon our senses is enormous—more than we
realize.

Escaping one's heritage is no easy task. We seem to be locked into
bits and pieces of our past. For instance, certain members of our society
cling to the notion that the only road to success is to go into business for

yourself; working for someone else leads nowhere. Others feel that working for yourself creates more problems than it solves and therefore advocate working for someone else.

The immigrants who settled here brought with them values that they passed on to their sons and daughters. The result is that these young men and women are often caught between the old and the new values. If you are of Irish, Greek, Italian, Jewish, German, French, Chinese, Indian, Polish, Spanish, Arab, or African descent, what career should you pursue? Should the values of the society from which your parents came take precedence over those advanced in this society? Again, it is no easy task escaping the influence of one's heritage.

DEVELOPING A POSITIVE CAREER PHILOSOPHY

A philosophy is a way of looking at something. Here we are looking at a career strategy that will work for you. Toward this end, you must see yourself as a gatherer, sifter, synthesizer, and interpreter of information. Your success and happiness will depend upon your ability to do this. Negative thoughts yield negative results; positive thoughts yield positive results. Such negative statements as "that field is overcrowded already" or "I don't want to start from the bottom" immediately place you at a disadvantage. People who are not success-minded imagine all kinds of obstacles, barriers, and roadblocks in their paths. Success-minded people, although they are aware of obstacles to be overcome, are neither disturbed nor discouraged by them. Instead, they see open doors, available positions, receptive employers, opportunity, growth, and advancement all around them.

A positive career philsophy is not an empty phrase. It is a state of mind, a way of setting yourself in relation to a goal. Aside from being a great source of envy, successful people possess certain definitive attitudes toward time, competition, courage, flexibility, self-worth, self-pity, and human interaction. Compare your attitudes with theirs.

Time

Time must be viewed as a friend, not an enemy. If you are given twenty-four hours to complete a job and half of that time has already elapsed, think in terms of there being twelve hours left, rather than the fact that you have lost twelve hours. Concentrate your energies on the present, using the past and future as guidelines. Avoid the advice of people who dwell on what used to be or how things will be in the future. Their opinions generally lack an important quality—immediacy, a sense of the here and now.

Competition

Some people dread competition; others thrive on it. Competition is the bloodstream of business. Without it, growth is virtually impossible. The saying "a road without obstacles leads nowhere" applies to business as well as personal growth. Whether or not you are willing to admit that there is competition out there, it does exist, and in full force. Success, in every field, will demand that you deal with things as they are, not as you would like them to be. Competition is one of those things. Rather than avoiding it, take it to task full strength, and build on what you learn from each of your encounters.

Courage

The person who never made a mistake never made anything. Most of us are endowed with liberal amounts of courage, which ofttimes is seriously dampened by the growing-up process. Young men and women, if left to their own devices, would make many mistakes. It is the older generation, in an effort to spare them the pain and suffering of such mistakes, that advises them not to take chances. There are among the elders, however, those few voices that urge them to take chances, run risks, and, by so doing, learn those invaluable lessons that life teaches.

Successful people have the courage to pick up a phone, write a letter, get on a plane, or ask an awkward question in any situation that could directly or indirectly affect their careers. The more timid-minded would mumble, "What if I call and the position is filled—what if I write and they don't answer my letter—what if I get there and someone else was hired?" So what! The total loss is a coin for the telephone, a postage stamp, or a plane ticket. Not a very large investment when it involves a career that could affect the rest of your life.

Anytime you translate career thoughts into action, it will require courage, and courage involves risk, and risks are what successful people seem to be willing to take. Thus, a career philosophy that lacks courage is certain to invite failure.

Self-Worth

With due respect to such universal values as honesty, humility, and sincerity, never say anything about yourself that can be taken negatively. Your chances of having a successful career will be much greater if you avoid giving other people ammunition they can use against you. For some

70

peculiar reason, people have a keener eye for what is wrong than for what is right. Negatives appear to attract more attention than positives. For proof of this, consult your daily newspaper.

Promise that the next time you are on the verge of saying something negative about yourself, you will *stop, rethink the thought,* and either say something positive—or say nothing at all. It is bad enough that deficiencies in your self-worth are occasionally betrayed by your non-verbal communication. Why remove all doubt by admitting them?

Flexibility

A healthy career philosophy must possess the capacity to deal with having its course interrupted, altered, or terminated. Due to ill health, a financial setback, or adverse stock market trends, many people have had their careers dramatically upset or ruined. But, because they possessed psychological flexibility, they picked themselves up and started to build again. This would have been impossible had they lacked an ability to adapt to change.

How do you react to having your plans upset? Do you throw your hands in the air and forget about the whole thing or do you learn what you can from the experience and try again? Fits of depression, emotional outbursts, and crying jags are all symptoms of an inability to cope with adversity. You must make an effort to bend with a situation and make a critical analysis of its nature. Such an approach will usually help lead to an early solution.

Self-Pity

If you think you are the only one having a rough time, you may be guilty of self-pity. A heart-to-heart talk with someone who is in the same position can do you a world of good. You will soon discover that what you are going through is not unique. They are probably going through the same thing. Just becoming aware of the fact that what you are thinking and feeling is perfectly normal will do a great deal to reduce the wear and tear on your nerves.

Having a positive career philosophy does not mean you have to do everything alone. It calls for a willingness to share your thoughts and feelings. Sharing is a marvelous calming agent and an excellent tonic for the ego. Feeling sorry for yourself not only pulls you down, it pulls those around you down as well. Self-pity must be fought with all your might. Begin vowing that whenever someone asks you how you are, you will answer, "Great! I never felt better in my life." Let it be rumored that you are a positive thinker.

71

Interaction

People aren't mind readers. Unless you tell them what you're thinking, they will be forced to rely upon other, less dependable sources of information-gathering, such as assumption, presumption, intuition, inference, and implication. Placing people in this position is a bad habit to develop. Deliberately not interacting with someone when an interaction is called for quickly undermines most verbal exchanges. Professionals don't like to play guessing games when it comes to communication. They want to know where you stand on an issue. Naturally, this requires that you interact. Keeping your lines of communication open is a luxury you cannot afford to ignore if you want to develop a career strategy that will work.

PEOPLE YOU SHOULD CONTACT

A sound career strategy will require that you talk with three types of people: (1) those currently working in the field; (2) those retired from the field; and (3) those whose job it is to help others with their careers.

Those Currently Working in the Field

While opinions may vary within any group of people working in the same field, there are usually certain things upon which they can all agree. It is the nature of this area of agreement that you should attempt to discover. Instead of trying to get it over the telephone, try for a personal interview. If you are permitted to tape the interview, do it. This will enable you to play it back several times at your own convenience and will give you an opportunity to more fully absorb and digest what was said.

There are several things for which you should watch and listen during the interview. Notice the person's facial expression (happy or sad), manner of dress, interaction with others, and whether the surroundings are calm or uptight. Take in all the information you can. Be prepared to ask specific questions and hold out for satisfactory answers. Don't be afraid that you will ask a stupid question, because the only stupid question is the one that *isn't* asked. While the question might seem stupid to you, the person you are interviewing might regard it as very perceptive and relevant.

Another thing to remember is to speak with more than one person. The more the better. After communicating with several members of any business or profession, you will find yourself slowly drawing certain conclusions about the field and the people in it. Whether the conclusions you draw are accurate or not will have to wait until you acquire some firsthand experience.

Speaking with someone who is currently working in your field of interest will provide you with an emotional insight that you will not be able to get from a career advisor or vocational counselor. Let's say you were interested in becoming a dentist. A visit to a neighborhood dentist's office would provide you with some specific information: the odors and sounds to which dentists are exposed, the number of hours they put in, the types of people with whom they must deal, the pains and aches to which they are susceptible, and the kinds of equipment they must know how to operate. Although you could probably read about these things in a career folder, it is not the same as being there in person, experiencing a dental office with your own senses.

Those Retired from the Field

Retired people aren't afraid of being fired or bawled out for what they say. Consequently, they tend to be refreshingly open and frank in their opinions about the field from which they have retired. For this very reason, it is essential that you speak with some of its elder statesmen or stateswomen.

Retired people generally enjoy having an opportunity to advise those who will listen. This willingness, if you take advantage of it, could be invaluable.

In preparing to visit with retired people, do not go empty-handed— that is, without a set of well-thought-out questions to which you want answers. Because long experience has allowed them to see the larger picture, they may lump together things that you, because of little or no experience, are obliged to take one at a time. Remember, their past might well make up bits and pieces of your future.

A final warning. Be patient and let the retirees talk. Remind yourself, regularly, that the reason you are there is to learn from their experience and not to tell them of yours.

Those Whose Job It Is to Help Others

How much do you actually know about being a law enforcement officer, accountant, astronaut, attorney, full-charge bookkeeper, real estate broker, or electrical engineer? Probably much less than you think. Prejudging a career on the basis of what you think you know about it could be extremely costly. You could easily drift away or miss out on an interesting career because the information you have about it is incorrect or misleading.

73

Vocational guidance and employment counselors are paid to know what you don't know about the field in which you are interested. If they don't know something, they know where to look to find the answer. While they may not be able to tell you what it feels like to be a doctor, watchmaker, or stuntman, that is not their function. They adequately fulfill their professional responsibility to you by communicating whatever relevant information they have at their disposal. You, in turn, have the option of accepting or rejecting their suggestions on the basis of your personal needs.

Sensing a Career

Every business and profession, aside from consisting of people gathered together to perform a particular function, occupies physical space—office buildings, industrial parks, professional centers, etc. It is one thing to see a picture of a plant or complex in a brochure or pamphlet, but quite another to make an on-the-spot visit to one.

In the section where you were advised to talk with someone who was currently in your field of interest, a dental practice was described. Here, we shall go further into sensing a career.

Words are poor substitutes for the information you get from your senses of seeing, hearing, tasting, touching, and smelling. Try describing, in words, the characteristic smell one usually finds in a hospital, lumberyard, slaughterhouse, plastics factory, or pig farm. No description in a career booklet could ever hope to compare with the actual experience of being there. You would be unwise to assume that you could handle any one of these sense experiences without checking it out beforehand.

Should you be unable to arrange getting inside a place to "sense" people at work, there is an alternative. You would be amazed at how much you can find out about what goes on inside a company building by observing it from the outside. Such things as its architecture, location, size, and the kinds of people going in and out all serve as non-verbal clues to the quality of life within.

Are the faces of the people entering and leaving the building sad, angry, bored, or blank? Is there much talking going on between them or are they walking in silence? Does the way they are dressed suggest personal pride or that they don't give a damn? If you can overhear what they are saying, are their conversations job-oriented?

Sensing the career in which you are interested is important. Don't be guided completely by what you read or what others tell you. Make it your business to visit places where your intended career can be observed in progress, where people are actively engaged in the work you may one day be doing.

DO YOU HAVE ANY EXPERIENCE?

Whether your intentions are to go into an entirely new field or switch careers, count on people being interested in your experience. The single biggest obstacle the newcomer to a field has to overcome is a lack of experience. Successfully graduated and armed with classroom knowledge, the average job-hunter is almost invariably shot down when asked, "Do you have any experience?" How can a person who has just graduated have any experience? The irony of it is that without experience, they won't give you the job, and without the job, you cannot get any experience. Unless, of course, someone is willing to hire you on the basis of your other qualifications.

There is no such thing as not having *any* experience. To be alive is to have experience. While you may not have the exact kind of experience a job calls for, you *do* have experience. You will recall that this book is based upon the premise that organizations and professions do not exist in any real or material sense—only as people communicating with people having common interests and goals. Consequently, any experience you have dealing with people provides you with a basis for dealing with them in the future.

An effective career strategy must stress *potential*—an individual's ability to learn and grow. Large corporations send out their scouts every year in search of young men and women with potential. In some cases, they will prefer someone without experience to someone with it. Their reasoning is that they can train the person in any way they wish and will not have to combat the way they did things on prior jobs. Thinking this way, you might consider not having any past experience an asset rather than a liability. At every possible opportunity, emphasize your potential, that you are a clear thinker and able to pick up new ideas, methods, and practices quickly. In short, substitute your potential for your lack of experience.

5

Surviving an Interview by Reducing the Element of Surprise

Why do most people dread being interviewed? Is it because they are afraid they will be asked questions they cannot answer, be made to appear ignorant, be rejected, or be compared with others? These possibilities exist in practically every interview. Perhaps being asked personal questions by a perfect stranger permits an intrusion into psychological areas you would prefer to have remain private. The damage is not usually done by such innocent questions as "Where did you work last?" "In what branch of the service were you?" or "Who was the supervisor on your last job?" It is done by questions that expose the deeper elements of your character, such as your attitude toward God, family, sex, and marriage. Then, should you not get the job, you have left someone you have never met before with all that personal information about yourself. Is it any wonder so many people are intimidated by interviews, especially if they want and need a job badly?

A fear of the unknown takes a tremendous toll on the nervous system of anyone being interviewed. Even though the person knows what the interview will cover, it continues to rate number one as an anxiety-producing experience. Recognizing the threat most interviews pose, this chapter will seek to reduce the unknown, minimize the anxiety, and, by so doing, increase your chances of surviving those interviews that lie ahead.

INTERVIEW PHOBIA

Just as claustrophobia is a morbid fear of being closed in, interview phobia is a morbid fear of being interviewed. With the exception of those who are very secure in their jobs or who have an extremely high degree of self-confidence, the majority of perfectly normal people are frightened of being interviewed for those reasons mentioned earlier. Listed below are some of the more commonly expressed fears. Read them and place a circle around the number that most accurately reflects the extent to which your own level of fear or apprehension is represented.

```
 1. I won't get the job.
    0   1   2   3   4   5
 2. I will be embarrassed or humiliated.
    0   1   2   3   4   5
 3. I will be asked questions I cannot answer.
    0   1   2   3   4   5
 4. The interviewer won't like my type of person.
    0   1   2   3   4   5
 5. I will be cross-examined.
    0   1   2   3   4   5
 6. I will say either too much or too little.
    0   1   2   3   4   5
 7. I will be very nervous.
    0   1   2   3   4   5
 8. I will be caught in a lie on my résumé.
    0   1   2   3   4   5
 9. I will forget what I had planned to say.
    0   1   2   3   4   5
10. I will make a bad impression.
    0   1   2   3   4   5
11. I will have to take some kind of practical test
    and, because of my nervousness, will fail it.
    0   1   2   3   4   5
12. I will have to compete with people who are better
    qualified.
    0   1   2   3   4   5
13. I will be kept waiting for a long time and
    chicken out.
    0   1   2   3   4   5
14. The interview will be held in a place where other
    people can overhear what I say and see how I act.
    0   1   2   3   4   5
```

15. The interviewer will see through me.
    0 1 2 3 4 5
16. I will be dressed inappropriately.
    0 1 2 3 4 5
17. The job will turn out to be different from the
    one for which I applied.
    0 1 2 3 4 5
18. I will be asked very personal questions.
    0 1 2 3 4 5
19. The job will pay too little.
    0 1 2 3 4 5
20. I will under- or oversell myself.
    0 1 2 3 4 5

Score yourself by adding up the numbers you have circled. The total will represent your Interview-Phobia Index. 80-100: Terrified; 60-79: Very Frightened; 40-59: Apprehensive; 20-39; Casual; 0-19: Unconcerned.

If you are psychologically ready to learn from yourself, how you scored on this quiz can be useful. Your response to each question could act as a clue to your thoughts and feelings about being questioned across a desk. For instance, if you scored Terrified or Unconcerned, don't throw up your hands in despair. Contrary to what you might think, being unconcerned about an interview is almost as bad as being terrified. A realistic attitude is one of due concern and reasonable preoccupation. People who dismiss a forthcoming interview with "It's nothing—a breeze, I'll do it standing on one foot" are behaving unrealistically and often fail to prepare appropriately. The other extreme in attitude is equally dangerous—"I'll never get through it. I just know I'll blow the whole thing."

Being terrified or being unconcerned both have a tendency to alienate you from reality and, in its place, substitute a distorted reality. Each reaction seriously reduces the possibility of your surviving an interview.

Allowing for individual variations in personality, most people are inclined to score Very Frightened, Apprehensive, or Casual on this quiz. Feeling threatened, however, may not necessarily show up in a person's external behavior. Some people have a tremendous capacity to come apart inside and look as cool as a cucumber on the outside. Unfortunately, few of us can do this convincingly. How we feel inside is often betrayed by the look in our eyes, how we sit or stand, our facial expressions and gestures. Only the most experienced interviewee can control or disguise these non-verbal displays.

Interview phobia can be cured. Its successful treatment depends upon

78

how much of the unknown can be eliminated from the interviewee's mind. If the unknown produces fear and anxiety, replacing it with knowledge and insight should generate the courage and self-confidence necessary for a complete recovery.

THE BIG MYTH

A widespread myth that has long circulated in the marketplace is that the best-qualified person gets the job. This simply is not always true. People are hired for a variety of reasons, and only *one* of those reasons is competency. Newcomers by the dozen enter interviews thoroughly convinced that the most qualified person will be hired. Failing to be hired, they come away with the erroneous impression that they weren't qualified. Nonsense! Their fractured logic tells them that if they were the best qualified, they should have gotten the job. Such needless psychological pain could be easily avoided if they would accept the fact that people are frequently hired for reasons having precious little to do with their competency.

In organizations, people hire people. It is impossible to hire "a skill." If a particular skill is needed to perform a particular task, a living, breathing human being possessing such a skill must be hired. People and their skills are inseparable. While it may seem childish to make so much of this point, it is not without purpose. According to Dr. Nathan Azrin, founder of Carbondale's Center for Human Development, "Employers make hiring choices on a skill-irrelevant basis." This does not mean that they ignore skills entirely. It means that in most instances they are more interested in the man or woman possessing the skill than in the skill itself. Naturally, this does not apply in those cases where a machine can perform the skill in question. The majority of employers, when interviewing, appear strongly influenced by such human factors as character, reliability, motivation, honesty, intelligence, politeness, creativity, appearance, etc. A serious deficiency in any one of these traits could easily eliminate an applicant with a high skill index.

Those who subscribe to the myth that they can walk into any interview and rely exclusively upon their skills are inviting disappointment. Preparing for any interview must include, in addition to any required skill proficiency, an awareness of the human factors for which most perceptive employers are on the lookout.

PROFILE OF AN INTERVIEW

Robert Goyer, an authority on interviewing, sees it as "a form of communication involving two parties, at least one of whom has a preconceived and serious purpose, and both of whom speak and listen from time to

79

time." A more colorful description depicts the participants of an interview as "corporate actors" programmed to mouth certain words according to some organizational script drafted by a giant computer. But, no matter how it is defined, it boils down to a pair of people exchanging information.

The participants of any interview invariably come to it with a headful of opinions. These opinions act as sounding boards and springboards from which information is bounced back and forth during the interview.

A psychologist once suggested that in most dialogues people are actually talking to themselves. An interview is no exception. While many individuals attempt to create the illusion that they are speaking and listening to another party, this is often untrue. While questioning others about their personal habits, they are indirectly advancing their own views on the subject. An example would be the question "You don't smoke, do you?" Our biases and prejudices are frequently revealed by the questions we ask others. Interviews may be filled with such disclosures.

Surviving an interview takes more than an open mind, honesty, and an ability to tell the difference between right and wrong. Though these qualities are certainly worthwhile, they need to be coupled with an ability to shift psychological gears quickly under any circumstance that might arise. With each subsequent interview, one learns how to cope a little better with the unexpected. Surprise tactics soon become relegated to the familiar, and getting caught off guard, a less frequent experience.

Questions are the heartbeat of an interview. Without them, an interview cannot exist. In this society, we have been conditioned to believe that answers are more important than questions. At school, heaven help the student who didn't know the answer to a question. Class after class confirmed the hysterical need to know answers. Students who asked questions were rarely rewarded. In fact, some of them were looked upon by their teachers as classroom pests. Perhaps this is why we have become an answer-oriented society. To get through school we must take examinations requiring answers; to become licensed by the city, state, or federal government—more examinations requiring answers. The list of situations that require answers is endless.

A serious consequence of this preoccupation with answers is that the art of asking a good question has never been adequately developed. Even worse is the fear many people have of asking questions. Although the majority of interviewers conclude with "do you have any questions?" it is the rare interviewee who asks any questions. Somehow, they have gotten the cockeyed notion that questions grow out of ignorance, misunderstanding, and inattention. In the back of their minds, they recall the classroom situation in which, after delivering a lecture, the teacher asked, "Are there any questions?" Those students who had questions were often accused of either not paying attention or having missed the teacher's point entirely. Very quickly, students learned to withhold their questions and, by so doing, became part of a conspiracy of silence.

To give you some idea of how this conspiracy of silence has carried over into adulthood, here is what happened to a young woman who went on a job interview with her friend. Mary had a two o'clock interview at a downtown law firm. A little nervous, she asked her friend Vanessa to go with her, and while she was upstairs being interviewed, Vanessa would wait in the corner coffee shop. After almost an hour, Mary came down from the interview. "Well, how did it go, Mary?" asked Vanessa. "Fine, it went just fine!" answered Mary. But Vanessa, being curious by nature, pressed Mary for more information about the job for which she had just been interviewed. Did you get the job? What was the salary? What kind of a job was it? Would it be a five- or a five-and-a-half-day week? How about vacations, benefits, and job security? Was it steady or part time? What happened to the person you would be replacing? Would you believe that Mary could not intelligently answer one of these questions? Whereas Mary's interviewer came away with a great deal of information about her, she came away with practically no information about the job for which she was interviewed. Why? Because she didn't ask any questions.

From where you are sitting, this story might sound a little extreme. You may not be willing to believe that anyone but a fool would walk away from an interview with so little information. Well, I regret to inform you that Mary's behavior is not that uncommon. It happens quite often with many young men and women who are inexperienced in the job market. They are very timid about asking questions.

Interviewers, by comparison, have no difficulty asking questions. Not only do they take pride in possessing a rich supply of questions but also they have the ability to launch them in a lively and interesting manner. Here are some of their favorite questions:

1. Tell me about yourself.
2. What are your strongest and weakest points?
3. What motivates you to put forth your greatest efforts?
4. Why did you leave your last position?
5. How do you determine or evaluate success?
6. What do you expect to be earning in five years?
7. What do you think you're worth?
8. How do you think one of your former teachers or a friend would describe you?

81

9. What are your short- and long-term goals?
10. What qualities do you think a good administrator, manager, or supervisor should possess?
11. If you were offered a choice between a raise in salary and a promotion, which would you choose? Why?
12. What subjects did you enjoy most at school? Why?
13. If you were hired for this job, what three things would concern you most?
14. What makes you think you would be happy in this job?
15. How do you think a person's worth should be judged? By whom?
16. How important is a sense of humor?
17. What positions of leadership have you held?

An interview is not a linear experience. Participants do not merely take turns speaking and listening—first one and then the other. From the standpoint of interpersonal communication, it is a circular experience. Information about the interviewer and the interviewee is constantly being exchanged. While one speaks, the other is communicating through such body language as head nodding, sitting postures, and facial expressions (see Chapter 2, "Advertising Yourself with Body Language").

Beyond being circular, an interview is also multidimensional. A number of things are going on at the same time. Verbal, non-verbal, and vocal signals are being transmitted and received in different combinations and at different levels of consciousness. In short, it would be a gross oversimplification to say that an interview is simply a situation in which people ask and answer questions.

A successful interview should be a synthesis—a blending of personalities in which there is a meaningful sharing of information and purpose. While either an interviewer or an interviewee may come away from an interview with a feeling of personal satisfaction, the truly successful interview should be one in which such a feeling is experienced equally by the two parties.

INTERVIEWS DIFFER

Just as people differ, so do interviews. Though most interviews have a number of things in common, their differences must not go unnoticed. They are usually designed to do three things: give information, get information, or solve problems. Another way of thinking of interviews is in terms of the response they are expected to elicit. When specific questions are asked and brief answers are given, the response is labeled as "limited." Where a greater amount of freedom is permitted and the nature and extent of any answer is left to the discretion of the interviewee, the response is "free." And finally, when the interviewer tries to maneuver the interviewee in such a way as to determine whether the individual can field a battery of questions under pressure, the response is called "defensive."

As with so many other situations, rarely does the communicative process occur in a pure state. Hence, with interviews, the majority are mixtures of these responses (limited, free, and defensive). A traditional interview, moving along in a neatly structured fashion, could be easily sidetracked by an unorthodox question or answer. The participants in any interview must therefore be able to adjust to a change immediately.

Similar adjustments must be made in accordance with the type of interview in use. As objectives differ, the means to achieve them must differ. Consequently, you will require a slightly different strategy in each of the following interviews.

Employment Interview

This is probably the best known and most widely used type of interview. At a specific time and place, an applicant meets with either an employer or an employer's representative. The objective of one is to get hired, and of the other, to hire the individual best suited for the position. The length of the interview will often depend upon the importance of the job; the more important the job, the longer the interview.

While an employment interview is far from perfect, it has the advantage of permitting both parties to observe one another at close range—in the flesh rather than through such impersonal items as a job prospectus, recommendation, résumé, photograph, or cover letter.

The kinds of questions used in this form of interview are usually rather direct. Successful interviewers using this method generally have a prearranged set of questions to which they adhere. Although they may depart from their format, if the situation calls for it, having definite guidelines to which they can return makes for a much more closely knit interview and a more wholesome exchange of information.

Regardless of how the employment interview is managed, there is always one overriding goal: to match up an individual with an organization to their mutual advantage.

Selection Interview

This one is also known as a recruiting interview. Although it has characteristics in common with the employment interview, it differs in that it seeks to select one individual from many. With the employment interview, it is possible to have only one applicant for a position, and a hiring decision may be based on that person's qualifications alone. With the selection interview, decisions are based upon the comparative qualifications of several people. This interview, therefore, has two purposes: (1) to select the person best qualified and (2) to motivate that person to accept the job.

Appraisal Interview

This interview is used to evaluate the progress of someone who is already on the job. It attempts to discover whether employees are fulfilling their potential, are being duly motivated, have the proper job attitude, or can be assigned greater responsibility. It also gives employees a chance to meet their superiors and discuss their performance. This procedure helps bring to the surface any disagreement that may exist between how employees evaluate their work and how their employers evaluate it.

Any growth-oriented organization must see to it that its employees get feedback from management as to how they are doing. If they are doing a good job, they must be made aware of it. If they aren't, they should be apprised of ways to improve. The appraisal interview makes such feedback possible.

Placement Interview

Unlike the employment interview, where a decision is made to hire or not to hire someone, the placement interview leads to a decision about where an individual should be placed in an organization. Positions are not always permanent. Employees are frequently moved around in a company, performing different jobs at different times. Instead of firing someone whose work is not up to certain company standards, management might elect to transfer that individual to another department or division.

Occasionally, an employee becomes handicapped because of an accident or illness. Rather than letting that person go, responsible management might search out another job within the company that the individual can do. A placement interview can serve this function.

Discipline Interview

The word *organization* implies rules. Some are written (company policy), others are unwritten (personal demands and expectations generated by those in charge). Employees not complying with such rules run the risk of being called in for a discipline interview. In it, they are told in a formal or informal way what they have done, why they shouldn't do it again, and what will happen to them if they do.

Not everyone can successfully conduct a discipline interview. It takes a

84

certain personality and a great deal of diplomacy. Those who conduct them seldom win popularity contests with their co-workers.

Board Interview

When an individual is interviewed by several people, it is termed a board interview. It is generally reserved for the hiring of people in upper-level management. In large corporations, where someone is being considered for a high-ranking position, the individual might be obliged to appear before a board of directors and be asked questions by its members.

After such an interview, where the board members have expressed positive interest in a candidate, they deliberate. Shortly thereafter, a decision is handed down concerning the fate of the candidate.

Group Interview

This type of interview is used when several individuals are being considered for a job. It is also known as the "oral performance test" and the "leaderless group discussion" technique. Seated in a circle, the candidates are given either a problem to solve or a subject to discuss. The person(s) who will make the hiring decision do not participate. They sit outside the circle. Competitors are judged on such qualities as initiative, flexibility, awareness, open-mindedness, politeness, sensitivity to group behavior, leadership, diplomacy, understandability, creativity, self-control, sense of humor, and assertiveness.

This type of interview has been proved quite successful by several large corporations. It takes less time and, overall, produces no unfavorable reactions. Another reason why it has found such widespread approval derives from the fact that it so closely resembles actual on-the-job situations: staff, departmental, committee, and divisional meetings or conferences. Any organization in which people in groups must arrive at a meeting of minds would benefit from the use of this kind of interview as a screening device.

Stress Interview

The function of the stress interview is to determine how well a person stands up under pressure. Some jobs, more than others, require nerves of steel. This type of interview was developed during World War II by the Office of Strategic Services to aid in the selection of candidates to be saboteurs, spies, propaganda experts, and resistance leaders. If they were caught by the enemy and interrogated for information, they had to be able to withstand tremendous mental strain. Closer to home is the stress interview conducted by a clever lawyer of someone on the witness stand in a court of law. Still another example can be seen in any local police precinct where a detective questions a suspected criminal. All of these interviews have one thing in common—stress.

A variation of the stress interview is the "chaotic interview." This is where an applicant is shuffled back and forth from one interviewer to another. Aside from the interviewee's being bombarded by one question after another, added stress is often contributed by environmental noise, telephone calls, and people walking in and out of the room.

Another variation is the "Freudian interview" in which a candidate's privacy is invaded by such questions as "Are you on the pill?" "What would you do if your employer made sexual advances?" or "Are you a homosexual?" Any one of these questions, even if the law prohibits it from being asked, could easily unnerve a susceptible applicant for a position to which he or she was not suited.

Exit Interview

No company wants to have its good name or reputation marred by a former employee wanting revenge for being fired. The company would prefer to have such an individual leave with fond, rather than foul, memories. The exit interview is designed to accomplish this end. The person being dismissed is called in by a superior and told why his services are no longer required and, if he wishes to do so, is given an opportunity to defend himself. Thus, an exit interview makes it possible for an employee and the company to part friends—with no hard feelings or grudges.

New employers often exhibit a keen interest in the circumstances under which a prior job was left. Letters of recommendation could be heavily influenced by the outcome of an exit interview. If angry words were exchanged, the letter could take on a negative tone. If the words were civilized and pleasant, a positive letter of recommendation could be the result.

A company stands to gain a great deal from conducting exit interviews. Employees who are leaving have been known to speak openly and frankly about the company and its employees. This provides management with an unthreatened opinion of the job and its duties from the perspective of an incumbent. It may also spark some new ideas for improving the job being vacated.

What the exit interview does is act as a bridge between past and future sources of employment and, as a result, alerts both employers and employees of how to best deal with the present.

Let's Discuss It over Lunch

What could be better than combining business with pleasure? Practically anything can be discussed over coffee, gin and tonic, scotch and soda, or a business lunch. Since the invention of expense accounts and credit cards, discussing business over lunch has in itself become "big business." A surprising number of executives build their business day around luncheon engagements.

As with the board interview, interviews over lunch generally involve upper-level management positions. Rarely will an interview for a file clerk or stock boy be conducted off the premises. An occasional exception will be made when the individual being interviewed will be working very closely with an administrator, manager, or supervisor.

What could be accomplished over a luncheon interview that could not be accomplished at the office? The answer is informality. After a drink and a good meal, a feeling of relaxation prompts most people to speak more freely. While this is pleasant indeed, it can be extremely tricky if one is not careful. An interviewee is inclined to be much more guarded in the formal setting of an office than in the comfortable surroundings of a well-appointed restaurant. Take the simple act of salting your food before tasting it. One corporation executive interprets salting food before tasting it as a sign of impetuousness. Not waiting to see whether one's food needs salt could suggest that such an individual makes hasty decisions. Although anyone who makes a decision about another person on the basis of whether food is salted before or after it has been tasted is equally impetuous, it is an example of the kind of judgment certain employers are prone to make from time to time. We all have pet quirks. Why should any employer be exempt from such a human frailty?

If you have already experienced a luncheon interview, you have some idea as to what it is like. For those of you who haven't had the experience, here is a list of things *not to do.*

1. Speak with your mouth full.
2. Be late.
3. Spread papers on the table.
4. Look at your wristwatch frequently.
5. Talk loudly enough so that you can be overheard by the people around you.
6. Order a heavy meal when the other person is eating a light one.
7. Monopolize the conversation.
8. Let the food appear to be more important than the interview.
9. Use profanity.
10. Smoke without asking if the other person minds.
11. Complain about the food, the restaurant, or the service.
12. Jump from subject to subject.

13. Ask personal questions.
14. Have more than one drink (two, only if you can definitely handle them).
15. Be intellectually dishonest.
16. Hoard the food.
17. Make noise when you eat.
18. Overdress in order to attract attention.
19. Be a know-it-all.
20. Be argumentative.

Here, now, is a list of things you *should do*.

1. Call, if you are going to be late.
2. Leave the interviewing to the interviewer.
3. Maintain good eye contact when the other person is talking.
4. Ask your host for a suggestion from the menu.
5. If you arrive first, alert the headwaiter or hostess that you are expecting to meet someone and give your name.
6. Let whatever your host orders be an indication of what you should order.
7. Look at the waiter when you order.
8. Maintain a pleasant look on your face.
9. Dress appropriately. Conservatism is the wisest choice.
10. Present an optimistic view of life.
11. Make the other person feel as though he or she were the only person in the room.
12. Speak clearly and distinctly.
13. When it is time to leave, don't linger. Leave promptly.
14. Graciously thank your host for the luncheon.
15. Be sure you leave your telephone number and address.
16. Use your host's name occasionally during the meal: "Yes, Mr. Jones, I agree with you completely on that point." Use an individual's first name only if invited to do so.
17. Show signs that you are listening by periodically restating what your interviewer has said—for example, "I think your idea of putting part-time workers into the pension plan is excellent."

Cross-Cultural Interview

As recently as 1940, the chances of your being interviewed by a non-white person were extremely slim. Today, that is no longer the case. People of African, Oriental, Latin, Indian, and Asian extraction have moved into middle- and upper-management positions throughout the United States.

As a result, we find ourselves in a position of having to communicate with people from different cultural backgrounds. America has the reputation of being a melting pot, a nation to which people from all parts of the world have immigrated. Millions who were born into other cultures now boast citizenship papers and proudly declare themselves Americans. Where foreigners once crowded the lowest rung of the working ladder, they now have begun to climb up that ladder.

Because people are able to get around so much more easily, the planet on which we live seems to be getting smaller and smaller. No longer are individuals born and reared in one culture destined to remain in it for the rest of their lives. Many have made the break successfully. But they have not done it without retaining certain cultural imprints made on them during their formative years. How many of the attitudes, values, and beliefs indigenous to their native culture still remain with them? Such a question strikes at the very heart of the cross-cultural interview.

Take something as basic as eye contact. Men and women who grew up in Latin cultures were taught that it is impolite, even rude, to engage someone in authority or of a higher status in direct eye contact. In the United States this does not seem to apply. People who avoid eye contact during an interview are often considered to suffer from low self-esteem, lack of self-confidence, and a deficiency in assertiveness. This is but one of the many culturally determined traits that might surface in an interview, particularly one in which those participating are culturally different. According to Glazer and Moynihan in their book *Beyond the Melting Pot*, "Ethnic groups beyond the second generation have retained many of the traits which their forbears brought with them from other cultures." Anthropologist Edward Hall adds additional force to this notion when he writes, "Superficially, these groups may look alike and sound alike but beneath the surface there lie manifold unstated, unformulated differences in the structuring of time, space, materials, and relationships." To appreciate some of these culture-specific traits, let us look at a few.

The Latin culture displays a slightly different attitude toward punctuality from that of the American. In Latin America, expect to spend hours waiting in outer offices. A forty-five-minute wait is not unusual—no more unusual than a five-minute wait would be in the United States. In the United States, a consistently late person would be labeled as undependable—but not by Latin American standards.

To the Latin, an acceptable interpersonal distance (from nose to nose in conversation) is less than to an American. While the Latin considers a distance of 12"–18" perfectly natural, Americans consider it a sign of pushiness. To the American, a more appropriate distance in conversation

89

would be about 18″–24″ from nose to nose; to the Latin, it would be considered a distance suggesting coldness and unfriendliness.

The Arab culture reveals still another conception of time. For example, mentioning a "deadline" to an Arab is like waving a red flag before a bull. In his culture, stressing a deadline has the same emotional effect on him that his backing you into a corner with a raised club would have on you.

Arabs also have a slightly different way of exerting pressure in order to get results. The usual way is one Americans would consider terribly bad manners. It is needling. If you haven't been needled by an Arab, you haven't been needled. An Arab businessman whose car broke down will give you some idea of what I mean by needling. Here is his explanation of what happened:

First, I go to the garage and tell the mechanic what is wrong with my car. I wouldn't want to give him the idea that I didn't know. After that, I leave the car and walk around the block. When I come back to the garage, I ask him if he has started to work yet. On my way home from lunch, I stop in and ask him how things are going. When I go back to the office, I stop by again. In the evening, I return and peer over his shoulder for a while. If I didn't keep this up, he'd be off working on someone else's car.

If this cultural practice were applied by an American businessman in an interview situation, he would seriously reduce his chances of getting the job. While assertiveness and perseverance are commendable traits in the American culture, the nature and extent of their application seem to vary considerably from those of the Arab culture.

There is also the matter of smell. In the United States, only the refreshing smell of a lively mouthwash is acceptable, and then only among intimates. In the Arab society, people often converse closely enough to smell one another's breath and body odor. They employ slight differences in odor to learn something about the emotions and personality of even casual acquaintances. Such face-to-face closeness would be considered downright vulgar in the United States and interpreted as a display of poor manners and bad upbringing.

The Arab culture endorses something else that Americans would regard as negative. Americans are largely a "hands off" culture in which physical contact is a clear sign of intimacy, except in certain stylized expressions of friendship (hugging and kissing associated with saying hello and good-bye, etc.). For Arabs, touching colleagues or even strangers in the street is perfectly permissible. Consequently, an Arab interviewee who proceeded to freely touch an American interviewer might not be hired and never know why. The American interviewer, by being unfamiliar with this culture-linked touching practice, would be inclined to consider it presumptuous and perhaps rude. This is but one example of a cross-cultural misunderstanding.

The Japanese culture has a different attitude toward time from the American. Americans are extremely impatient and the Japanese know it. The head of one Japanese firm commented: "You Americans have a terrible weakness. We Japanese know about it and exploit it every chance we get. You are impatient. We have learned that if we just make you wait long enough, you'll agree to anything."

In the United States, an individual would never go to see about a job with a group or into an interview with one or two other people. Unless otherwise stipulated, most interviews involve only the candidate and the interviewer. This does not apply in Japan. There, the importance of the occasion, and of the man, is measured by whom he takes along. Two young Japanese once asked an older American, widely respected in Tokyo, to accompany them so that they could "stand on his face." He was not expected to enter into the negotiations; his function was simply to be present as an indication of their serious intentions. Whereas Americans would not think twice about doing some name-dropping, they would not take the liberty of bringing uninvited people to an interview so that they could "stand on their faces."

Every culture has its own behavioral norms. You have just read about a few that are common to Americans, Latins, Arabs, and Japanese. There are a great many others with which members of the business and professional community must become familiar if they are to engage in productive interpersonal communication. This need is not five, ten, or fifteen years away. It exists—right now! In large cities throughout the world, cultures are already clashing and giving rise to serious problems in communication. Only by recognizing that they exist can we ever hope to effect a remedy. And what better place to begin than with the interview?

As if the omission of cross-cultural interviewing from most books were not enough, subcultural interviewing can be observed to receive even less attention. A subculture refers to a group of people who have found commonality among themselves. In slightly broader terms, subcultural communication is a process whereby one gains and maintains the ability to communicate effectively and meaningfully with a group's members.

Senior citizens, homosexuals, ex-mental patients, ex-offenders, the handicapped, alcoholics, prostitutes, and vegetarians are all examples of subcultures. Each group has its own specific problems, which are seldom known outside the group. For example, not only are the average interviewers ignorant of the ex-offender's or ex-mental patient's needs and frustrations, they make little or no effort to become aware of them.

It has been reported that people on the street tend to avoid making direct eye contact with those who are handicapped. This same avoidance behavior applies to others outside the mainstream of society. Imagine your own reaction if, during an interview, the person you were interviewing confessed to being a homosexual, an epileptic, an ex-mental patient, an ex-addict, an ex-alcoholic, or a transsexual. Do you think you would be able to continue along the same line of questioning? You may think you would remain objective and unmoved by such a confession, but that is highly unlikely. Your difficulty in dealing with such people would probably arise not from your ignorance of their predicament but from the many misconceptions you have about it.

Both the interviewer and the person being interviewed must be prepared to cope with the widest possible number of circumstances. Surprises must be reduced to a minimum. To help achieve this end, certain things must be taken into consideration.

REMINDERS TO THE INTERVIEWER

1. Make every effort to prevent the interviewee from leaving the interview with partially or completely unanswered questions. At some point near the end of the interview, ask, "Do you have any questions, or is there something about which you are still not clear?"
2. Avoid value judgments.
3. Don't become emotional.
4. Ask one question at a time and patiently await an answer.
5. Make no promises that cannot be kept.
6. Let your appearance set a visual example for the interviewee.
7. Don't bad-mouth another organization.
8. If interruptions get out of hand, instruct the secretary, in front of the interviewee, that you don't wish to be disturbed for the remainder of the interview.
9. Choose the best possible location for this interview.
10. Carefully review the applicant's file.
11. Allow enough time for the interview.
12. Be sure to be in a proper frame of mind to conduct a good interview.
13. Remember to listen more and talk less, since the primary purpose of the interview is to get information.
14. Make certain that this interviewee is being interviewed for the position he or she applied for.
15. Remember it's easiest to get more information about the interviewee with open-ended questions than with direct ones.

REMINDERS TO THE INTERVIEWEE

1. Be confident—look as though you already have the position.
2. As quickly as possible, look around the interviewer's office for clues to his or her personality and interests (e.g., pictures, trophies, books, furniture, decor, desk size).
3. Stay on the subject. It reflects a disciplined mind.
4. Avoid answering questions with a simple yes or no. Elaborate whenever possible.
5. Try to be yourself at all times.
6. Without staring, maintain good eye contact.
7. Be unafraid to ask relevant questions.
8. Listen carefully for clues to what the interviewer is really after.
9. If you fail to get the position. Do not feel personally rejected. Bear in mind that there may be other factors involved here.
10. Make every effort to prevent the interviewer from rattling your nerves.
11. Without going to an extreme, match the interviewer's speech speed. If he speaks slowly, speak slowly; if he speaks rapidly, speak rapidly.
12. Don't interrupt.
13. Be courteous at all times.
14. Permit the interviewer to determine when the interview is over.
15. When in doubt, dress conservatively.

A wise person once suggested that "chance favors the prepared mind." The reminders you have just read are intended to increase your level of preparedness and, by so doing, help you survive an interview. To help even further, here are some positive and negative verbal and non-verbal cues you might remember during your next interview.

POSITIVE VERBAL CUES

1. "That's very interesting. Please, tell me more about it."
2. "Yes, I see exactly what you mean."
3. "I would really appreciate that. Thank you."
4. "You are very kind."
5. "I never realized how important that was."
6. "You make it sound so simple."

POSITIVE NON-VERBAL CUES

1. Occasionally nod your head affirmatively.
2. Sit up straight in your chair.

3. Lean slightly forward from time to time to communicate interest.
4. Smile appropriately.
5. Sit with your hands and feet unfolded.

NEGATIVE VERBAL CUES

1. "That may be true, but I never heard of it."
2. "We did it differently on my last job."
3. "I'm terribly sorry, I didn't catch what you said."
4. "Is that really so important?"
5. "What has that got to do with the job?"

NEGATIVE NON-VERBAL CUES

1. Frowning
2. Drumming your fingers on the desk or tapping your foot.
3. Squirming around in your seat.
4. Playing with some object (briefcase, pencil or pen, clothing, etc.).
5. Checking your wristwatch periodically.
6. Looking out of the window while the other person is speaking.

Finding a Common Denominator

People prepare for an interview differently. Most of them find it extremely difficult because they are not quite sure what to expect. All they know, with any degree of certainty, is that they will be asked questions that they had better be able to answer. Beyond being questioned, they generally have only the vaguest idea of what to expect. Preparation, therefore, consists primarily of trying to second-guess the interviewer. And, since mind reading has yet to be proven in the scientific community, guessing is not much better than a crap shoot.

Finding a common denominator pertaining to any business or profession involves doing some calculated generalizing. Picture yourself in a hypothetical interview for a position with an accounting firm. What fairly responsible generalizations could you make about either the accounting field or accountants as a group? You could reason this way:

1. Accounting demands precision when dealing with figures. Therefore, I will make it a point to include in my answers information that reflects my concern for exactitude.
2. Because organizations usually adhere to tight schedules and demanding timetables, I will invest my answers with information suggesting a well-established respect for deadlines.

94

3. Realizing that such qualities as honesty and ethics are essential to the accounting field, I will be sure to communicate that I possess such traits.

With a little patience, you could probably generalize about practically every field. Concentrate on what attitudes, values, and beliefs are essential to a particular business or profession; what special qualities, mental and physical, must people in that field possess in order to excel? For example, *show business*—talent and determination; *teaching*—an ability to communicate what one knows to students: *sales*—an ability to persuade others, self-confidence, and assertiveness.

While such generalizing will by no means guarantee sailing through an interview without a hitch, it will set your mind working in a given direction. Not only will it help create the proper psychological mood for an interview, it will also signal the interviewer that you are sensitive to the climate of interest surrounding a particular business or profession. In short, it is an attempt to zero in on your interviewer's wavelength.

6

Listen, Damn It!

I know that you believe you understand what you think I said, but I am not sure you realize that what you heard is not what I meant.

There is more to listening than meets the ear. This is the premise of Chapter 6. Reading it will not only give you a better understanding of why experts consider faulty listening to be the number one cause of breakdowns in communication on the job, but it will also add insight into the listening process. Taking the Listening Quiz with which the chapter opens will provide you with an opportunity to test your present grasp of the subject. The balance of this section will alert you to such aspects of listening as (1) the types of people who listen, (2) why people listen, (3) the different kinds of listening, (4) what it means to "pay attention," and (5) the nature of what might be termed a "listening philosophy."

Although most people would argue that we live in a speech-centered society, a small percentage would disagree. Norbert Wiener, the father of cybernetics, states, "Speech is a joint game between the talker and the listener against the forces of confusion," and while the physical barriers to communication have all but disappeared, the psychological barriers remain. It is with the inner self that most of us must grapple—especially on the job. Only after we are able to listen to ourselves can we ever hope to listen effectively to others. Perhaps we should strive to become a listening-centered society.

Neither this chapter nor any other words on a printed

page will ever make you a good listener. Only you
can do that. You must, however, be ready to listen.
Perhaps you are too busy talking to listen; perhaps
you have several more years of talking to do before
you reach the listening stage of your life. Some
people never reach this stage. They seem to talk
from the womb to the tomb. Take the following listening quiz to discover your own listening status.

LISTENING QUIZ

Instructions: Read each of the following statements
and, on the basis of your judgment, place the word
true or false in the appropriate spaces:

_____ 1. Listening is simply a matter of being
quiet and looking at whoever is speaking
to you.

_____ 2. More intelligent people listen better.

_____ 3. People cannot be taught how to improve
their listening ability.

_____ 4. The older you get, the better you are able
to listen.

_____ 5. Listening is just a matter of understanding language.

_____ 6. The average person does more talking
than listening.

_____ 7. When you learned to read, you learned to
listen at the same time.

_____ 8. Speaking is more important than listening
in the communication process.

_____ 9. It takes no effort to listen.

_____ 10. The better you hear, the better you
listen.

If you placed the word *false* next to all ten statements, you have
reached the listening stage of your life, and you should read this chapter
to learn what to do about it. If you marked some of the statements *true*
and the rest *false,* you have not quite reached your listening stage, but you
should read the chapter because you are not far from it. If you marked all
statements *true*, you are not ready for this chapter and should skip over it
for the present and return to it later.

Realizing that the statements in this quiz may have more than one
interpretation, perhaps a brief comment on each would be helpful.

Listening is simply a matter of being quiet and looking at the speaker.

Have you ever found yourself speaking to someone and felt that the person was not listening to a word you were saying? How can you tell whether someone is really listening to you? Apparently, being quiet and looking into your eyes is no guarantee. An occasional nod of the head, smile, and uh-huh can also be misleading. Determining whether someone is listening is even more difficult on the telephone. Without visual feedback, all you have to go on is the person's vocal activity—or lack of it. Long periods of silence are met with, "Hello, are you there? Are you listening?" Whether face to face or on the phone, of one thing you can be sure: listening is *not* simply a matter of being quiet or looking directly at a speaker.

More intelligent people listen better.

People listen for different reasons. Do you think intelligent people have better reasons for listening than those who are not so intelligent? Of course not. The problem word here is *better.* Just as it would be ridiculous to say that intelligent people have better hearing than less intelligent people, it is equally ridiculous to say that intelligent people have better reasons for listening than unintelligent people. What can be said, however, is that intelligent people, because they manipulate ideas a certain way, listen in a slightly different manner. But do not be misled. Listening differently does not mean listening better. More intelligent people *do not* listen better, only differently.

People cannot be taught to improve their listening ability.

Not true! Whether you are a good listener and think you aren't, or a poor listener and think you are, the bottom line is that you can become a better listener. In a special program, 1,400 Michigan State college freshmen were tested before and after a listening program. Poor to above-average listeners before training improved the most. Listening-trained students improved from 9 percent to 12 percent over non-listening-trained students. While there is some truth to the belief that certain people make better listeners than others without training, everyone stands to benefit from taking a responsible and well-thought-out listening program. Listening is more an art than a gift with which a person is born. Listening skills *can* be learned and, with practice, can be significantly improved.

The older you get, the better you can listen.

In addition to being an art, listening can be habit-forming. If you didn't develop the listening habit when you were young, chances are you will not automatically develop it when you are older. Like many other personality traits, listening habits tend to remain the same throughout a person's life. An exception to this generalization might be when someone has a setback in his mental or physical health. It is also possible, in special cases, for time to convince a person of the importance of good listening. But, given these exceptions to the rule, you would be wise to abandon the myth suggesting that listening improves with age, and begin cultivating it whenever you can. It is a talent that will last a lifetime.

Listening is just a matter of understanding language.

Do you think that knowing the alphabet will automatically make you a good speller? Or perhaps you believe that knowing a great many words will automatically make you a good writer or storyteller. The answer is no in both cases. As you were told at the beginning of this chapter, there is more to listening than meets the ear. Successful listening involves taking the words you hear, decoding them in your brain, and weaving them into meaningful units of negotiable thoughts. The meaning, therefore, is not in the language but in the people using the language.

The average person does more talking than listening.

Average adults, under average circumstances, spend approximately 7 percent of their time writing, 10 percent reading, 35 percent speaking, and 48 percent listening. And, since the advent of television, they spend even more of their time listening. To this we must add the listening demands made upon them by such media as radio, tapes, concerts, theater, and films. The only exception to these figures are those people whose occupations require that they "talk for a living" (teachers, auctioneers, actors, radio announcers, salespersons, etc.).

The net result is that, although it might appear that the average adult does more talking than listening, this is untrue. The listening that is done is clearly inferior in nature.

When you learned to read, you learned to listen at the same time.

Wrong again! Reading and listening are separate and distinct processes. They involve different areas of the brain. Although it was necessary for you to hear a supervisor or manager explain a specific word on an invoice, it taught you precious little about the art of listening. As you will soon discover, there is a great deal of difference between listening and hearing. For instance, there are those who are excellent readers but poor listeners. Why, when they learned to read, didn't they simultaneously learn to listen?

Speaking is more important than listening in the communication process.

From childhood, most of us remember being told how important it is to "speak up!" Then, in the same breath, we were reminded that "silence is golden." Knowing when to speak and when to be silent was no easy chore for even the cleverest child, much less an adult. In today's society, the ability to speak up continues to be regarded as a most desirable trait, one that is often envied. Consequently, a great deal of talking goes on with a disproportionately small number of listeners. So enormous is the need for listeners that professional listening services are beginning to crop up in the marketplace. You can now hire people to listen to you. Nevertheless, whether hired or not, for communication to have meaning and purpose, it requires feedback. Listening, as a major source of feedback, acts as the radar by which most speakers are guided. Without responsible listening, most speaking proceeds rather aimlessly.

It takes no effort to listen.

Anyone who has ever taken a course in chemistry, statistics, or Euclidian geometry knows that it is an effort to listen. This is especially true if the instructor is a poor speaker. It takes the patience of Job to listen when the instructor and the subject are equally boring. But, let us be generous and assume that you have the good fortune to hit upon both a good teacher and an interesting subject. Would it take less effort to listen? Yes, but without knowing *how* to listen, it would continue to be an effort. Good listening leads to understanding. Hence, one way of judging how well you listen might be to examine your understanding of the subject. While effortless listening will by no means guarantee understanding, it will certainly increase your desire for it.

The better you hear, the better you listen.

As suggested earlier, many people confuse hearing with listening. They are not the same thing. Hearing is the process by which sound from the environment is carried to the brain by the auditory mechanism; it is a physiological process. Listening is an emotional and intellectual process by which meaning is made out of what a person hears. Again, care must be taken not to assume that whatever a person hears is automatically understood. Although every time people listen, they hear, the opposite is not necessarily true; when people hear, they have not necessarily listened. In short, listening competency does not increase proportionately with hearing competency.

WHY PEOPLE LISTEN

While you may be able to conceal many of your negative traits, being a poor listener is not apt to be one of them. Most people expect responses when they speak—appropriate responses. When you arrive at work each day and say "good morning" to various co-workers, you expect a similiar reply. When you ask a question, you expect an answer, not to be ignored. Few things on the job can make you feel like a non-person more quickly than being ignored when you speak. It is interesting to speculate what might have happened in the Garden of Eden had Adam not listened to Eve. Or, what course history might have taken had Caesar not listened to Cleopatra,

Romeo to Juliet, Samson to Delilah, Queen Isabella to Columbus, and the German people to Adolf Hitler. Thus, whether it be in the realm of world affairs, on the job, or at a personal level, listening has the power to alter the meaning of any message.

People listen for different reasons and at different levels. Have you ever found yourself speaking to someone and he appears to be looking through you? By the look in his eyes, you get the feeling he is daydreaming, and when you confront him by saying, "Are you listening to me?" he snaps back with, "Sure, go ahead. I'm listening!" As we make our way through this chapter, you will come to realize that most people, at their best, are fuzzy listeners. Even worse is the fact that they are not aware that they are fuzzy listeners.

Basically, listening is a selfish act. People usually listen because they want something. It could be information, attention, understanding, clarification, or money. Whatever their motive, it is selfish in nature. Rarely do people listen solely for the benefit of others. Eliminate their superficial motive and beneath it you will usually find a deeper, selfish motive.

Whether it is their car radio, television, or a dear friend, people tend to listen to that which interests them the most. If you are interested in how to make more money, you will be drawn to radio and television programming that addresses itself to the subject of investments, etc. If your prime interest is cooking, you will seek out programs featuring cooking hints. In practically every case, your motive will be selfish.

Another tendency people have is to listen to those things that agree with what they already believe. If two political candidates are debating an issue on television, chances are you will listen more attentively to the candidate expressing your view on the subject. This same principle can be found to operate on the job. People with similar opinions on any subject are drawn to one another because of their listening preferences.

The unexpected is another source of increased listening. The more often you hear something, the less inclined you are to listen to it. With a reasonable amount of accuracy, you could probably guess what each of your co-workers will say at the next business meeting you attend. Their favorite topic will inevitably creep into the conversation. Though not word for word, not only will you probably be able to predict what they will say, you will also be less willing to listen to them. However, let one of your colleagues suddenly deviate from the usual remarks and your ears will be more apt to perk up with interest. The unexpected is what makes the difference. As a general rule, our attention becomes numbed by the familiar and re-charged by the unfamiliar.

Let us now look at each of the reasons why people listen.

Information

In any business or profession, there is a body of information with which people in that field must become familiar. From the first day on the job, the newcomer begins to gather this information by listening to others. Infrequently, such information is acquired by reading brochures, pamphlets, or data sheets. While such sources of information exist and are often helpful, they constitute only a small part of learning a business or profession. The majority of learning comes from listening.

More personally, finding out how you are doing on a new or old job can be determined by feedback from others. This, of course, involves listening—listening carefully to whatever information comes your way.

Pleasure

Among the many forms of pleasure that reach us, listening to compliments about ourselves occupies a high priority. Other forms of pleasure include listening to a good joke, a rumor that you are getting a raise in salary or a well-deserved promotion, or that your department has topped all other departments in service or sales. The human ear seems to have an affinity for information that yields pleasure to the listener. It likewise has the capacity to tune out unpleasant information.

Recognition

We all like to be noticed, to be complimented when we do a good job. Because it makes us feel good, we listen more attentively when such notices or compliments are bestowed upon us. Regrettably, they aren't issued often enough. The hunger for recognition in some individuals is so great that they actually solicit it by inquiring, for example, "Did I do a good job on that last deal, Phil?" No one is without a need for recognition to some extent. Both the chairman of the board and the stock clerk alike listen when they are being noticed or complimented. Saying positive things about people turns on the listening switch in their heads; saying negative things turns it off.

Understanding

Upward mobility demands an understanding of what is going on around you. This demands that you listen carefully to what you are told by responsible individuals. Understanding is a process by which your brain translates bits and pieces of information into meaningful units of thought. Unfortunately, the importance of such understanding on certain jobs is lessening. With the advent of machines that do the thinking (computers), much human understanding is often bypassed. People who are expected to behave like machines seem to be listening less, as less understanding is required of them. Like robots, they are told, "You are not being paid to think. Just do your job." The individuals who resent being treated like human robots continue to thirst for understanding and, as a result, will continue to listen. They realize that without listening, personal growth is almost impossible.

Opinions

Clinging to an unshared opinion can be very lonely. By comparison, opinions that are shared can be extremely comforting, psychologically. Without being aware of it, many of us spend a great deal of time listening to others for thoughts and feelings we have had. Surely someone at work has approached you and asked, "Listen, Charlie, how do you feel about the new administrative assistant in the front office?" What such an individual wants to hear is a confirmation of his own opinion of the new administrative assistant. If he doesn't get it, he will continue asking people until he does. In short, people continuously listen for opinions that match their own.

Reassurance

Compliments are few and far between on most jobs. As a result, many of us experience some self-doubt after a while. The fact that we are not criticized for doing something wrong is no consolation. We have to be told in plain language that we are doing a fine job. Consciously and unconsciously, healthy, well-adjusted people constantly listen for reassurance that they are being appreciated and performing their jobs a cut above the next person.

Gossip

Although you may not be the type of person who listens to idle gossip, the majority of people do. By nature, humans are a curious lot—always ready to accept an earful about someone with whom they work. Few organizations are without a well-oiled grapevine, ready to carry any and all information at a moment's notice. It requires but one thing—people to talk and people to listen to what they say.

Money

When money talks, everybody listens. While it may take more money to get certain people to listen than others, it is money that triggers their listening. Whether it is in the form of salary, raises, bonuses, commissions, bonds, percentages, or royalties, most people pay close attention to people who use such terms in their favor.

DIFFERENT KINDS OF LISTENING

Do you know what a *duologue* is? It is a term I bring to you from the mind of Abraham Kaplan, a distinguished professor of philosophy at the University of Michigan. A duologue characterizes a way in which people listen that, I believe, gets at the essence of the phenomenon we call listening. Kaplan explains a duologue as "a monologue mounted before a glazed and exquisitely indifferent audience." In a business setting, it would go something like this: The boss talks and the employee doesn't listen; then the employee talks and the boss doesn't listen. Each gives the other certain verbal and non-verbal signals when it is his turn to talk. These include a polite vertical nodding of the head, an occasional smile, a well-placed uh-huh, or an artificial laugh at something that is said. It is phony listening, at its civilized best. Professor Kaplan feels that the word *duologue* should be applied to those occasions in which "everyone talks and nobody listens."

Ideally, the kind of listening we should all seek to develop is where what the other party is saying acts as a basis for what we say in response. In the duologue, this does not happen. Each participant is impervious to what the other is saying or trying to say. A perfect example of a duologue would be two TV sets tuned in and facing each other. How many times have you felt like one of these TV sets, talking to someone tuned to a completely different channel?

The way people listen is not consistent. Depending upon the time, place, circumstance, subject matter, past experience, and mood of the moment, people listen a little differently.

Selective Listening

When you listen selectively, you zero in on only those things that interest you. All else is filtered out. You do this when you listen to radio and television commercials or when an employer's pet lecture or admonition begins to sound like a broken record. You listen best whenever your favorite subject comes up. For example, if you are anxious to get ahead on a job, you will be on a constant "listening alert" for any information dealing with promotions; if you are interested in finding a mate, your ears will be selectively tuned to any mention of meeting new and interesting people.

Critical or Evaluative Listening

At practically every level of organizational life, you will discover people trying to persuade you to think, feel, or do something differently. Some of what they say will make sense, some nonsense. It is your task to separate the sense from the nonsense and, to do this, critical or evaluative listening is required.

This type of listening also demands that you be as objective as possible. Objectivity means to keep your emotions down and your reasoning up. Your attention must be almost exclusively limited to things that can be tested or verified by others, i.e., facts, evidence, proof, logical reasoning.

Defensive Listening

On almost every job, there are certain people who are uptight, walking around with a chip on their shoulder, and waiting for someone to say something with which they can take issue. You probably know someone to whom you simply cannot say certain things. Take the case of an individual who is always late for everything. Rest assured that he has probably been lectured many times about the virtues of punctuality. He knows perfectly well when he is late without others repeatedly saying, "Well, George, you're late again!" People like George listen defensively whenever the subject of lateness comes up in a conversation.

An understanding of defensive listening requires knowing, beforehand, a person's sore spots. Unfortunately, these sore spots cannot be known until they surface in a conversation. Once their identity becomes common knowledge, proper precautions can be taken by those with whom they must communicate; e.g., don't mention a raise to Helen, marriage to Bill, or overtime to Marty. Realizing that certain people do listen defensively can be an excellent means of avoiding needless altercations with them on the job.

Authoritative Listening

Those in authority often feel they know more about their field than those in their charge. Whether or not this is true does not apply here. The important thing is that most superiors *think* they know more than their subordinates and, consequently, listen to them accordingly. Authorities also have a tendency to believe that, because they worked their way up to their present position, they possess a more comprehensive view of things than their subordinates. This attitude, along with the knowledge that they can back up what they think by the power vested in them by the organization, further inclines them to listen with half an ear. And, the longer they hold their positions of authority, the more they tend to become victims of authoritarian listening.

Non-directive Listening

The national sales manager of a large corporation was troubled by a recent policy change. He had some definite ideas on the subject that he wanted to get off his chest. He decided to have a chat with one of his more efficient regional sales managers, who happened to be in town. They met in his office and he let off steam for twenty minutes. Aside from asking an occasional question or making a brief comment, the regional sales manager said practically nothing. The conversation was clearly one-sided. After the regional sales manager left, the national manager said to himself, *Boy, that Phil Donaghey sure knows what he's talking about.* Although Donaghey spent almost the entire meeting listening, his behavior was regarded as conversational by his superior.

Professional counselors and psychiatrists often use non-directive listening. Their reason for employing it is to "hear the other person out." As a result, a patient will occasionally say to them after a particularly good session, "Gee, Doc, it sure was nice talking with you today." In spite of the fact that the doctor, like the regional sales manager, listened substantially more than he spoke, the patient came away with the feeling that a two-way conversation had taken place.

We have all been in situations where we wished we had someone with whom to talk—someone who would listen patiently and seriously try to understand what was on our mind. The reason so many people appreciate non-directive listeners is that they can be relied upon to withhold any personal value judgments or criticisms. A good supervisor or manager who is sensitive to the needs of his subordinates will find non-directional listening an invaluable tool on the job. There are times, for instance, when an employee who asks a simple question does not want a pat answer, but an opportunity to chat about something on his mind without running the risk of having it criticized or evaluated.

Non-directive listening is by no means the exclusive domain of management. The need for it can be felt at every level of an organization. As an excellent means of keeping lines of communication open, non-directive listening allows people to feel "listened to" rather than "listened at."

Empathic Listening

Empathy means sharing someone else's feelings or emotions. It is different from sympathy. When you see a group of workers on strike, you may be sympathetic to their cause and understand the economic nature of their problem, but not be empathic. To experience empathy, you must be able to project your own personality into the personality of those on strike —to share their feelings and emotions.

Empathic listeners seek to fully understand what a speaker is trying to communicate and, as a result, take appropriate action. They make a concerted effort to keep their own feelings and ideas separate from those of the speaker. The empathic listener also assumes good intentions on the part of a speaker until shown otherwise. By making such an assumption, the bias and prejudice that so often contaminate listening can be avoided.

In plain language, the empathic listener is one who truly "gives a damn" about what you have to say and, if need be, does something.

THREE TYPES OF LISTENERS

Having described several different kinds of listening practices, here are three types of listeners. Since most of us are a mixture of these types, you will rarely find one of the following in a pure state.

Additive Listener

These are individuals who expand or exaggerate whatever they hear. If you tell them that everyone in your department is going to get a $50 Christmas bonus, they will tell others that it will be $250. The extent to which they exaggerate will depend, naturally, upon their personality and psychological makeup.

Subtractive Listener

In contrast with the additive listener, these individuals make less out of what they hear. Instead of saying that the bonus will be $50, they will repeat that it will be $10 or $25. They tend to underplay and undersay everything they hear.

Distortive Listener

Here you have a type of listener who routinely alters what is heard so that it differs significantly from what was originally said. In the case of the Christmas bonus, rather than inflating or deflating the amount, they might distort the information entirely. For example, they might say that instead of a bonus, everyone in the department will get a free, all-expense-paid vacation in Bermuda. Their talent is to mask what was said so that it cannot be recognized.

WHAT IT MEANS TO PAY ATTENTION

Without an ability to pay attention, to concentrate on what is being said, listening is nearly impossible. Just as poor readers must go back periodically and reread passages in a book because of faulty concentration, poor listeners likewise suffer from periods of inattention. One of the most common signs of a listener suffering from an inability to pay close attention to what is being said is the tendency to ask speakers to repeat themselves. Whereas a failure to concentrate while reading involves only the reader, a similar failure in a listening situation could involve other people as well.

Asking someone to repeat a statement, question, or order can have serious repercussions. Employees who do not pick up on what they are told the first time soon acquire a reputation of being dull, preoccupied, uninterested in their work, poorly motivated, and lacking in potential. Naturally, the more often this happens, the worse such a reputation becomes. So, if you are interested in one of the most effective ways of infuriating a superior, don't pay attention when he speaks to you.

The average person's attention span is much shorter than you think. It has been suggested that it seldom lasts more than a few seconds. While listening, your attention is constantly wandering and decreasing in strength. In most instances, it can only cope with four or five objects at a time through your sense of sight, and five to eight objects through your sense of hearing.

Imagine yourself being lectured by an instructor in a sales training program. Unless the instructor is exceptional, your mind is sure to wander off, with different thoughts constantly vying for your attention. Because you want to succeed in your job, you strive to pay close attention to what is being said by the instructor. But how does one pay attention? Unlike arithmetic or grammar, the art of paying attention was never taught in school. Your parents probably demanded attention but failed to tell you how to pay it. What, exactly, does one do in order to pay attention? Is it a matter of concentration, imagination, interpretation, reasoning, or good old-fashioned common sense?

In his book *Listening: Key to Communication,* Ernest Mills recommends that those who want to improve their ability to concentrate or pay attention do the following: (1) dispose of distractions, (2) focus your listening, (3) be sincerely interested, (4) listen for interesting statements, (5) put yourself in the speaker's place, and (6) involve yourself in what is being said. Let's take a closer look at some of these recommendations.

Dispose of Distractions

Many things are capable of distracting you from listening. A common distraction is a poor public address system where the microphone periodically squeaks and squeals. Then, there is the person next to you chewing gum frantically, sucking a candy, fidgeting in his seat, or smoking an obnoxious-smelling cigar. Any of these could easily distract your attention from a speaker. Other distractions might include a room that is either too hot or too cold, has uncomfortable seats, is overcrowded, or does not enable the speaker to be clearly seen.

Aside from these external distractions, there are also those distractions that arise from within you. These could be a throbbing headache, dyspepsia from overeating, or an emotional problem. Because of the mental and physical changes people experience from day to day, their ability to listen also fluctuates occasionally from hour to hour, from minute to minute. Thus, at best, listening is susceptible to a wide variety of distractions.

Focus Your Listening

There can be no doubt in your mind that someone involved in the delicate process of disarming a bomb must give it his undivided attention. One minor distraction could mean the end. People working with radioactive materials, constructing a building 100 stories high, or performing intricate brain surgery must all master the art of paying close attention to what they are doing.

Listening, likewise, requires focusing. Picture yourself as an employee in a tower at a local airport. It is very overcast, and you have to "talk down" a pilot whose aircraft has malfunctioned. You talk to the pilot and he listens; then he talks and you listen. Should either of you fail to remain sharply focused on what is being said, it could spell disaster for the aircraft.

Less serious examples of poorly focused listening are numerous on the job. Employees are continually being told what to do and how to do it. The successful performance of these tasks often depends upon accurate focusing. In return, management must maintain a similiar focus if the feedback it requires is to be accurate and reliable.

Be Sincerely Interested

A barrier to any listening situation is a lack of interest. Management is constantly faulting labor for its lack of interest, for not realizing how important things really are. Labor, in turn, indicts management for overstating the importance of things. As a result, each faction listens according to the extent and nature of its own bias. Then there are salespeople who listen with greater interest to their customers than to their peers. Whoever is doing the listening, whether labor or management, salesperson or customer, the quality of listening is apt to be better if the person doing the listening is truly interested in what is being said. Most job promotions, for instance, are proportional to the interest a worker displays in either a product, the process, or the people involved—that is, the willingness to listen to specific job talk.

Listen for Interesting Statements

Few subjects are interesting in their every detail. A singer's repertoire, for example, might contain some songs you like and some you dislike. Therefore, you are more inclined to listen to those things you like and ignore those you do not. This same selectivity applies to listening. While listening to a lecture, you must not dwell on those aspects of it that bore you. Instead, concentrate on those aspects of the lecture that you find interesting. It is a matter of mental emphasis on your part. By listening for that which is positive, you will help sustain your own interest and, by so doing, improve your listening technique.

Put Yourself in the Speaker's Place

Try to get inside a speaker's head. Ask yourself why a particular subject is being brought up, and why it is being treated in a given way. Speculate on how you might have done it. Wonder about such things as a speaker's use of visual aids, sequence of presenting lecture material, dress, gestures, and vocal technique. You will find that by becoming involved with what a speaker is doing, by putting yourself in the speaker's place, you will increase substantially your understanding and appreciation of what is going on.

Involve Yourself with What Is Being Said

Since you and every speaker share a common humanity, it takes little effort to build a psychological bridge between you. Whatever sense experiences a speaker might mention, rest assured that you have had similar ones. It is these similarities that will enable you to involve yourself with what is being said.

Using the awareness afforded by these needs, you can meet any speaker to whom you are listening halfway on the psychological bridge you have constructed in your mind.

Lumping all of these recommendations together against a background of what it means to pay attention, you should be slowly gaining a more sophisticated understanding of why it is misleading to think of listening as something simple—that anyone can do. Here are some common listening barriers. Many have already been mentioned in previous pages, but, in case you weren't paying attention, here is a checklist:

1. unintelligible speech (accent, dialect, mispronunciation)
2. uninteresting topic
3. closed-mindedness
4. purposeless gesturing
5. distracting noise, odors, temperature, decor
6. disorganized material
7. poor eye contact
8. inappropriate dress of speaker
9. uncomfortable seating
10. mind wandering
11. excessive detail

12. flowery language
13. poor scheduling
14. ill-advised humor
15. excessive long-windedness
16. faulty reasoning

A LISTENING PHILOSOPHY

Granting that listening is not simple, how does one go about developing good listening habits? To begin with, resign yourself to the fact that effective listening demands patience. If you are impatient by nature, expect to run into difficulty. Impatient people seldom make good listeners. While others talk, they are busy thinking of what they are going to say when their turn comes. Too often, they cannot wait their turn and interrupt without warning. Good advice to such people is to repeat these sentences: "I must not interrupt. I must wait until others are finished before speaking."

Another characteristic of a sound listening philosophy is the willingness to assume that what the other person has to say may also be important. Just as you may feel that what you have to say is important, extend others the same courtesy. A happening last summer clearly illustrates this point. A college professor, returning to campus after a summer vacation, met a colleague. The colleague asked, "What's new? . . ." Without hesitation, the professor readied himself to describe a whole array of summer activity. But, before he could say a word, his colleague finished his thought with "that would be of interest to me?" Whereas most people, out of politeness, may pretend to be interested in what others are thinking and doing, their prime interest is in what they themselves are thinking and doing. Thus, to be an effective listener, you must recognze that most of the people with whom you speak will have only a secondary interest in what you have to say. While there are, of course, those who are genuinely interested in others, they are few and far between. Since most people are self-centered, they have a ready ear for anything to do with *their* world. They are interested in yours only as it relates to theirs.

People like to be asked, not told things. Developing an effective listening philosophy should encourage the habit of asking more and telling less. If you must tell someone something, you might consider putting it in question form. For example, instead of saying, "Partnerships are a dangerous business," try asking, "What do you think the chances are of a partnership succeeding in today's market?" Questions, if properly asked, suggest respect for the person being asked and encourage responsive listening.

As was suggested in Chapter 1, people are not "whats" but "whos." This means they have a specific identity separate and apart from everyone else. To ignore this individuality is to dismiss them as non-persons. They have names and like to be called by them. To refer to someone whose name you cannot remember as honey, sweetie, ole buddy, or pal is to invite rejection. And this rejection often induces tokenistic listening. Depending upon how offended people are by your forgetting their names, they will listen accordingly.

At work, when a superior asks you a question and addresses you by name, chances are you will listen more attentively than if you are referred to by one of the all-purpose substitutes mentioned in the preceding paragraph. The reverse is also true. Your superiors will pay closer attention to what you say if you refer to them by name.

Good eye contact is another helpmate in developing a positive listening philosophy. Just as people listen better when you address them by name, they respond the same way when you engage them in direct eye contact. Without staring, looking at the person talking to you is an excellent means of telling him that you are listening to what he has to say—that you are interested. Conversely, when you want him to listen to you, tell him so with your eyes.

A final word of advice is carried forward from Chapter 2, "Advertising Yourself with Body Language." It involves the relationship between body langauge and positive listening. Whether you are speaking from a platform or to someone in a showroom, you will be getting feedback. Most of it will come in a nonverbal form. Certain facial expressions and postures are means of letting you know whether or not people are listening. Frowns, head nodding from side to side, slumping and squirming in a seat communicate disinterest and sluggish listening. Eyes open and in good contact with the speaker, an erect or forward-leaning posture, smiles, and affirmative head nodding all communicate high interest and lively listening. Be aware of how you look when you listen; be aware of how people look while listening to you. Learn to recognize an "interested look" in others and develop it in yourself. It is a giant step toward positive listening.

Into whatever field or profession you should go, bad listening habits could be disastrous. Patients are forever complaining that their doctors don't listen; teachers complain their students don't listen; parents complain their children don't listen; the list is endless. If everyone is talking, who in the world is listening? Listening expert Larry Barker has this to say on the subject: "A failure to listen probably creates more interpersonal problems than any other aspect of human behavior." Therefore, to insure against such problems, persuade yourself that good listeners bring a high price the world over. To learn, you must listen, for listening is the prerequisite of successful communication on the job.

7
Communicating with Others on the Job

No matter what job you ever hold, you will be expected to get along with others. Regardless of how intelligent or skilled you are, the inability to work smoothly with other people may result, sooner or later, in your demotion or dismissal.

The days of the rugged individualist are gone. No longer does an organization rise or fall because of one person. Today, the watchword is teamwork, with everyone ideally pulling in the same direction. It is not only dangerous but foolish for any employee to think that he or she is indispensible. As proof of this, read the following poem:

Indispensible?

Sometime, when you're feeling important,
Sometime, when your ego's in bloom,
Sometime, when you take it for granted
You're the best qualified in the room.
Sometime when you feel that your going
Would leave an unfillable hole,
Just follow this simple instruction
And see how it humbles your soul.
Take a bucket and fill it with water,
Put your hand in it up to the wrist,
Pull it out and the hole that's remaining
Is the measure of how you'll be missed.
You may splash all you please when you enter,
You can stir up the water galore,

But stop, and you'll find in a minute
That it looks quite the same as before.
The moral of this quaint example
Is to do just the best that you can,
Be proud of yourself, but remember,
There is no indispensible man (or woman).

—Anonymous

You will probably spend the greater part of your
productive years working with others. To help you
prepare for such togetherness, this chapter will
introduce you to the nature of group life and the
various types of people you are apt to encounter,
and will recommend ways of communicating with them
more effectively.

THINGS YOU SHOULD KNOW ABOUT GROUPS

Attitudes toward Groups

Most people are either loners or joiners. They either like groups or hate them. While there are those who have no definite feeling one way or another about group life, the majority of working people consider "belonging" extremely important. Open your wallet or handbag and see how many membership cards you carry. Look for evidence suggesting that you belong to school, church, library, athletic, social, professional, or political organizations. Also notice how many credit cards you have.

In today's world, belonging to various groups is no longer an option. It is a necessity. In addition to being caught up in the Space Age, we are also caught in what might be called a Group Age—a time when doing things by yourself runs the risk of being considered somewhat deviant behavior. Remarks like "You don't mean to tell me that you are going on vacation by yourself?" or "Really, you live all alone?" are examples of how society views independent behavior or status. If you are a *groupophiliac* (a compulsive joiner of groups), you consider the unshared life not worth living. By contrast, if you suffer from *groupophobia* (a fear of belonging to groups), you perceive sharing as a potential threat to your identity.

This attitude toward grouping, or togetherness, was not always this intense. In bygone years, independent businesses flourished. There was the neighborhood grocer, tailor, cobbler, baker, physician, lawyer, or barber. However, as we rounded the corner of the twentieth century, things began to change; the Industrial Revolution launched the concept of people work-

114

ing together. Factories consisted of hundreds of people all doing the same thing. Manufacturing any product required that scores of workers busy themselves under one roof. Human emotions had to be suppressed during working hours, feelings about the work being done and the people with whom one had to work needed to be kept under strict control. Like gigantic flesh machines with many moving parts, businesses of every description concentrated on but one thing—productivity.

The second half of the twentieth century spawned some new ideas about the nature of group life in the marketplace. Psychologists and sociologists began taking serious interest in how people felt and behaved in various kinds of groups. They recognized that all businesses were best served by the establishment of ways to improve and maintain the mental and physical health of people working together. The old-fashioned notion that business and pleasure didn't mix came under renewed suspicion. Researchers began to discover that, in many cases, it was not the work that caused people to be unhappy on the job, but rather the people with whom they had to work. Social scientists came to realize that the majority of employees—white-, blue-, and pink-collar workers alike—knew precious little about group dynamics, that is, how to get along with others on the job. While some were endowed with a natural gift for dealing with people, the greater majority muddled through each day, functioning at a gut level, substituting feelings for reason and logic. The need for knowing how to communicate with others on the job grew steadily. The nature of group life in industry and the professions had begun to attract large sums of grant money. Big business wanted to know how to make their employees happy and, at the same time, warrant their best work effort. The importance of company morale began taking on new meaning to management. One Japanese firm set a good example of this. In a room directly adjacent to the office of its president, a large picture of him was put up on a wall. When employees were unhappy with their jobs, they could go into this room and throw darts at the president's picture.

To Join or Not to Join

People join groups for different reasons. Each joins a group hoping it will fill a particular need. Loneliness, a desire to be of service, to comply with company policy, to satisfy the request of a friend or co-worker, and the pursuit of status, money, power, security, and recognition are some of the more familiar reasons why people join groups. Regardless of the reasons they give for joining, that joining can usually be traced to some real or imagined need.

Our basic needs haven't changed much since the days of the cave dwellers. Perhaps it is because our anatomy and physiology haven't changed. While we can satisfy some of our needs without the help of others, most of them require outside assistance. Just as the cave dwellers discovered that their chances of survival were better when they lived, hunted, and traveled together, today's apartment dweller has come to recognize the survival value of living together (condominiums), working together (companies, corporations, industrial parks, medical centers), and traveling together (group flights, vacations, tours). The list of things modern men and women do together is staggering. Fat people, tall people, short people, divorced people, single people, lonely people—people of every description have formed groups. Beyond a shadow of a doubt, we are solidly locked into the Group Age. Joiners are in; non-joiners are out.

Experience has probably taught you that job competency alone is no guarantee of job security. People who are liked by their superiors and co-workers, but whose competency leaves something to be desired, are more apt to be retained than those who are disliked by their superiors and co-workers, but whose proficiency is extremely high. While there are certain jobs in which an individual's personality and character play little or no part, the majority of jobs are not that impersonal.

Since any reasonably large organization consists of many smaller units (departments, divisions, sections, bureaus, branches), it is nearly impossible to avoid becoming part of one group or another. Thus, to grow in a job, you must recognize the importance of becoming a joiner. Having done this, you must then learn to survive the trials and tribulations of group life. A failure to get along with other members of any group on the job could easily result in a serious setback.

Exactly What Is a Group?

When does a collection of people become a group? Does the fact that a dozen individuals sit around a table talking at one another make it a group? Would you consider five executives having a conference call a group? How about four sales managers gathered in their boss's office to discuss plans for a national sales campaign? Three of the four are out to impress their boss with their acumen and wit. The fourth seeks to ingratiate himself with the boss by going through the motions of discussing plans for the campaign. Does this scene constitute a group?

There is more to a group than simply being a collection of people. If this were not true, mobs, gangs, cliques, and claques would automatically qualify as groups. Taken in a stricter sense, groups must meet certain requirements. Consider the following definition: "A group is a body composed of individuals who occupy or assume various roles and status positions and who share a common purpose in the accomplishment of which they establish and enforce group norms and interact verbally and non-verbally."[1]

Boiled down, this definition of a group suggests three things: first, that a group should consist of people who assume various roles, namely, president, chairperson, leader, vice-president, secretary, treasurer, and sergeant at arms; second, that the group should have a common purpose mutually known to all of its members; and finally, that each member of the group should be given an opportunity to interact freely with every other member of the group—preferably, face to face.

Wherever you encounter a group, either on or off the job, you will find it conforming to these three criteria. The degree to which it fails to conform shall be the degree to which it fails to qualify as a group. No business can afford the luxury of supporting malfunctioning groups under its roof. With members pulling in different directions due to conflicting goals, personal axes to grind, or fragmented egos to defend, organizational interests are rarely served. Thus, if we define a goal as a human desire toward which one is willing to work, a group having such a commitment stands the best chance of reaching its goal.

Types of Groups

Since groups have purposes, it is your responsibility to become familiar with those purposes. The better an individual understands why a particular group was formed, the better that individual can serve its needs. Some groups, for example, demand specialized knowledge. How could you intelligently participate in a group whose express purpose is to develop a nationwide advertising program without ever having worked in the advertising field? You can be certain that in any lively discussion involving people who eat, sleep, and breathe advertising, you will soon be exposed as someone who doesn't belong there. The best insurance against being caught in such an embarrassing position is to know beforehand the kind of a group into which you are getting.

Groups are generally classified according to what they do. Name a function and you will find a group dedicated to that function. Basically, there are three group functions: task-oriented, maintenance-oriented, and self-oriented. In the preceding paragraph, you encountered a task-oriented group whose function it was to develop a nationwide advertising program. Its members were obliged to initiate new ideas and procedures, make relevant information available, evaluate information, and coordinate any efforts growing out of the application of that information. In addition, they

1. Abné M. Eisenberg and Joseph A. Ilardo, *Argument: An Alternative to Violence* (Englewood Cliffs, N.J.: Prentice-Hall, Inc., 1972), p. 118.

117

had to elaborate on any contributions made by other members of the group.

Members of a maintenance group must supervise its operation and seek ways and means of keeping the group going. They must also support and encourage a free exchange of ideas, reduce or eliminate any tension that might arise, and, overall, keep the communication process free from any unnecessary interference.

Self-oriented groups must be dedicated to the needs of the individual. These needs are usually irrelevant to the group task and negatively oriented to the growth and maintenance of the group as a whole. Since each individual tends to bring to any group a personal set of attitudes, values, and beliefs, and since these traits are capable of producing varying degrees of interference or conflict, it is the function of the self-oriented group to exercise a protective influence over its membership.

Another method of identifying a group is to determine whether it is formal or informal. If it is formal, expect to find it having a definite goal or objective and consisting of people in specifically traditional roles, such as president, secretary, treasurer, etc. If it is an informal group, it will probably be smaller in size. Its members will be more familiar with one another and more relaxed. The flow of communiction will be considerably less restricted.

A list of the types of groups you will find in the business and professional community is rather extensive. By knowing what function each of them performs and the needs they serve, you should gain a better understanding of the people involved and the company of which they are a part. Could you, for instance, tell anything about the companies that sponsor each of the following interest areas: human relations, personal growth laboratories, sociodrama, psychodrama, sensory awareness, organizational development, creativity workshops, and team building? While many of these groups do exhibit overlapping functions, a conversation with those who administrate them will often disclose some rather concrete job-related activities: persuasion, problem solving, conflict resolution, personnel interaction, and decision making. All of these communication processes can be found to operate fully in any active business or profession.

Cohesiveness

When people stick together, are interested in one another, have common interests, and enjoy each other's company, they are said to have a cohesive relationship. On most jobs, the people brought together by management have little to say about it. If they are lucky, their co-workers will be decent human beings; if they are not, there is generally little that can be done about it. While concerned management makes every effort to bring compatible people together, this is not always possible. The result is that employees are often forced to work side by side with people they can't stand, or who bore them to death.

When people are brought together who are similar to one another, it is called *homophily*; when they are different from one another, it is called *heterophily*. In most cases, the more homophilous group members are, the more cohesive will be their relationship. The basis for their similarities might be race, color, creed, affiliation, knowledge, education, cultural background, personality, or socioeconomic status. Any one or a combination of these characteristics could increase their cohesiveness. In reverse, their differences could decrease their cohesiveness.

As suggested earlier, the business world is currently bringing more and more people with different inherent and acquired characteristics together on the job. While at first these differences might appear to be rather dramatic, after a period of time has passed, similarities begin to arise. Because they are bound to each other by a common purpose—the job—they begin to realize that every human being wants to be liked, to become more efficient, and to climb higher on the ladder of success. It is then their degree of perceived "alikeness" begins to increase. Differences slowly begin to fade and take on lesser importance. This phenomenon was conspicuous during wartime when mixtures of people were thrown together in the armed forces and expected to get along with one another for their country's sake. Granting that there were some who simply could not adjust to such heterophily, the majority did. By deferring to the greater cause (winning the war), they were able to maintain a more sensible attitude in dealing with those lesser causes that constituted their differences.

Corporations often demand a similar commitment of their employees. They expect them to put aside personal differences and defer to the corporation's best interest. To management, a high level of cohesiveness among personnel means better morale, increased productivity, greater group loyalty and trust, plus a noticeable openness in their daily interaction.

Group Size

The number of people with which an individual can cope in a group varies. Not only will it vary from individual to individual, but from situation to situation. For some, more than six people represent a threat; others feel perfectly comfortable in a room with thirty-five people. While there are several other psychological factors that could influence how a person reacts to being in a group (e.g., inferiority complex, egocentrism, prior experience involving trauma in a group situation, childhood conditioning), most people can be relied upon to behave rather predictably. At the risk of oversimplification, there are those who dislike groups, those who love them, and those who can easily adjust to practically any situation. The reason why this three-way split is an oversimplification derives from the fact that many people will not admit how they feel in a group setting. Frequently, if they are unhappy and feel uncomfortable, they will pretend that everything is all right and pray for the meeting to end. Their true mind-state, however, is often betrayed by certain non-verbal clues such as long periods of silence, a tensed posture, erratic eye movements, nervous hand/foot movements, and increased sitting distance from the center of group activity.

A young lady in a management training program offered by a leading department store chain once displayed some curious behavior. As part of the program, participants were divided into several five-member discussion groups. Regardless of which group she was in, she remained silent. The administrator of the program was disturbed by her consistent unwillingness to speak in any group. She was an attractive, intelligent, and dedicated young woman with only one drawback—she refused to speak when in a group. On a one-to-one basis, she spoke freely and with enthusiasm, but as soon as she was put in a group, she clammed up. The administrator decided to try an experiment. He divided the class into the usual five-member groups, but with one exception. He paired the young lady in question with one other member of the class and seated them apart from the other groups. The young lady had absolutely no difficulty. She engaged her partner in a lovely and highly animated conversation. Then, the administrator told another member of the group to join the pair in conversation. Now there were three of them and the conversation continued to flourish. Five minutes passed and the administrator sent over a fourth person to join them. A curious thing happened. The moment the fourth person joined the group, the young lady *stopped talking*. Whereas she could handle communicating with two people, she could not handle three.

The size of a group, according to communication experts, can affect not only its individual members but also the group as a whole. As the size of a group increases, its complexity likewise increases. Also, as the number of people in a group increases arithmetically, the number of interpersonal relationships increases geometrically. For example, a two-people group constitutes 1 interpersonal relationship; a group of three people have 3 interpersonal relationships; a group of five people have 10; a group of ten people have 45; a group of twenty people have a possible 190 interpersonal relationships, and so on.[2]

2. Loosely adapted from Ernest G. Bormann and Nancy C. Bormann, *Effective Small Group Communication* (Minneapolis, Minn.: Burgess Publishing Company, 1972), pp. 32–38.

Another consequence of size is that the more people involved, the less opportunity the individual has to speak and influence others. This, in turn, may produce frustration and disappointment with the entire group and its objectives. Large groups tend to turn off the more timid individual—the person who simply refuses to raise his or her voice to get a word in edgewise. As a result, the large group is usually dominated by the more forceful speaker or, occasionally, by those who rudely interrupt others and muscle their way into the limelight by their verbal diarrhea and loudness.

Group control also suffers as the number of members increases. Leaders seem to have greater difficulty maintaining order; the continuity of any ideas advanced by group members tends to become splintered or lost entirely. And, lastly, the larger the group, the greater the likelihood that cliques will develop within it.

The importance of group size must not be glossed over. It can make the difference between a constructive and a destructive experience. This is especially important on the job where the outcome of a committee, department, or division meeting could result in a successful season, beating a competitor to the punch, or electing a particularly gifted individual to a position of power or influence. Ideal group size (six to twelve) serves a double purpose: it facilitates individual growth and development and, at the same time, enriches the organization of which it is a part.

Cooperative Behavior

A group can be helped or hindered by the behavior of one or several of its members. It is not difficult to tell whether someone is behaving in a cooperative or obstructive manner. You can judge by *what they say, how they say it,* and *how they look while saying it*—i.e., their verbal, vocal, and non-verbal behavior. Here is a partial list of these communications. Let us begin with those that are cooperative in nature.

VERBAL

1. Refer to people by their names.
2. Use simple and straightforward language.
3. Exercise courtesy at all times.
4. Allow people to finish what they are saying.
5. Encourage those who are shy and retiring to speak.
6. Compliment people when they deserve it.
7. Ask questions if you are not clear on something.
8. Give others the benefit of the doubt whenever possible.
9. Substitute such words as *we, us,* and *our* for *I, me,* and *my.*
10. Try to build up, not tear down, what others say.

1. Speak up so that you can be heard.
2. Stress all important words and ideas.
3. Use a pleasant tone of voice.
4. Make every effort not to use *ers*, *ahs*, and *uh-huhs* while speaking.
5. Don't mumble.

NON-VERBAL

1. Look at the people to whom you are speaking or listening.
2. Wear clothes that indicate that you care about the group you are attending.
3. Occasionally nod or smile agreeably.
4. Keep your hands, feet, and arms uncrossed and unfolded to suggest open-mindedness.
5. Sit as though you are interested—upright or leaning slightly forward.

Obstructive Behavior

Here, in contrast, are some negative behaviors that serve to detract from the quality of group life.

VERBAL

1. Using foul language.
2. Repeating yourself in a way that serves no useful purpose.
3. Cracking jokes and horsing around.
4. Monopolizing the conversation.
5. Humiliating or intimidating others.
6. Changing the subject for no good reason.
7. Using big words to show off.
8. Making self-centered remarks.
9. Cutting people off in the middle of a sentence.
10. Raising unpopular issues.

VOCAL

1. Talking too fast or too slowly.
2. Speaking in a monotone.
3. Talking too loudly or too softly.
4. Using a high-pitched voice, which grates on people's nerves.
5. Mispronouncing everyday words.

1. Nodding your head from side to side while someone is trying to make a point.
2. Fidgeting in your seat.
3. Displaying negative gestures and facial expressions while communicating with others.
4. Playing with pencils, keys, coins, and clothing while someone is talking.

THINGS YOU SHOULD KNOW ABOUT THE PEOPLE YOU MEET IN GROUPS

Having discussed the various types of groups in which you may find yourself on the job, it is now appropriate to talk about the types of people with whom you will have to get along. They will range from those whom you will dislike with a passion to those who will become lifelong friends. Between these extremes, you will encounter a wide variety of personalities. Knowing how to get along with each of them is an art you must learn. The sooner you start studying people and how to communicate with them, the better your chances will be of succeeding in your chosen line of work.

Whatever your attitude may be toward another individual, it is seldom an attitude that considers the person as a whole. Our likes and dislikes usually focus on one or perhaps two mental or physical traits. Surely you know someone who is fantastic in every way—except one. The objectionable trait might be bad breath, poor manners, foul language, or snobbishness. This phenomenon could also work the other way around. The person might have several objectionable traits and a single good one. Regardless of whether the single trait is good or bad, there is a human tendency to treat it as though it represented the entire individual. Put another way, we tend to think of people in parts. In some instances, five bad parts may be outweighed by one good part; then again, five good parts may outweigh one bad part. Only rarely do we meet someone who is all good or all bad. People, it seems, are mixtures of one another and, as a result, frequently see reflections of themselves in those around them.

Many of us, from childhood, have had a deep-seated desire to be unique—just a little bit different from the others. We tried to accomplish this in a number of ways. These include getting the highest marks in school, performing well in some sport, being voted class president or the graduate most likely to succeed. Whatever method we chose, the goal was usually the same—to be just a little bit different from the rest. Unfortunately, only a few of us excelled in the ways just mentioned. Alternative methods of distinguishing ourselves had to be found that, on occasion, turned out to be somewhat less gratifying than we would have wanted.

The prospect of being liked by *everyone*, while seeming to be a worthwhile goal on the surface, often proved otherwise in actual practice. Although our parents and teachers considered us more manageable when we looked and acted according to some conventional standard, that desire to be different was always there, pulling at us from the inside. And, quite understandably, some of us felt this pull more than others.

The types of people described in the balance of this chapter were selected because they possess some unique trait that distinguishes them from the rest, some behavior that attracts attention in a group situation. Since it is impossible to examine them individually, we shall collect and discuss those with similar traits as units. Along the way, you will probably run into a personality trait or two of your own. It is also possible that you will discover yourself possessing a combination of traits being described. Whatever your reaction, out of fairness to the personality types to be described (since they cannot be here to defend themselves), declare yourself by taking the following quiz. Be aware, however, that the questions being asked do not have a right or wrong answer, nor is the quiz based upon any heavily documented scientific evidence. All that it may do is provide you with some insight into the way your mind operates in relation to others.

ARE YOU THE KIND OF PERSON WHO:

	Yes	No
1. Catches yourself repeating what others have said?	—	—
2. Doesn't say much at most social or business functions?	—	—
3. Giggles a lot?	—	—
4. Is surprised at what most people say?	—	—
5. Thinks you know more than the average person when it comes to general knowledge?	—	—
6. Helps people who cannot express themselves?	—	—
7. Always seems to find yourself caught in the middle?	—	—
8. Likes to write things down?	—	—
9. Demands that people be specific when they discuss a particular subject?	—	—

10. Is annoyed by people who do not let
    other people finish what they are saying? ___ __
11. Insists that people stick to whatever
    subject they are discussing?
12. Is always quoting famous people? ___ __
13. Can't resist telling others what you
    have just learned or read? ___ __
14. Studies very hard for every little ex-
    amination or quiz? ___ __
15. Doesn't take an umbrella even though
    the weather bureau forecasts rain? ___ __
16. Has the reputation of explaining what
    other people mean? ___ __
17. Often finds yourself saying just the
    opposite of what others have said? ___ __
18. Tends to throw cold water on other
    people's ideas? ___ __
19. Is inclined to tell others what they can
    look forward to? ___ __
20. Seems to be very concerned about how
    things used to be? ___ __

If you are an honest and sincere person, anxious and willing to find
out how you can improve yourself, you probably responded to these
questions in an open and straightforward manner. But there is a small
problem. Most people do not see themselves as they really are, but rather
how they learned to see themselves. Consciously or unconsciously, they
make regular adjustments of their self-image to conform to how they were
conditioned to look or behave.

Another item worthwhile bearing in mind is that, while people do behave differently from time to time, their behavior tends to form patterns.
For example, people who speak in loud voices can be heard to speak that
way most of the time. People who touch others during conversations tend
to do it most of the time. Therefore, to a large extent, personality patterns
can often be predicted with a reasonable amount of accuracy. The charac-
ters you are about to meet were conceived on the basis of such patterns.
Perhaps, by providing you with some insight into their behavior, you will
be able to communicate with them more effectively, should they cross your
path.

The Hostile Ones

Those individuals whom we shall refer to as *blockers*, for some psychological reason(s), have an irresistible urge to sabotage all forms of communication. They go out of their way to label ideas that are not their own as

misguided, irrelevant, and unworkable. They are also quick to indict any plan as ill-conceived and riddled with deficiencies. And, to round out their hostility, they have the reputation of dismissing most people as stupid, incompetent, and naïve. By whatever means they can devise, their express goal is to block human communication in any group of which they become a part.

It is important to realize that someone who asks sensible questions at company meetings, makes valuable points of reference, and initiates qualification whenever necessary should not be labeled as a blocker. The blocker has a compulsion to throw a monkey wrench into any effort by group members who share meaning and exchange information.

To illustrate how blockers ply their trade, imagine this scene: You are working for a large department store chain and attend a monthly sales meeting. At some point, you say, "Why don't we advertise our fall line in one of those foreign-language newspapers?" The blocker, sitting opposite you, would probably butt in and say, "Are you kidding? That would be a complete waste of time and money. The people who read those newspapers are as poor as church mice." In a characteristically negative, hostile, and argumentative tone, the blocker has spoken.

Someone who behaves similarly to the blocker is called a *contrary*. This individual gets pleasure out of saying *up* when you say *down*, *in* when you say *out*. No matter what contraries hear, they chime in with a diametrically opposite statement.

And finally, there is one other obstructive type who falls into this category: the *district attorney*. This type finds it necessary to cross-examine any group member who has advanced an opinion or idea. Interestingly, district attorneys rarely have an opinion or idea of their own; their stock in trade consists of attacking other people's views.

Whether you are dealing with a blocker, a contrary, or a district attorney, be aware that they are all in the same business—hostility. They will attempt to upset and unnerve you whenever, wherever, and however they can.

Bloomers 'n' Gloomers

In this grouping, you will find *optimists* and *pessimists*. The optimist views the world as a bowl of cherries, while the pessimist views it as a bowl of pits—doubt, despair, and misery. Whereas the optimist has mastered the art of positive thinking, the pessimist has mastered the opposite—the art of negative thinking.

If, in fact, how people believe does strongly influence their behavior, it behooves every company to find out whether important members of its staff are optimists or pessimists. Such knowledge can definitely affect a company's growth and development. Predictions can often be made as to how a particular individual will think or behave in a given situation. Optimists will usually regard a six-ounce glass of water with three ounces of water in it as "half full"; pessimists will usually regard it as "half empty." What is more, each of these types has the capacity to influence the thinking of other personnel. Frequently, a case of devout optimism or pessimism can be contagious and infect anyone who comes into contact with it.

When discussing optimistic or pessimistic philosophies on the job, a qualification should be made. Occasionally, you will encounter people who say one thing and do another. Saying what they think others want to hear, they verbally express a negative or positive point of view, and then proceed to do just the opposite. A chairman of the board, sensitive to the likes and dislikes of his colleagues, might voice a popular opinion to their faces and and privately do just the opposite. Though such contradictory behavior is the exception, it nevertheless can and does happen.

In itself, being a cockeyed optimist or a pessimist is no serious offense. It is only when our leaning in either direction becomes so intense that it interferes with our judgment, and others expect us to think or act a certain way. If an open and flexible mind is a pre-requisite to success in business, an extreme commitment to either optimism or pessimism should be taken to represent a liability, not an asset.

Know-It-Alls

May I now present the *qualifiers* and the *oracles*? Both act as if they have a hot line to God; information passes directly from God's mouth to their ears. No matter what anybody says, they take it upon themselves to let them know that they know all there is to know on the subject.

Jumping into a conversation to explain the meaning of what someone else has just said is the M.O. (modus operandi) of the qualifier. If a bank officer has just said, "Ladies and gentlemen, this is the first time in six years that our branch has received a commendation from the home office," the qualifier might interrupt and say, "What George is really trying to say is. . . ." Perhaps, out of some misguided sense of being helpful, this qualifier feels that if he or she didn't come to George's rescue, the rest of the staff might not correctly understand his meaning.

Supplying a group with endless commentaries is the express preoccupation of the qualifiers. While their intentions may be sincere and quite honorable, their actions run a high risk of being misunderstood. After all, few of us like to think that we are so incapable of expressing ourselves that we need an uninvited interpreter.

127

Oracles suffer from a similar superiority complex. Thinking that they know it all, they take every opportunity to remind us of it. Both the oracles and the qualifiers swim through life convinced that what others believe is utter nonsense and it is their solemn duty to set things right. A heavy responsibility, to say the least—especially when nobody asked them.

Time-Bounders

On practically every job, you will meet those who are continually looking backward and those who are looking ahead, i.e., how things used to be and how things are going to be. These people are locked into either the past or the future. We therefore will refer to those who look backward as *historians* and those who look forward as *prophets*. In more conversational terms, the historians can often be overheard saying such things as, "I remember when ———," "If only they would bring back the ———," and "They just don't make them like they did in the good ole days." In contrast, the prophets make such statements as "You watch, in the next ten years, there will be socialized medicine in this country," or "By the year two thousand A.D., the dollar won't be worth the paper it's printed on."

If reduced to the absurd, neither the historian nor the prophet seems to be living in the present. Any remark they make sounds locked into the past or future. It is an effort for them to speak about the here and now—what is going on today! If, by chance, they are pressured into talking about contemporary events, it won't be long before they drift backward or forward in time in search of an event with which the present can be compared.

Whether they are time-bounders or any of the other types being mentioned, you must not get the impression that people fall into neatly arranged slots. None of them are pure blockers, contraries, district attorneys, qualifiers, oracles, optimists, pessimists, historians, or prophets. The only justification for assigning them such labels is to alert you to the fact that each possesses some unique personality trait that differentiates him from the others.

Limelighters

In every group, there are individuals who require more attention than others. How they get the attention they need is very interesting. Some do it by telling jokes, uttering silly remarks, or making amusing facial expressions or gestures. We shall call this type the *playboy* or *playgirl*. Then there are those called *martyrs*, who get attention by playing the role of an injured party. If the whole group expresses a desire to have a company or department picnic and the martyr doesn't like picnics, he or she will say something like "Gee, I really don't like picnics, but don't let me spoil your fun. You all go ahead without me and have a good time. I'll find something to do by myself."

Still another means of getting into the limelight of a group is to be a *situationist*. They get attention by using their own special little gimmick. No matter what anyone says, they say, "Well, that really depends upon the situation." As an attention-getter, it almost never fails because it fits practically any set of circumstances.

As a group, situationists are harmless. They bid for attention, give their reasons why something depends upon something else, and patiently wait for an opportunity to do it again. Martyrs can be a little more annoying if they overdo their bid for pity. Playboys and playgirls run a similar risk of incurring group resentment if they overwork their jokes, wisecracks, and fooling around. While their respective behavior can be tolerated in small doses, the deciding factor is usually a matter of discretion.

Town Criers

Driven by some unseen force, the *information-giver* must, like a walking encyclopedia, pass on certain ideas, opinions, and information. Without being asked, the information-giver will give out any kind of information, regardless of who said it. From books, newspapers, magazine articles—you name it, these people relay what was said or written in a machinelike fashion.

Similar to, but not identical with, the information-giver is the *according-to freak*. This type of individual attracts attention by quoting others. With very few opinions of their own, according-to freaks repeatedly cite the words and works of others. An example would be, "According to Freud, dreams play an important role in our lives." Or, "According to Aristotle, 'As is the mind, so is the form.' " In short, while the information-giver is preoccupied with the dispensing of information, the according-to freak, in addition to the information, compulsively dwells on who said it.

Regulators

Three types of people fall into this category: *gatekeepers, police officers,* and *leaders*. They all have something in common—the need to influence what others say, think, and do. Let's look at them individually.

At every meeting, there is a certain amount of disorder—i.e., people talking while others are talking, an unwillingness to comply with parliamentary procedure, etc. Whatever the disturbance, it must be attended. It is the function of the police officer to regulate such misbehavior. Whereas, in the more formal group setting, a sergeant at arms is duly appointed, such a person is frequently self-appointed in the informal groups. This is some-

129

one who, when the group gets too noisy or unruly, calls out, "All right, everyone, let's have a little quiet now, OK?" This type seldom makes any profound contribution to the group aside from keeping the peace.

Also by self-appointment, the gatekeeper springs into action whenever a member of the group strays from the topic under discussion. Some people have a tendency to ramble or drift when participating in a group discussion. Staying on the subject is an art and it takes a disciplined mind. The need for a gatekeeper is almost always present. The question is: Who should perform that function? Since a gatekeeper is not specifically designated in an informal group, there is a tendency for the self-appointed gatekeeper to occasionally intimidate certain members. The presumptive gatekeeper might, therefore, say something like, "Just hold on a minute. We're talking about Christmas vacations and you bring up the responsibilities of a shop steward."

Little need be said about the leader type. Traditionally, leaders have a way of emerging whenever people come together—especially when they congregate for a purpose. If a leader is not elected or appointed, one (or perhaps more than one) generally assumes the role of guiding the direction of the group. Leaders assert themselves by either stepping to the front of the group, seating themselves in the center of the group, or sitting at the head of a conference table when no prior seating arrangements have been made. In addition, leader types come in all shapes and sizes and exert their leadership differently. Some do it softly, others by a show of strength.

In practically every group, there is at least one regulator, whether it be gatekeeper, police officer, or leader. Occasionally, two functions are served by one person. No matter what role they assume, all three take it upon themselves to manipulate others in some way. It would be improper to say that regulators are good or bad, helpful or destructive. Their value will generally be proportional to the needs they satisfy in any group to which they belong.

Transferites

Suppose you were at a meeting and sitting across the table from you was a manager with whom you were angry. During the course of the meeting, it became necessary for you to direct a remark to that manager. How would you do it? If you decided to tell someone else to tell that manager what you had in mind, the person who relayed your message would be a *go-between*.

People who are extremely timid about making open remarks in groups are occasionally observed to ask someone seated at their side to speak for them. "Harry, ask the chairperson why the meeting was called on a Saturday." When they are told that they should ask the question themselves if they really want to know the answer, they generally retire into silence. Those who are willing to do their bidding, that is, transfer a message from one person to another, bring to mind the game we used to play as kids, called "telephone." It consisted of one child whispering something to another, and so on.

The word *transferites*, as used here, applies to people whose major interest is passing on information. It is a way of getting involved and, at the same time, not getting involved. While transferites may be accused of distorting the information they pass, they can usually blame the source of the information. Barring such a complication, it is essentially a low-risk group role.

Recorders are people possessed with a compelling urge to jot things down. They are forever asking others for a piece of paper and a pencil. They make great notetakers because of an unwillingness to trust anything to memory. While having someone like this in a group generally serves a useful purpose, it occasionally creates an annoyance when they write slowly. By continuously interrupting the flow of conversation in order to "get things down," they have a tendency to compromise any spontaneity that might exist. Neither recorders nor go-betweens represent a serious threat to the group. The only thing that bears watching when dealing with them is that they accurately relate the information they receive.

Out-to-Lunchers

Have you ever had the feeling while talking with someone that he was not really with you—sort of out to lunch? Be on the lookout for these four types: intellectual virgins, gigglers, mannequins, and parrots. Each possesses a unique personality trait that, when experienced, will leave you with mixed emotions.

The intellectual virgin (male or female) rarely has an opinion on anything. Whatever you ask or tell them comes as a revelation. If you say that cotton is cooler than polyester, they usually respond with, "Wow, that's really fantastic—wow, cotton is cooler than polyester—wow!" Their entire vocabulary seems to consist of little more than a series of wows, gee whizzes, gollys, and no kiddings. They often seem surprised to learn that the world is round and that bees can fly. If you ask them whether they prefer to travel by bus, train, or plane, they become completely confused and mumble things like, "Gee, I never really thought of that. I don't know—gosh, that's a good question."

Gigglers do just that, they giggle instead of speaking. While the reason for their giggling may be a matter of stupidity, ignorance, or nervous tension, they giggle at practically everything.

Mannequins haven't any opinions and don't giggle. Like store-window dummies, they sit or stand in silence. They can go through an entire evening sitting in the same chair at a social function. If you ask whether they are having a good time, they usually smile and, if they are in a festive mood, occasionally nod affirmatively. If you ask if they want a sandwich, they might utter a clipped yes or a reasonable facsimile. Some mannequins are smilers, others are frowners, and still others make no motion at all. Mind you, these people are not necessarily retarded or unintelligent. Their behavior generally is a result of some personality problem.

Carefully watched, mannequins can be observed to make some very definite non-verbal statements in a group. A raised eyebrow, direct or indirect eye contact, limb positioning, or trunk posturing could each have a meaning missed by those who limit their concept of communication to talking. Unfortunately, our society is still a little reluctant to recognize non-verbal participation in a group as a legitimate medium of exchange. The notion that the person who doesn't speak isn't participating still prevails.

Parrots are people who repeat portions of what they hear. If I say, "Well, it's getting late. I think I'll go home," a parrot type would say, "—hmm—late, go home." You must have encountered people who repeat the last part of what you have just said. If I were a parrot person and you just told me that it was hot outside, I would mutter "—hot outside." Being around such people makes you feel as if you are in some kind of echo chamber.

THINGS YOU SHOULD KNOW ABOUT DEALING WITH PEOPLE IN GROUPS

It is one thing to name and describe the types of people you are apt to meet in various groups, but quite another to know how to deal with them. This part of the chapter will supply you with some suggestions and recommendations that, if applied, will prove useful. Be mindful of the fact, however, that each of the group types just presented was deliberately portrayed in an exaggerated form in order to illustrate a specific personality trait.

Dealing with the Hostile Ones

℞ Dealing with blockers, contraries, and district attorneys on the job is a tricky business. While dismissing, warning, suspending, and admonishing them are available as last resorts, there is a more tactful or strategic approach. It involves understanding how the hostile one's mind operates. Essentially, it thrives on attention and, almost invariably, spits out remarks that lack anything even remotely resembling a sound foundation. Therefore, to rob the hostile ones of their incentive or motivation, you must pay as little attention as possible to what they have to say and, every chance you get, press them for explanations to support their remarks.

Whenever you are attacked by a hostile one, it is important to remember that the hostility being displayed may be a displaced hostility. This means that whatever the individual is hostile about may have little or nothing to do with you personally. The real object of hostility might be the person's husband, wife, boss, girl or boyfriend, children, or relatives. Or, closer to the situation at hand, it might be the job or people related to the job. The point is, you must not do what most people do when they are attacked—that is, think that the attack was provoked by something you either said or did.

By snapping at whatever the hostile one is using as bait, such as an *obstructive remark* ("What? You've got to be kidding, George. That idea has no more a chance of working than a snowball has of surviving in Hell."), a *contrary statement* ("I disagree, Joan. I think it would be better to have our next state convention in the fall, not the spring."), or an *argumentative attack* ("Just hold on a second, Phil. Where did you get those statistics you just threw at us?"), you are walking into a trap. However, by recognizing it as an attempt to get attention, you deprive the hostile one of any payoff. It's not unlike getting rid of ants in your kitchen. Once you have removed whatever the ants came for, they will cease and desist. Most hostile ones, if handled this way a couple of times, will get off your back and seek other less suspecting and more susceptible victims.

Dealing with Bloomers 'n' Gloomers

If you should meet an optimist or a pessimist in a group, try not to browbeat him into believing what you believe to be realistic or rational. Once you have discovered whether the person with whom you are dealing is an optimist or a pessimist, it isn't too difficult to predict how he will approach any given subject. The problem is to decide the best way of dealing with him on the job. One basic rule is to try and get at *why* the optimist or pessimist believes as he does. Don't think for a moment that his way of behaving developed overnight; it probably took years. It would be foolish for you to think that you can straighten such people out in a matter of minutes.

One effective method of dealing with optimists or pessimists is to anticipate their frame of reference—that is, where they are coming from. For instance, in responding to an optimist's remark, you might begin by saying, "Even though I fully realize that everything is going to turn out just great . . ."—and then, continue with the rest of what you were going to

133

say. While such an optimistic opening statement may not completely satisfy the optimist's need to see the world through rose-colored glasses, it will at least serve to identify you as someone who is also ready, willing, and able to engage in the art of positive thinking.

For the pessimist, use the same technique in reverse. Say, "I am fully aware of the fact that all of this work is a waste of time, but. . . ." With optimists and pessimists alike, your remarks will put them on notice that you are aware of their philosophy toward life, and sensitive to how someone subscribing to that philosophy thinks and feels.

This method of dealing with optimists and pessimists should not in any way be taken to compromise your own way of looking at things. All it should do is establish the fact that you are willing to communicate with someone having a different orientation, and not permit the difference to act as an obstacle. If successful, an attitude like this can act as a baseline or starting point from which both parties can enjoy a free and meaningful exchange of information.

Dealing with Know-It-Alls

B. Coping with people who fancy themselves as know-it-alls takes some doing. If what they say is ignored or taken too lightly, they sometimes attack with even greater vigor. Their weakest point (Achilles heel) seems to be their credibility. They experience their greatest communication setbacks when what they say is treated as stupid, inane, or inappropriate. This characteristic is a major clue to dealing with them. You must try to discredit whatever claims they make—challenge their contentions as rigorously as possible. If know-it-alls can be made to realize that their lofty claims and unsupported opinions will be met with criticism and doubt, they will think twice before airing them the next time. Their continued success in any group can often be traced to the fact that, more often than not, their remarks go unchallenged.

One more thing you should know about know-it-alls is that, after years of pontificating on practically everything, they are inclined to take themselves too seriously. This makes it increasingly difficult for them to separate their remarks from their emotions. They tend to interpret any attack against *what* they say as a personal attack against *who* they are. This tendency, if overdone, could make them even more difficult to communicate with on the job.

Dealing with Time-Bounders

B. The problem you will have in dealing with historians and prophets is to get them to talk about what is going on in the world *right now*.

Pretend that a historian with whom you work has just said, "I remember when a hot dog was only a nickel." How would you deal with such a statement? You might consider asking how the value of a dollar in those days compares with the value of a dollar today.

If the historian's counterpart, the prophet, were to speculate that in five years, a hot dog will be two dollars, how would you respond? You might say, "What conditions in today's market could account for the price of a hot dog going up to two dollars five years from now?"

In both cases, your goal should be to get each of them to speak in terms of the way things are today, not how they used to be or how they will be in the future. Only allow references to the past and future as a means of getting them to relate to the present—that is, as a means of comparison.

Dealing with Limelighters

℞ Not unlike some of the others just described, limelighters (playboys, playgirls, and situationists) have a strong need to be noticed. The only difference seems to be *how* they solicit attention. Although, at times, their behavior can result in the reduction of group tension, it usually increases the tension by blocking constructive interpersonal communication.

These individuals will continue their antics as long as they are tolerated. Objections to their behavior by one or perhaps two members of the group generally fail to stop them. However, if the entire group should register a complaint, they will usually behave themselves.

Another technique for dealing with limelighters is to ignore them. At first, being ignored will incite the more determined ones, but as soon as they see that the group means business, they will usually quiet down. Others, recognizing that the group no longer has anything to offer them, will leave.

In a strict sense, situationists are not full-fledged limelighters. Through trial and error, they have learned that by saying, "That depends upon the situation," after almost any given statement, they will cause eyes to be turned in their direction. Not terribly interested in where their comment will take the conversation, their concern is limited to being recognized as a member of a group. They are not a malicious type and require little in the way of psychological nourishment. Unless they demonstrate that their comment will be followed by some constructive thought, it should be acknowledged and casually glossed over.

Dealing with Town Criers

℞ Dealing with the information-giver or according-to freak depends, to a large extent, upon your own personality. You may be someone who is unable to tolerate show-offs, people who either flaunt their knowledge or repeatedly name-drop. If this is your temperament, you might derive some genuine pleasure from exposing such people as phonies or pseudo-intellectuals. A more tolerant personality might, however, remain undisturbed by their conduct.

Since there is no need to advise those who are unaffected by town criers, here is a suggestion for those who are annoyed by them. As quickly as possible, the information-giver or according-to freak must be put on the defensive. Do this by asking them such questions as: How does what you are telling me relate to what we are discussing? What is your point? Did the person you just quoted say anything else that might contradict what you have just said? How can I be sure that your quote is accurate? Do you want me to accept what you just said on faith or are you prepared to give me additional proof?

Questions like these have a way of quickly placing people on the defensive. Needless to say, they should only be used if you find it necessary to defend yourself against one of these types of people.

Dealing with Regulators

℞ Since these individuals fancy themselves destined to influence others, they require the cooperation of those who will allow themselves to be influenced. Most people have been conditioned to take orders and therefore do not have much difficulty honoring authority. Up through the years, parents, older brothers and sisters, teachers, and a variety of people designated by society have been giving them orders. Consequently, the role of the regulator comes as no surprise in group life. There are some, however, who resent being told what to do, where to sit, and when to speak. Unless they themselves occupy a position of authority in a group, they must learn how to deal with it in others.

Regulators can either be submitted to, ignored, or opposed. If they are duly appointed by the group, they are seldom resisted. It is when they are self-appointed that the trouble usually begins. Occasionally, those whose personalities are of equal strength will clash, and there is a vying for power in the group.

One of the more common methods of dealing with an unpopular or unwanted regulator is to enlist the support of other members of the group. Another technique is to confront the would-be leader, gatekeeper, or police officer and demand to know the reasons why he or she should have such authority and not the others. A final suggestion is to insist upon taking a vote to determine whether the self-appointed regulator has the support and confidence of the membership.

136

Dealing with Transferites

[B] Getting along with recorders and go-betweens is usually uncomplicated. The only real danger arises when they fail to accurately relate the information they are given. Messages, under the best of circumstances, are often misunderstood. Therefore, whenever you are in a situation where someone is responsible for communicating what you mean to someone else, be absolutely certain that you check it out beforehand. For example, any executive who dictates a letter to his secretary and neglects to read it carefully before it is mailed may run into trouble on the other end. Secretaries are not mind readers, nor are they privy to the larger picture. It is almost impossible for anyone to know exactly what another person has in mind. At best, people who act as go-betweens or recorders arrive at an approximation of what was said or meant by those they represent.

The successful monitoring of transferites means to carefully screen what they write for such items as word choice, sentence structure, punctuation, and correctness of names, dates, and places. If the information being relayed is oral, in addition to monitoring its verbal content, its nonverbal content (facial expressions, gestures, and body movements) and paralinguistic delivery (tone of voice, speech speed, emphasis, and phrasing) must also be considered. While taking all of these precautions will substantially reduce the chance of communication being distorted by the transferite, it is still far from a foolproof method.

Dealing with Out-to-Lunchers

[B] Intellectual virgins, gigglers, mannequins, and parrots are the types of people who make up this category. Dealing with them in groups is more a matter of understanding and patience than of confrontation. With few exceptions, they are people who have made an unsatisfactory adjustment to getting along with people in groups. Because they feel threatened by collections of people, they have developed ways of coping that, for them, represent a means of survival.

Although out-to-lunchers seldom achieve management status, there are the occasional exceptions. These occur when the son or daughter of a family-owned business is placed in a position of responsibility with which he or she cannot cope. Another case in point would be where an executive, showing favoritism, elevates some unqualified person to a managerial or supervisory position.

If you find yourself having to deal with out-to-lunchers on the job, it can be very frustrating. Most of them, with few exceptions, cannot be reasoned with on a serious and logical basis. The situation also runs the risk of being further complicated by their emotional disposition. Your best bet will be to appeal to their immediate superiors. If this is not feasible, you have two choices: tolerate them or find another position. Of one thing you can be sure: the probability of an out-to-luncher ever shaping up is extremely unlikely.

8

Getting Others to See Things Your Way

Regardless of how advanced you are in your career, an ability to influence others is essential. Whether buying or selling a product or vying for a promotion on the job, you must get your customer, client, or employer to see things your way. This same principle applies if you are trying to sell yourself. You must get whomever you are trying to impress to see you in a particular way.

Several words can be used to describe the process of getting people to see things your way. These include <u>brainwashing</u>, <u>propaganda</u>, <u>coercion</u>, <u>seduction</u>, <u>manipulation</u>, <u>influence</u>, <u>inducement</u>, and <u>persuasion</u>. Although each of them employs communication to reach its goal, their reputations vary. To some people, <u>propaganda</u>, <u>brainwashing</u>, and <u>manipulation</u> are dirty words. Terms such as <u>influence</u> and <u>inducement</u>, by contrast, enjoy much greater respectability.

With deference to the adage "It's not <u>what</u> you know, but <u>who</u> you know," the pages ahead will attempt to displace such a notion and, in its place, leave you with the opinion that "who" you know may be of little value unless you can exert some positive influence on that person.

We are living in a country with the greatest "influencing density" in the world. Manufacturing and manipulating public opinion and behavior are big business. Whether you like it or not, to compete, you must become a part of that business. To hide or

behave as though it doesn't exist can only lead to a
weak and vulnerable state. Too many of us have
already declared ourselves helpless victims of an
overbearing society. A submissive attitude like this
is not only wrong, it is unnecessary. If you understand how and why you influence others as well as
how and why they influence you, your ability to communicate will be substantially enriched. This, in
time, will better enable others to see things your
way and, by so doing, help you become successful.

GENESIS OF INFLUENCE

To be human is to be susceptible to influence. The fact that we live, love, and work together demands that we develop an ability to cope with what- ever positive or negative influences we encounter.

As children, we found it difficult to avoid the influence of our parents. They told us when to get up in the morning, when to go to sleep at night, when to eat, what to wear, which programs we could watch on television, and with whom we could play after school. Their influence, on many oc- casions, came dangerously close to being absolute during any given twenty- four-hour period. And, to make matters worse, their influence was further compounded by the influence exerted by grandparents, uncles, aunts, brothers, and sisters. All, for whatever reasons they deemed appropriate, tried to get us to see things their way.

The impact of the influence to which we were exposed as children did not disappear when we became teen-agers. Instead, it was supple- mented by our teachers, friends, and peers. Teachers, for example, fre- quently tried to convince us that their subject was the most important one in the entire curriculum. Self-serving friends and peers protected their egos and interests by enlisting our undying loyalty and friendship. But, because we could no longer childishly respond to their influence with crying spells and temper tantrums, managing our reactions became increasingly difficult.

The realization that our lives were not our own became most evident when we entered the job market. We were confronted by strangers who began telling us what to do, when to do it, and how they wanted it done. Outside influence grew steadily. This, we were told, was the nature of "working for a living." For a salary, we would be obliged to submit to the influence of others, that is, to see and do things their way, whether we like it or not.

Today, people are preoccupied with influencing others. This is evidenced by our rapidly growing knowledge about controlling human behavior. The mass media have a paramount objective—to influence how people think, feel, and behave. Magazines, books, newspapers, films, tapes, records, and television all play their parts in this influential process. Whatever word you may choose to describe such "influencing"—the bottom line is power, the power to influence!

Since the serpent successfully influenced Eve to eat the forbidden fruit in the Garden of Eden, history could be measured by carefully noting who influenced whom, and what they did about it. Such influence opened and closed minds, encouraged and discouraged new ideas, and helped vote into public office both qualified and unqualified politicians. The lesson to be learned from these events is this: without an opportunity to influence or persuade one another, our personal and public growth depreciates rapidly.

Persuading Others

Behind every effort to get others to see things your way, there is usually a motive. Regardless of whether it is intentional or unintentional, rational or irrational, real or imagined—there is, nevertheless, a motive. The same goes for those trying to influence you. In either case, knowing *why* someone is trying to influence you or why you are trying to influence someone can be extremely important. It could provide a deeper insight into the influential process. For instance, if you had a job and wanted a raise in salary, you might try being especially nice to your boss; offer to work overtime without expecting to be paid for it, or do certain things you would not normally do on the job. But what would you do if your boss became suspicious and asked you why you were being so nice? You could deny any special behavior and claim that it is your natural way, or openly declare that you are bucking for a raise. Your employer's reaction might take many forms, depending upon her mood, your past performance, how well the business was doing, her preconceived notions about the kind of behavior that warrants a raise, or the reason you gave for wanting one. Whatever the situation, knowing the reason behind it can make a significant difference in the attitude of the people involved.

Anyone with practical experience in the field knows how unwilling most people are to reveal their true motives. Whereas someone angling for a raise might behave in a number of different ways, he would probably deny it if you confronted him with the question "Are you bucking for a raise?" It is the rare individual who freely admits an ulterior motive for doing something. Most motives have to be guessed at or inferred from what people say or do. Perhaps it is because certain members of our culture frown on actions based upon such motives as greed, power, status, and control. Too often, admitting that you are motivated by these traits leads

141

to embarrassment. There are, of course, circles in which such motivational attitudes are held in high regard, and even bragged about.

In the business and professional world, success is a common motive. But the term *success* is an abstraction that means different things to different people. While financial growth is usually a leading symbol of success, it is not the only qualification. A man who has built a successful toy company may have more than one motive for continuing: (1) to remain its president or (2) to have the business prosper so that his son can take over after he retires.

Motives may be overt or covert. Telling others that you want to be a physician so you can help relieve human suffering is an overt motive. However, secretly wanting to become a physician to fulfill your parents' dream would be a covert motive—one that you might not feel like telling others.

Another sample of overt motivation would be the desire to become an attorney to protect the poor from excessive abuse in the courts. Covert motivation to become an attorney might be a secret desire to outdo a brother or sister.

Wanting to influence others is perfectly normal—providing the desire is honest, ethical, moral, and legal. From the standpoint of communication, it demonstrates an awareness of others, a willingness to satisfy their needs, or to create a situation that will arouse in them a sense of need.

Arthur Schlesinger, talking to this point, said, "If man or machine were infallible, there would be no need for persuasion; but because they are not, the discipline of consent is indispensible to civilized society." We humans appear to need some form of control or influence over one another. As an inescapable part of living, we must find ways and means of getting others to think and act in accord with our wishes. This is the mainspring of progress whether it be in the home, on the campaign trail, selling flowers in the park, or supervising thirty men on a construction site. In each case, there should be trusting openness to the process of influence, and a willingness to accept, reject, or hold in abeyance any consequences it might deliver.

THIS BUSINESS OF BELIEVING

Why People Believe

Why do you believe anything? A day in your life doesn't go by without your being bombarded with information by the mass media. Your clock radio awakens you with the weather forecast, time, and early morning news. If rain is predicted, do you believe it and reach for an umbrella? If a voice announces the correct time, do you immediately reset your wrist-watch? If you hear reports of torrential rains in southern California, do you pick up your phone and call relatives who live in the area to find out if they are all right? Of all the information that floods your senses, how on earth do you know what to believe and what not to believe?

For centuries, statesmen, philosophers, educators, industrialists, and military leaders have tried to figure out why people believe some things and not others. The strongest reason for such interest seems to stem from the fact that people's beliefs usually dictate their behavior. If they believe there are sharks in the water, they stay on the beach; if they believe the Earth is flat, they stay away from the edge, and so on. Therefore, crucial to any study of how to best influence others—that is, to get them to see things your way—is to find out as much as you can about their belief system.

There are three ways of influencing people: through emotions, logic, and status.

There are people who, given a sob story, will believe practically anything. This is clearly seen on the streets of any large city where con games operate. Would you believe that one con artist collected over two thousand dollars in one day for the "widow of the Unknown Soldier"? The kinds of far-out things people will believe is staggering. Whether they have a psychological need to believe, are not too street-wise, or have a deep compassion for their fellow human beings is not at issue here. The important thing for you to realize is that their need to believe is largely based on the type of influence exerted upon them. One of these methods operates through their emotions.

Most of us learned to respect logic early in life; i.e., if something is logical, it is probably right and should be believed. Little else seems to matter to those who worship logic. Let all forms of evidence reek of deception except logic, and these people will believe whatever idea is being advanced. They fail to recognize that something can be logically valid but materially untrue. Consider these two statements leading to a conclusion:

Major Premise: All dogs have two heads.

Minor Premise: Spotty is a dog.

Conclusion: Spotty has two heads.

Whereas this form of reasoning conforms to the rules of logic and is, therefore, valid—it is materially untrue because in the real world, *all dogs do not have two heads.*

Regardless of this qualification, there are those who will continue to believe anything that is logical. These same people are also inclined to believe anything supported by statistical or mathematical proof.

143

Emotional or logical appeals have little or no effect upon those who are impressed by status. Messages from people in high places (governmental officials, celebrities of the sports world, and stars of radio, stage, and screen) are readily believed because of their status. No matter how far out or off the wall their opinions may be, those who are influenced by status will believe them.

True or False

In almost every work situation, you will find people who are preoccupied with whether something is true or false. When asked to explain why they feel this way, they say, "Because it helps me decide what to think and how to act." Considerations such as style, economy, correctness, public appeal, and convenience play secondary roles in their reasoning. What they seem unable to understand or unwilling to accept is that most transactions on the job are based on assumptions, presumptions, inferences, faith, and intuition. If all of the decisions made at the office depended upon whether the information on which they were based was true or false, many would never be made.

Unlike the temperature of water (which can be measured with any reliable thermometer), the width of a carton (which can be measured with any reliable ruler or tape measure), or the weight of a man (which can be determined by any reliable scale), most decisions or judgments involving human traits such as motivation, integrity, loyalty, dependablity, sincerity, and aggressiveness cannot be as easily tested.

Assume, if you will, that you are working for an employer whose notion of true dedication to a job demands a perfect attendance record. In his mind, your chances of getting a raise or promotion would be extremely slim if you were out sick every Tuesday and Thursday. Despite the fact that you are an excellent worker in every other regard, your employer would not consider you to have a *true* dedication to your job.

To such an employer, deciding if your dedication to your job is true or false will probably hinge on your attendance record. The equation is simple: Good attendance = True dedication. The fact that the world *true* is highly abstract and requires careful definition does not seem to bother such employers. In an arbitrary and capricious manner, they seize upon some human characteristic and, on the basis of it, decide an employee's worth. An attendance record is but one such preoccupation. There are also punctuality, dress, politeness, attitude, neatness, truthfulness, assertiveness, etc.

No respectable discussion on the subject of whether something is true or false would be complete without mentioning a very sensitive phenomenon—*lying*. To define a lie by saying it is something that is not true is about as meaningless as defining a cat by saying that it is not a dog. And yet, millions of people in business lie to one another 365 days a year. If caught in the act, they defend themselves by redefining the word *lie* by calling what they did strategy, diplomacy, cunning, shrewdness, or gamesmanship.

Regardless of how people manipulate their words to influence others, public opinion toward lying is predominantly negative. In some organizations, lying is punishable by immediate dismissal. In others, a more tolerant attitude consists of an attempt to determine the circumstances surrounding the alleged lie—i.e., the intent behind the lie, the nature of the lie itself, and any consequences resulting from the lie.

Practically all forms of influence depend upon what people believe. Thus, your ability to persuade anyone of anything will be based, to a large extent, upon how closely your beliefs agree with theirs. Most people will persuade themselves if they are provided with information that agrees with what they already believe.

Propaganda

For many of us, the word *propaganda* brings to mind visions of spies, secret police, wartime aircraft dropping leaflets from the sky, and rabble-rousers distributing pamphlets on street corners. All have the same purpose —to get you to see things their way. But propaganda need not be negative. It can be used for good purposes as well. According to William Hunnel and Keith Huntress in their book *The Analysis of Propaganda*, "The motives and the ends are the important parts of any campaign; propaganda for products. . . . But the same methods are used to . . . win support for the Red Cross, to obtain help for crippled children. The aims are different, but the methods are the same."

Propaganda has sold everything from sex to farm equipment to birth control in India. There are few things any of us do each day that cannot be traced back to some form of propaganda. The moment we set foot on a new job, we begin to experience the propaganda devised by management. Many of the notions we harbor from previous positions must be unlearned; we must be deprogrammed. Most companies fancy themselves unique and waste no time telling you, "Forget what you did in the last place you worked! We do things a little differently here." With admonitions like this, the propaganda process begins.

In a sense, all propagandists are missionaries. They are missionaries for an idea, an action, or an attitude. Thus defined, every business and profession selling a service or product has its staff of missionaries (salespersons). They go out among the people and spread the word. If it is to survive, an organization must grow. To do this, its propagandists must communicate its worth to the public.

Information comes to us from learned members of our society: mathematicians, physicists, physicians, bacteriologists, geologists, astronomers, etc. They tell us that serious problems can be solved with mathematics, it takes eight minutes for light from the sun to reach us, red blood cells pass through capillary walls, bacteria give off toxins, earthquakes are caused by faults in the earth, and planets in our solar system revolve around the sun. We accept what they tell us without being able to personally verify their statements. What all this means is that most of our information comes to us secondhand.

If you are willing to accept on faith what the experts tell you, and what you see and hear from the mass media, there should be absolutely no reason why you can't accept yourself on faith. See yourself as a propagandist whose express purpose in life is to get others to believe in you. Begin by setting a good example and believe in yourself.

Brainwashing

Propaganda is child's play compared to brainwashing. Whereas both are methods of getting people to change their beliefs or behavior, they employ different techniques. For example, brainwashing utilizes such techniques as starvation, freezing, psychological and physical abuse, and isolation. Victims are continuously annoyed and questioned until the only way they can gain any relief from their brainwashers is to yield to their bidding.

Referring to them by any other name and using them in a variety of more subtle ways, certain organizations practice lesser forms of brainwashing capable of effecting changes in the beliefs and behavior of their employees. These include removing certain privileges from those who step out of line and rewarding those who render the company some special service. Tattling on a fellow employee may be encouraged by management, suggesting that it is in the best interest of the company. Personal feelings must take a back seat to what is best for the company. The employee is often torn between self-interests and company interests. The result is frequently some degree of behavior modification, that is, doing whatever you are told by those who pay your salary.

Rumors: Spreaders and Believers

Rumors consist of information passed from person to person, and the human chain along which it passes is called a grapevine. Like propaganda, rumors are generally considered to have a negative connotation. This, how-

146

ever, is not consistently true. They may serve a constructive purpose if they reflect an interest in the work, in the people doing it, and in the organization for which the work is being done. They can be destructive when they result in a betrayal of company secrets, poison someone's reputation, lower morale, or distract people from their work. Whatever their impact, constructive or destructive, rumors do exert a definite influence within the organization.

People are attracted to and often fascinated by rumors. This is especially true when they are anxious about the outcome of a particular event or action. The more anxious or frustrated they are, the more willing they are to accept practically any explanation or version of it. Suppose a rumor got out that the company for which you were working was going to be taken over by some big conglomerate. Most employees, hungry to find out how such a takeover would affect them personally, would probably be quick to believe a number of different interpretations of what was going to happen.

Another reason why so many people believe rumors pertaining to their jobs is that knowing something, even though it is not accurate or backed up by solid evidence, is better than knowing nothing at all. In this sense, rumors can be said to reduce tension by satisfying those who are cursed with a burning curiosity.

Contrary to popular opinion, few people have the compelling desire to "spread the word." The average person on the job is a passive receiver of rumors. Those having a psychological need to spread rumors—to tell others things they didn't ask to hear—are known as "change agents." Along with fancying themselves as serving the best interest of those whom they tell, they also perceive themselves as playing an important role within the company.

People on a grapevine are usually job-centered and, as such, can be extremely useful to alert managers, supervisors, and administrators. Instead of being viewed as something to be censored, the grapevine should be taken full advantage of and treated as an asset to communication. For example, great care should be exercised in seeing to it that rumor-spreaders are supplied with accurate information. It is bad enough that the information they spread suffers from varying degrees of distortion as it passes from mouth to ear.

Other means by which management can exert an influence on rumors include: (1) maintaining a constant alert to what employees are saying; (2) keeping inter-office information up to date; (3) correcting any misinformation that is currently being circulated on the grapevine; and (4) making certain that all company communication is as clear as possible before it is dispatched.

Rumors travel rapidly, efficiently, and without regard for truth or consequence. The exact nature of what is passed from person to person depends upon the people themselves. Some, upon receiving negative information, enthusiastically pass it along; others refuse to pass on anything negative. Then there are those who don't give a damn one way or the other and will pass on anything they hear. Finally, there are those who, under any circumstance, flatly refuse to participate in any rumor-spreading activity. In all, those who constitute the grapevine in any company are a mixed bunch—each operating from an individual set of psychological needs.

The next time someone approaches you with a red-hot rumor, notice your own response. Do you immediately walk away, stay and listen, ask for more information, reprimand the rumor-spreader, or wonder why the person is telling you all this? Explore your reactions to a grapevine on the job and the kinds of people it attracts.

ANALYZING YOUR AUDIENCE

Getting one person to see things your way has a great deal in common with persuading many to do it. While there are some distinctions to be made regarding the technique used, basic principles are the same.

Earlier, you were told that meaning is in people, not in their words or actions. This factor alone makes knowing how to analyze your audience an invaluable tool in such situations as sales meetings, conferences, training programs, negotiations, seminars, union rallies, and briefings. Whether your works requires you to influence a group or an individual, the response will usually be based on whatever meanings are assigned to your words and actions. Also to be borne in mind is that making a good speech or presentation, by itself, does not always yield success. But a good speech or presentation buttressed by a carefully planned audience analysis frequently does.

Orientation

One of the most common mistakes you can make in preparing to influence an audience is to think of it as separate and apart from yourself. You must, instead, think of yourself and your audience as a whole—that is, two halves of something continuously supplying each other with positive or negative feedback. At no time should you think of yourself or your audience as independent of each other.

Experienced actors and actresses are sensitive to their audiences. Backstage, you frequently hear them asking, "What's the audience like out there tonight?" Such characteristics as friendly, restless, hostile, receptive, or apathetic are often assigned to particular audiences. On the basis of these judgments, some performers can predict with incredible accuracy the kind of feedback they can expect. So, you see, audiences are not merely blobs of feelingless humanity. They register their reactions to speakers, and whatever affects them as an audience is relayed to the speaker as feedback.

Like chemical compounds, audiences are composed of different elements. Alone or in combination with others, these elements determine the ultimate outcome of any interaction between speaker and audience. Hence, the success of any speech will depend heavily upon how well an audience has been analyzed by a speaker. Perhaps you are familiar with the expression "the operation was successful, but the patient died." Its moral can be applied to the art of persuasion. The best speech in the world is doomed to failure if the audience to which it is delivered does not respond appropriately.

Another mistake is to think that audiences remain the same. They don't. Beyond having the ability to change from time to time, an audience can change while a speech is in progress. Audiences have been known to start out in a quiet and orderly manner and, in minutes, become extremely agitated and hostile. Then again, hostile audiences can suddenly become quiet and manageable.

The best safeguard against losing control of an audience is to have as clear an understanding of its nature as possible. Bear in mind, however, that there is no such thing as an ironclad guarantee when it comes to predicting an audience's behavior. Only by finding out all you can about an audience will you increase your chances of getting others to see things your way. Here are some characteristics of an audience you will find worth considering.

Size

The size of an audience is important. Depending upon the kind of business or profession you are in, you will have to deal with either large or small audiences. Each type will require a slightly different approach. For example, should your audience be large, appropriate seating arrangements must be made. You will have to decide whether to have the chairs arranged in a circle, in a horseshoe shape, or in traditional rows. If people are seated so they can see one another easily, they will be more apt to behave responsively. In addition, the reactions of an audience have a contagious nature. Laughter, applause, smiles, cheers, comments, and boos have been known to spread rapidly from person to person. Because of this tendency,

149

your enthusiasm and effectiveness as a speaker may be increased or decreased.

You must also consider the physical comfort of your audience. People who make up a large audience are more inclined to experience physical discomfort than those constituting a small audience. This is because large numbers of people generate more body heat and make a room warmer, plus the fact that by consuming more oxygen, they give off more carbon dioxide, which makes them somewhat irritable. The availability of a good ventilating system would, understandably, reduce the extent of their discomfort. A general rule to be borne in mind, therefore, is that audience discomfort increases resistance to a speaker's message, whereas audience comfort decreases it.

Resistance to a message being presented is further compounded by the fact that a large audience often fails to get the full benefit of a speaker's body language. While they may hear what is being said, many members of that audience cannot clearly see the speaker's body movements, gestures, and facial expressions. To compensate for this visual deficiency, it is essential that a good public address system be used—one that doesn't squeal when you pick it up or echo when you talk into it.

Small audiences are easier to manage. Aside from the fact that a more informal speaker/audience atmosphere can be created with less difficulty, the people constituting a small audience can be positioned and repositioned with less effort. Should you ever be faced with the need to address a large audience, try to break it down into smaller groups, if possible, and address each of them separately. Since more persuasion is achieved through the emotions than through the intellect, small audiences are preferable. Another advantage of the small audience is that the personal identities of its members tend to remain more clearly defined. Although experienced speakers can usually handle both large and small audiences, their greatest effectiveness most often occurs with the smaller ones.

Intelligence

To misjudge the intelligence of your audience is to invite unnecessary resistance. Talking down to people or over their heads is an error you cannot afford to make. Of the two, the less damaging error is to talk over an audience's head. People seem to be somewhat less resentful of a speaker who gives them credit for having more intelligence than they actually have than one who does not.

Unless you know the approximate level of intelligence of your audience beforehand, you will have to make an on-the-spot judgment from the speaker's platform. Relying upon such things as your common sense, power of observation, and intuition, you will have to make a guesstimate of how intelligent the people sitting before you are. The clues you use will have to include the way they are dressed, the look in their eyes, their postures, facial expressions, and general body movements. At best, you will be grasping at straws. Which of us has not met individuals who looked intelligent and turned out to be dullards, and those who looked like dullards but turned out to be intelligent? In spite of the risks associated with relying on our first impressions of people, we continue to take them.

It is also essential to recognize the difference between those who are intelligent and those who are knowledgeable. A person can be very intelligent and not knowledgeable or extremely knowledgeable and not too intelligent. Without going into a lengthy discussion of the subject, let us say that intelligent people have the potential to learn and the ability to manipulate ideas, whereas the knowledgeable individual is simply one who possesses a great deal of information.

The reason for making this distinction between intelligent and knowledgeable people is that it will help you decide how to deal with them more effectively. For example, it would make little sense for you to expect a not-so-intelligent audience to follow a complicated line of reasoning or to make subtle inferences from your remarks. If your audience were composed of knowledgeable, but not overly intelligent people, your best plan would be to stick with what you believe them to know and thereby ease them around to your point of view. To repeat, when dealing with a knowledgeable (but not too intelligent) audience, confine yourself to the familiar; when dealing with an intelligent (but not too knowledgeable) audience, attempt to engage their minds through logical and creative thought.

Language

Bridging the gap between theory and practice is not always easy. Those involved with management trainee programs should be able to appreciate the truth of this statement. In Chapter 3, "Advertising Yourself with What You Say and How You Say It," you were introduced to the use and abuse of language. In this chapter, those foundational elements of speech and language are applied to analyzing an audience.

There are several things about your language that can either help or hinder your getting an audience to see things your way. A poor choice of words, foreign expressions, unfamiliar terms, and flowery language are each capable of confusing or rubbing people the wrong way. The degree to which you offend them will, of course, depend upon their attitude toward language.

It is difficult to believe that in this day and age so many of us are still having difficulty separating people from their words. If someone uses dirty words, that person is dirty; if people use old-fashioned words, they are old-fashioned, and so on. Therefore, it is essential that you choose your words well. When in doubt, use words that have well-established meanings in the public mind.

Another suggestion is to avoid using foreign phrases or expressions with which your audience is unfamiliar: *raison d'être, sine qua non, sub rosa, modus operandi*. It is equally unwise, if you have only a superficial knowledge of a language, to throw in a phrase here and there to impress your audience. Speakers have been known to open their address to a Japanese or Hispanic audience with a few remarks in Japanese or Spanish. While this may impress a few people, it is generally considered to be both patronizing and unnecessary. Unless you speak the language of your audience fluently, avoid any obvious attempt to ingratiate yourself in this way.

Sesquipedality is also to be discouraged where alternatives exits. It means to use big words—words with many syllables (like *sesquipedality*). Not only will the use of flowery language go over the heads of most people in your audience, it will also serve to alienate them. If you know a simpler word, use it. If you must use an uncommonly big word, insert an illustration or explanation of its meaning into your speech without being too conspicuous.

Sex

Not long ago, it was safe for you to assume that members of your audience were either males or females. Today, this is no longer a completely reliable assumption. Progress in the fields of psychology and psychiatry dealing with homosexuality have brought to our attention new ways of looking at sexual identification. We know, for example, that certain homosexual males perceive themselves as "a woman trapped in a male's body." Likewise, there are homosexual females who perceive themselves as "a man trapped in a female's body." Although the chances of your having large numbers of such individuals in your audience is small, the chance nevertheless exists. When it does occur, you may have women thinking like men and men thinking like women.

Although the number of transsexuals (those who have undergone sex-change operations) in this country is small, it appears to be growing slowly but surely. It is now possible for people to have a sex-change operation if they meet certain mental and physical requirements. Consequently, in addition to the males and females in your audience, the males who think like females and the females who think like males, you may also have males who were once females and females who were once males.

Without trying to figure out the best way of communicating with these atypical members of your audience, just knowing that they exist is in itself an advantage. With the controversy over sex-change operations still being argued, there continues to be something called a "man's point of view" or a "woman's point of view." Male speakers addressing a completely male audience tend to talk a little differently from the way they would if they were addressing a completely female audience. Perhaps it has something to do with the way little boys and girls were socialized as children. Such notions as: boys are stronger than girls; boys play with trucks, kick footballs, and dress up in cowboy suits; girls play with dolls, sew, and want to be nurses when they grow up. The list of stereotypical roles that has been assigned to males and females in society is lengthy. How strongly these roles have affected the members of your audience will be difficult to know until they begin asking you questions or enter into a more extended dialogue. As they become more involved, their line of reasoning will help you decide how you can best relate to them.

With such labels as "male chauvinist" and "sexist" being hurled at certain speakers recently, it would be a good idea to check your own speech for stereotyping that might invite such criticism. Why give them ammunition to use against you when it can be avoided? A final word of advice. Whatever the sexual composition of your audience, avoid behaving as if people fall neatly into two clearly defined groups—men and women. Attempt to communicate to your audience that you possess a much broader understanding of human sexuality.

Health

Since you cannot know the health status of your audience, you will have to make some inquiries beforehand. If such information is unavailable, use your power of observation. In most instances, you don't have to be a doctor to tell whether people look healthy or sick.

People who are not well often behave differently. They are usually preoccupied with whatever is troubling them. Depending upon how serious their particular health problem is, they will perceive their environment in terms of their specific ailment. Those with heart trouble see the world as being made up of two types of people: those with heart trouble and those without it. Their everyday thoughts and actions are influenced by their symptoms. If you were a hospital administrator and were asked to say a few words to a newly admitted group of cardiac patients, would the fact that they all shared a common health problem influence the nature of your remarks? Or, in the field of social work, addressing a group of disabled men in a veterans' hospital, would your speech possess any special characteristics? How closely would you zero in on their individual or combined health needs?

153

Whether you are working in the field of health services or not, it is important that you take the general health of your audience into consideration and reflect that awareness in your speech. If you demonstrate such an awareness, your audience will be better able to relate to what you are saying.

Affiliation

If birds of a feather do flock together, knowing something about your audience's affiliations could be a valuable aid in preparing your speech. A joke about blood transfusions would be out of order if the majority of your audience were going to be Jehovah's Witnesses, or that a woman's place is in the home if the better part of your audience were members of the women's liberation movement. In this age of "belonging," people often betray their bias on any subject by disclosing the type of group with which they are affiliated. This is probably why so many politicians have their speech writers and aides thoroughly research the affiliations of those from whom they seek votes.

Being publicly known to affiliate with a particular group or organization represents a commitment. The more public the commitment, the more dedicated the individual who made that commitment will tend to be. Whereas somebody belonging to an unpopular social or political group might be willing to assume a more flexible position in a private conversation, he would not be inclined to display such flexibility in public. Thus, by knowing your audience's affiliations, you can anticipate in which areas they will be receptive to persuasion, and in which areas they will be stubborn.

You now have some idea of what to look for when making your audience analysis. The items treated in this section are but a few of the considerations you should make. I hope they will alert you to the importance of analyzing your audience. Delivering a speech without making such an analysis is like piloting an airplane without a map or a compass. Not to know anything about your audience's size, intelligence, attitude toward language, sexual composition, health, and affiliation is to needlessly disadvantage yourself. No speaker can afford to run such a risk.

STANDING UP TO AN AUDIENCE

A Positive Attitude toward Public Speaking

A number of jobs require that you make a speech or presentation. Regardless of what it is called, it involves getting up and speaking before a group. Although you may have all the other qualifications called for in a position, not being able to make a speech or presentation could mean not getting, holding, or growing in a job.

If you can speak, you can make a speech. Over the years, more people than you can imagine have overcome the fear of speechmaking. Your first move is to persuade yourself that you too *can* do it.

Having analyzed your audience according to the elements discussed in the preceding section, you now have some insurance. A solid audience analysis is the best safeguard against failure. You know more about your audience than it knows about you. You must use this knowledge to your best advantage. A first rule to remember is that audiences are responsive to speakers who are understanding and who are sympathetic to their wants and needs. This means choosing a topic in which they are interested and presenting it like a storyteller. People appreciate being told about "a man" or "a woman"—not about mankind or womankind. Whenever possible, talk about specific things, not things in general. Accentuate the positive in whatever you say, not the negative. Look at your audience when you speak, not down at the floor or out of a window. Tell them with your eyes that you are interested in what they think and insist upon having their attention. These are some of the factors that help develop a more positive attitude toward speechmaking.

Stage Fright

Most of the things you worry about with regard to making a speech seldom happen. These include being laughed at, forgetting what you were going to say, boring your audience, having someone ask you questions you can't answer, making a mistake, or having people walk out on you. Although a remote possibility exists that one of these things will happen, the probability is small. Most audiences are patient, reasonable, and sympathetic with a speaker unless some controversial issue—busing, zoning, rent control, or mass transit fares—surrounds the topic of the speech. In such cases, an audience comes with an ax to grind.

One thing that will increase your stage fright is reading from your notes. Instead of liberating you as a speaker, they will make you a prisoner of the paper from which you are reading. Audiences demand a speaker's undivided attention and resent sharing it with a book or a set of notes. This makes them less receptive and more uneasy. Speakers sense this mood in an audience, and it in turn increases their nervousness.

There is no surefire cure for stage fright. It is a matter of making speeches over and over and, in the process, coming to realize that whatever you imagined or feared didn't happen. Or, if it did happen, you were able to cope with it. There are also certain things you can do to speed up the process. Buy a tape recorder and tape some speeches. Listen to yourself repeatedly until you have a clear understanding and feeling about your own voice. Experiment with your voice by talking faster, slower, louder, and softer. Bring your speech under control by making your words convey a variety of meanings. Say the following sentence nine times. Each time, place the emphasis on the underlined word.

Is this the face that launched a thousand ships?
Is this the face that launched a thousand ships?
Is this the face that launched a thousand ships?
Is this the face that launched a thousand ships?
Is this the face that launched a thousand ships?
Is this the face that launched a thousand ships?
Is this the face that launched a thousand ships?
Is this the face that launched a thousand ships?
Is this the face that launched a thousand ships?

The object of this speech exercise is to increase your self-control. The more predictable your speech, the less fear will creep into your body and cause dryness of the mouth, profuse perspiration, shaky knees, trembling hands, irregular breathing, and the desire to urinate frequently.

Some Tips to Remember while Speechmaking

Many of us, when we were in high school or college, were told by a speech teacher to look at some point at the back of the classroom while speaking, and to move as little as possible. Consequently, those of us who were taught this technique often looked more dead than alive. Almost the entire speech was focused on its verbal content. While this approach was by no means universal, it did represent the thinking of certain people in the field at the time.

The approach to speechmaking today goes well beyond a speaker's words. It seeks to employ a more comprehensive technique in which the speaker utilizes not only verbal skills but also nonverbal and paralinguistic (vocal) skills. The result is a completely animated speaking individual.

Something that all nervous speakers dread is *silence*. They come unglued when they forget a word or a line from their speech and the room suddenly becomes deathly quiet. They never learned how to use silence as a positive tool. Have you ever noticed guests on a TV talk show holding a pipe, a pair of eyeglasses, or a cigarette? When they are asked a tricky or embarrassing question they can't answer and need more time to think, they immediately fill their pipe, clean their glasses, or light up a cigarette. In silence, they do something. This gives them time to think and the audience something to watch them do. By nature, audiences are a curious lot. They are willing to stand by patiently while someone puts on lipstick, fixes a bra strap, gets into a wet suit, or eats a sandwich. It is the American pastime called people-watching.

A good speaker must take advantage of an audience's tendencies. When you walk out onto a stage or into a conference room before a group of people, their main interest is who you are and what you are going to say. Fill this need as quickly as possible by telling them who you are and what you are going to talk about. Their next tendency is to compare what they know and expect you to say with what you actually say. Anticipate this by telling them what you think they think about your topic. While talking (and this is important), look at as many members of your audience as possible. People listen more attentively to speakers who look at them than to speakers who do not. Another tip is to come out from behind a desk or lectern and move closer to your audience. Some speakers hide behind such props and create a barrier between them and their audience. When you remain behind a desk or lectern, your audience can see only half of you. There is an implied honesty and openness when you place yourself in full view of your audience.

You may remember from Chapter 2, "Advertising Yourself with Body Language," that there are purposeful and purposeless gestures. That information applies here. While speaking, purposeless gestures are those that distract an audience from what you are saying. Purposeful gestures reinforce what you are saying. Whenever gestures are used, you must ask yourself: "How does this gesture add meaning to what I am saying?" If you cannot answer positively, drop the gesture from your speech.

How you dress as a speaker cannot be stressed too forcefully. First impressions continue to make a significant difference in how a speaker is received by an audience. You cannot afford the luxury of dressing inappropriately when making a speech or presentation. Don't rationalize why you should have to dress a particular way, just do it! You won't be sorry.

And, finally, try—whenever possible—not to memorize a speech. Audiences know in moments whether a speaker has memorized the speech. It sounds stiff, dry, dull, and manufactured. If you are forced by circumstances to do it, rehearse it as often as necessary so that it doesn't sound mechanical. Unless you are an actor and can make a memorized script come to life, steer clear of the memorized speech. Instead, construct a well-organized outline to guide you through your topic.

RESISTING THE INFLUENCE OF OTHERS

Because someone is good at influencing others, it doesn't mean that such a person is equally good at resisting influence. The faulty assumption most of us make is that people who are good at selling are equally good at resisting a good sales pitch.

How well do you resist the influence of others? Do the various ploys used by street beggars and panhandlers get to you? Are you a sitting duck for salespeople in department stores? Are you known to your family, friends, and co-workers as an "easy mark"? Although you may think this is a genetic weakness about which you can do nothing, that is not true. While you may not be able to develop the ability to resist all forms of influence, you can learn to stop thinking of yourself as a chronic victim.

In building up your resistance to influence, the point to be re-emphasized and remembered is that most attempts at influencing are aimed at feelings rather than intellect. Where sound logic, disciplined reasoning, and common sense are certainly the reliable tools of those who exert influence, they seldom are a match for a well-placed appeal to the heart of a subject's emotions. If properly managed, feelings can influence the most sophisticated executive as well as the hardworking stock clerk. The conscientious persuader, therefore, seeks to find ways and means of getting at your feelings. Words are but one way, actions are another. You must develop defenses against both.

People are always selling something, whether it is themselves, a product, a service, or an idea. To resist their persuasion, carefully consider the following recommendations:

1. Dispel from your mind the belief that opportunity only knocks once.
2. Play down the value of whatever you are being sold.
3. Do not discuss issues that are contrary to your existing beliefs, or entertain questions leading to such issues.
4. Avoid dealing with what you are being told as one idea or concept; break it down into several smaller ideas or concepts.
5. Think of the person before you in suspicious terms.
6. Question whether the way you are seeing or hearing things actually is the way you are perceiving them.
7. Wonder why *you* are being offered this opportunity.
8. Bring up as much information as you can that conflicts with what you are being told by the persuader.
9. Establish that you have another appointment. Specify the time.

10. Put the persuader on the defensive by asking for definitions, illustrations, clarifications, and justifications.

To further strengthen your resistance, here are some additional techniques you might want to apply the next time someone tries to influence you.

Keep Your Distance

Every person seems to have a "persuading distance." While it may vary from person to person and situation to situation, it generally amounts to a given number of inches. Some people persuade at close range, others tend to stand back and give their targets more room. By significantly altering this persuading distance, you can break the psychological balance of the persuader—i.e, the effective nose-to-nose distance at which a person persuades best.

A popular technique among many successful persuaders is to get their subject at a persuading distance and into a comfortable position—preferably sitting down. You must counter these attempts by moving away if they move in, and stand if they try to get you to sit. Avoid allowing yourself to be seated while the person trying to persuade you stands. If the situation calls for both of you to be seated, however, sit opposite, not next to or diagonally across from the persuader.

Eye Contact

Making or breaking eye contact with someone who is trying to influence you could be very important. Whereas initially maintaining good eye contact with a persuader is often interpreted as interest, this impression can be reversed by continuing the eye contact. Though experienced persuaders have generally mastered the art of making eye contact, they sometimes have failed to develop the art of resisting it in others. This can be used to your advantage.

Most people with low resistance to persuasion tend to look away from people trying to persuade them. A typical sales situation in a retail department store illustrates this. The salesperson approaches the customer, asks if assistance is needed, and proceeds to show various merchandise. The disinterested customer will usually look away or walk away. If the customer stands still and continues to look at the merchandise or at the salesperson, the sales talk will continue. The inexperienced salesperson will tend to avoid customer eye contact and look at the merchandise; the more experienced salesperson will seek to maintain good eye contact with the customer.

Most people in our society are self-conscious when others look at them. If the look is continued, they might ask, "What's the matter? Is there any-

159

thing wrong?" Capitalize on this tendency when you find yourself the object of persuasion. Make the other person feel uncomfortable by looking him squarely in the eyes. With eye contact, give him the impression that you are a mind reader. Pretend that you know exactly what he is thinking.

Safety in Numbers

Change agents, another name for people who seek to influence others, would love to get you alone. The fewer people around when they make their pitch, the better they like it. The more people around, the more opinions are apt to get in their way. This means that your chances of resisting their influence are greater if you take a friend or two along. This is especially advisable if you are quiet by nature and your friend is a talker. So, as another means of self-defense, increase your resistance by adhering to the principle that there is safety in numbers. Avoid going by yourself to places where you might be exposed to uninvited influence.

Avoid Personal Pronouns

Egocentric language is "self talk" and might be viewed as the backbone of the persuasive process. If persuaders can get you talking about yourself, they are halfway to their goal. You can prevent them from getting there by avoiding the use of such words as *I, me, my.*

You have already been told that your feelings or emotions are more vulnerable to influence than your intellect. And what better way to reach your feelings or emotions than through the use of personal pronouns. By temporarily dropping the words, *I, me,* and *my* from your vocabulary, you block those wordways leading to your feeling state. Pretend that a stockbroker has just asked, "How do you feel about Shell Oil as an investment?" Or, a family counselor asks, "How do you feel about retirement?" The temptation to answer these questions beginning with a personal pronoun is extremely high. Don't do it! Instead, make every effort to speak objectively. Eliminate your feelings and emotions from the conversation as much as possible.

Be Prepared

Those out to influence you count heavily on your ignorance—not your stupidity, mind you, but your lack of information on particular subjects. The last thing in the world a persuader wants is for you to be knowledgeable. Marketing problems seem to increase as the consumer becomes more educated on subjects like pricing, packaging, shipping, advertising, and the construction and content of various merchandise. The more people know about a product, the more difficult they are to deceive.

Because of people like Ralph Nader, the general public is far less willing than it used to be to accept blindly what it is sold or told. As a result, people are slowly becoming more resistant to persuasion. Join them by entering all persuasive situations with as much information as possible on the subject. In short, resist by being prepared.

Prior Commitment

Making a prior commitment as to how much you will pay for something or where you will draw the line on a particular matter is an excellent form of resistance. The commitment is even stronger when you have made it to more than one person, or before an entire group. Research has shown that the more heavily you have committed yourself, the less likely you are to reverse your position on the subject. Incorporate this principle by telling others beforehand what you plan to say or do on a subject. It will help you stand your ground, stick to your guns, and maintain your position under all kinds of persuasive pressures.

Suspicious Environment

Beware of soft background music, a sumptuous meal, and beautiful surroundings. They could lower your resistance to persuasion. The clever influencer knows one thing: to get you comfortable and contented. Eating a big meal, for example, will decrease the blood supply to your brain and could reduce your ability to think clearly. Counter this strategy by eating less and moving the conversation to a less relaxing environment. If possible, try to find a place with which you are familiar so that you will not be distracted from what is being said.

Sleep on It

While there are situations that require immediate action, the majority can wait another day without any great loss. Successful business people know this and, when made a proposition, usually take some time to sleep on it. They rarely snap at the bait the first time around. This would be a good policy for you to adopt. Tell the person attempting to persuade you that you would like to sleep on it. Contrary to the "opportunity only knocks once" philosophy, many successful individuals will argue that opportunity is always knocking. The problem is more a question of who is ready, willing, and able to move on it. As a first step in this direction, promise yourself not to leave a persuasive situation with your mind completely made up in one way or another. Take your time with the decision-making process and you will find it an excellent form of resistance against the influence of others.

9

Why Can't People Follow Simple Instructions?

Learning about any business or profession involves the transfer of information from those who know to those who don't know. Problems exist on both sides of the experience. Those doing the instructing often complain that the people they are obliged to teach are either not very bright, lack motivation, have little or no background, or resent being placed in a learning situation. Conversely, learners or trainees complain that instructors often are impatient or unqualified, have unrealistic expectations, talk down to them, and make unfounded assumptions.

Today, training programs are big business. Millions are spent each year on systems to develop reliable ways of training people quickly and efficiently. This endeavor requires considerably more than a casual knowledge of show and tell. In practice, it draws upon a number of disciplines: psychology, philosophy, sociology, education, English, and the art of communication.

To advance in any field, you will be required to either teach those who know less than you do or learn from those who know more. In both roles, you will have to possess a knowledge of instructional communication. This will involve understanding the difference between written and oral instruction, the stages of instruction, the kinds of people who write instructions, those factors that cause instructions to succeed or fail, and some of the theoretical

principles underlying instructional communication.
In short, you should come away from this chapter
realizing that giving or taking instruction, in all
of its forms, is but an effort to assist or shape
the growth of others and, in the process, shape your
own growth as well.

IT'S EASY, ALL YOU DO IS. . . .

A popular myth that shows no signs of yielding to the sophistication of the twentieth century is the belief that people who know how to do certain things can automatically teach others to do them. If you haven't challenged the validity of this myth, please do it now.

Do you remember who taught you to drive a car? It was probably a member of the family or a friend. If you are at all similar to most people, the experience was frustrating—especially, if the car had a stick shift. The fact that you were an intelligent person and understood everything you were told seemed to have little or nothing whatever to do with your inability to coordinate hand and foot movements. Somehow, it didn't make any sense. You were smart and yet you did dumb things.

In addition to your own attitude and behavior, there was the attitude and behavior of the person instructing you. The interaction was reciprocal. When the instructor got impatient, you got impatient; when you got emotional, the instructor got emotional. Unless you were being taught by a professional who knew how to remain detached and in constant control of the situation, the tendency to get emotionally upset lurked around every corner. The fact that your friend or relative was as intelligent as you didn't make as much of a difference as you thought it would.

Ironically, this same situation exists in the business and professional world. There are people who know a great deal about their subject but can't, for the life of them, communicate what they know to others. Memories of our school days can usually bring to mind teachers who were brilliant, but who couldn't teach. Even more peculiar is the fact that there are people instructing others to do things that they themselves cannot do (the obese physician whose practice is limited to diet programs and weight loss, the bald barber who gives advice on how to keep the hair healthy, and the voice teacher who cannot sing). It is refreshing to find someone who knows how to do something well and can communicate that knowledge to others. Yet, in spite of this dilemma, millions of people who know how to do certain things well say to those who cannot, "It's easy, all you do is. . . ." Perhaps it is because they have a slightly different attitude toward an understanding of the learning process.

Attitude toward Learning

Not only do people have different attitudes toward learning what they don't know, they also learn differently. Some individuals have trouble getting past the first stage—admitting that they don't know something and have to be taught or shown. Surely you have been in a large department store with someone, become lost, and observed that your friend stubbornly refused to ask anyone for directions. Then, after walking in circles for an hour, the friend asked for directions and refused to believe them. Being open and willing to accept instructions is the first step toward understanding them.

Another attitude involves those giving the instructions. They must exercise genuine patience and concern for those whom they are instructing. Too frequently, many instructors fail to appreciate the difficulties confronting a learner. For example, those who know how to do things generally think in broader terms than those who do not. Take the learning-to-drive situation, mentioned earlier. To the trained driver, where the ignition key is inserted, which side of the key is up, in which direction it is turned, where the ignition is located, how long the key should be held in the turned position, where the accelerator is located, and how hard to press on it are all lumped together in the expression "start 'er up." To the learner, they are all separate and distinct steps, which need to be explained one at a time. Thus, this tendency on the part of instructors to think in larger chunks than learners must be an attitude guarded against in every instructional situation.

People learn in two ways: through understanding (cognition) and doing (psychomotor activity). Many instructors think that someone who can achieve a high score on a written examination can translate that understanding into practice. Countless firms give prospective employees written examinations to determine how much they know about a particular subject and, if they do well, make the assumption that they can probably do well on the job. This leap from understanding to doing is more complicated than most people realize. Understanding a process is in no way a guarantee of being able to communicate such understanding to someone else.

There are times when learning involves unlearning. Does the statement "Well, I did this differently on my last job" sound familiar? Few things are more annoying to the person trying to teach you something than being told how you used to do it on a previous job. This raises not one, but two obstacles for an instructor to overcome: (1) to try to teach you his or her way of doing something and (2) to persuade you to forget how you did it in the past. Although past experience is certainly a valuable asset, it could be a liability if it conflicts with the situation at hand.

COIK Principle

This is perhaps one of the most important principles associated with instructional communication. The letters *COIK* stand for *Clear Only If Known*. With relatively few exceptions, trainers make assumptions about the people they teach. These assumptions may center on their language, intelligence, knowledge, perception, motivation, and temperament. Any one or a combination of these faculties could be responsible for an unsatisfactory learning experience.

In his book *Communication Vibrations*, Larry Barker illustrates how the COIK principle operates. He describes a scene involving a conversation between an avid baseball fan and an Englishman who is seeing his first baseball game. The Englishman asked, "What is a pitcher?" "He's the man down there pitching the ball to the catcher." "But," said the Englishman, "all of the players pitch the ball and all of them catch the ball. There aren't just two persons who pitch and catch." Later, the Englishman asked, "How many strikes do you get before you are out?" The baseball fan said, "Three." "But," replied the Englishman, "that man struck at the ball five times before he was out."

Only if you know the rules of baseball can you understand the Englishman's frustration. The explanations given to him by the fan would have been perfectly clear had the Englishman been familiar with the rules of the game.

The COIK principle exists whenever and wherever information is being shared. Rarely will you find two people involved in a teaching/learning experience with identical references. Too often, those doing the teaching make an assumption about what a learner knows, or should know. This kind of assumption can easily throw a monkey wrench into the works. Hold on a minute! I just committed a COIK when I used the phrase "monkey wrench into the works." Unless you are familiar with its meaning, I have made an erroneous assumption about what you know or should know.

The succcess or failure of any training program can often be determined by the number of COIKs it generates. Learning involves bridging a gap between the minds of those to be taught and those doing the teaching. To use words, references, or concepts with which the learner is unfamiliar is to invite failure. COIK constitutes such an invitation.

Take something as fundamental as the body's appendix. What if you were hired by an airline requiring that you take a first-aid course as part of your training? During the first class, you are told by your instructor how to treat a suspected ruptured appendix. In telling you to apply ice to the area, your instructor assumes that you know where the appendix is located in the body. The assumption will result in a COIK if you aren't sure whether the appendix is on the right or left side of the abdomen. Although the exact location of the appendix was clearly established in your instructor's mind, your understanding of where to apply the ice bag could not begin until it was equally well established in your mind.

This applied example of COIK is but one of thousands committed every minute in organizations across the nation. Instructions on how to answer a telephone properly, operate a lathe, address a customer, arrange a business conference, or conduct a routine employment interview can easily be sabotaged by a failure to mention some seemingly unimportant item, or by an unwarranted assumption about the person being instructed.

Who Writes Instructions?

No doubt you have bought a number of items that came with instructions. Have you ever wondered who writes them? These instructions are particularly insulting when they tell you that a child could follow them. I recently bought an all-purpose wristwatch with a stopwatch, alarm, calendar, automatic winding device, and a light that illuminates its face. The box contained operating instructions in seven languages. I spent almost an entire week playing engineer—trying to tame the watch. At first, I thought it was my ignorance that prevented me from understanding what the manufacturer called "simple operating instructions." After asking several of my more intelligent friends whether they had had similar experiences, I became convinced that it was not my ignorance that kept me from following the instructions. It had something to do with the way the instructions were written.

In an effort to find out who writes the instructions that accompany cake mixes, do-it-yourself furniture, electrical appliances, children's toys, and office supplies, I contacted several manufacturers. Their responses were rather interesting. Would you believe that certain companies were actually indignant? They were reluctant to tell me who wrote their instructions. Aside from the firms which explained that the person who wrote their instructions was out to lunch, the types of individuals who were mentioned included engineers, consultants, home economists, psychologists, technical writers, designers, copywriters, production managers, or people who had majored in English. Not once did they mention anyone trained in communication theory. The overall impression I got from their responses was that a command of the English language and some common sense were all that someone needed to write these instructions—except in highly technical areas. Here is an example of the kind of letter I received:

Dear Sir:

Other than a good background in English and an ability to understand what's going on, the people who write game instructions do not require special skills or qualifications. Working together with researchers, the person in charge of instructions must be able to say as much as possible in a few words, find and stop misconceptions before they happen, and use illustrations whenever possible.

Sincerely,

The tone and content of this letter again raises the question: What qualifications, if any, should the people who write instructions have? Is it sufficient to have a command of the English language, a working knowledge of a product, or perhaps a flair for merchandising? Does an understanding of the design and construction of a product constitute an ability to explain, in clear and understandable terms, how to assemble and operate it? The next few pages will illustrate why instructional communication involves more than a good knowledge of the English language and some common sense.

GETTING INSTRUCTIONS TO MAKE MORE SENSE

Instructions frequently disregard proper audience identification. Many times, the same set of instructions is offered for college students, distribution dealers, sales personnel, seasoned executives, and property owners. It is foolhardy to think that all of these audiences will possess the same background, training, ability, and understanding. There can be no doubt that proper audience identification is the best form of insurance for getting one's message across in any set of instructions. A classic example of this "shotgun approach" to audience identification comes to us every year from the I.R.S. As you know, the instructions that accompany these tax forms are easy to follow, whether you are a college professor, cab driver, dump truck operator, theatrical agent, cashier, secretary, research chemist, or opera singer. At least, the government says they are easy to follow. I wonder who writes the instructions used by the Internal Revenue Service. One West Coast professor struck a blow for the kind of tax reform taxpayers would

167

like to see most—*clarity*! Using twelve excerpts taken from a 1973 Form 1040, he asked thirty-five graduate students to apply the principles it advanced to twelve sample situations. The average student got less than six of the examples right. Should you not think too highly of today's college students, test your skill against theirs at understanding the following excerpt:

It may pay you to use the "averaging method" if after subtracting 3,000 dollars from your 1973 taxable income (line 48), the balance is over 30% of the total of your taxable income for the last four years (1969 through 1972).

Combining business with pleasure, this next set of directions was mailed to five executives telling them how to get to a popular restaurant on Long Island. It later became known that these directions were Xeroxed and routinely used by the company because the people involved were very fond of the restaurant. These same directions were dispatched, regardless of who was invited to attend the luncheon—a clear-cut abuse of audience identification. These were the actual directions.

Follow the signs to East Meadow. If there aren't any, look for signs to Canyon or Valley Junction which are bigger but you don't want to go as far as Canyon or Valley Junction because you want to make a sharp left near East Meadow onto Route 122 (or 221?). It's one of those funny towns you can go through without knowing it but you'll see a funny old store with a wooden Indian outside—or is it a totem pole? Anyway, that's the place.

The only thing more amusing than these confusing instructions is the fact that the person who wrote them closes with, "It's easy to get there, all you do is follow these simple directions." Both illustrations, this one and the one drawn from the tax form, demonstrate the chaos that can result from a faulty audience identification. Those who write instructions must be perfectly clear as to the audience for whom they are writing. They must adjust to the fact not only that audiences will vary but also that within any given audience, the following factors can dictate how well a set of instructions will be understood: stages, language, environment, sequence, time allotment, sense appeal, feedback, proportion, and safety.

Stages

Whether instructions are written or oral, they involve three stages. In the first stage, you are engaged in making the necessary preparations. This consists of gathering together all of the information and equipment

168

that will be needed in order to carry out the task to be performed. The second stage, that of development, serves to bridge the gap between what you have and what you want to accomplish. By outlining each step, your directions should enable the learner to do something he or she couldn't do before or improve upon how it was done in the past. In this phase, the outcome of each step in the instructions should be analyzed for its effectiveness and accuracy. The final stage is concerned with improvement. Unless instructions are updated, they may lose their relevance. Techniques, such as mixing cake ingredients by hand, have become almost obsolete and replaced by mixing with blenders; passé expressions must be replaced by current ones; and occupations and professions that are now defunct must be put to rest.

Although the stages of any set of instructions will vary with the individual project and the depth to which the instructor wishes to take the learner, some stages of organization are necessary. They provide everyone concerned with fixed guidelines to which they can easily refer.

Language

The words you use may or may not trigger pictures in the minds of those who read them. Words, without the ability to conjure up such mental pictures, communicate poorly. Just as two sides of a zipper should interlock neatly, so should words and mind pictures mesh. The language to be used in any instructions, therefore, should contain as few abstract words as possible. Words like *definitely*, *purposely*, *discretion*, and *carefully* generate no mental images. In their places, concrete words such as *house, pitcher, tree, table, key,* and *refrigerator* should be used. Whereas the mental pictures of these objects may differ somewhat from person to person or country to country, they do share certain recognizable characteristics.

There is also a question of technical jargon and name-dropping. Instructions containing them make most learners feel nervous and frustrated. Should you ever be tempted to use such technical words as *physiognomy, hemostat, syncope,* or *prima facie*—don't do it! Find more simple terms by enlisting a thesaurus to help you. Ask yourself: "How will using these words, names, or phrases make my instructions easier to understand?"

A final thought related to instructional language concerns the use of questionable grammar. Watch out for these pitfalls: (1) incomplete sentences (leaving out a subject or predicate, the object of a transitive verb, or a definite or indefinite article); (2) sentences longer than seventeen to twenty words; (3) excessive colons, semicolons, dashes, parentheses, commas, and underscoring of words; and (4) beginning sentences with conjunctions such as *and* or *but*.

169

Environment

Many instructions neglect to mention where they should be carried out. The surroundings of an individual trying to follow a set of instructions can definitely affect how well they are understood. Some people concentrate best with absolute silence. Others can think clearly with children yelling and screaming, trains and buses going by, or the television blaring. Then there is the question of proper lighting and acoustics. Regardless of how good your eyesight or hearing is, it must not be strained. Ample elbow room is still another consideration. Does the area where the instructions are being followed provide enough room for the necessary materials to be comfortably laid out? Will the instructions be executed in the house or in the yard? Some people work better indoors, others prefer working out of doors.

The nature of the task to be performed will usually determine the environment best suited to it. However, in all cases, the environment must be conducive to concentration. Distractions must be reduced to a minimum.

Sequence

The order in which various instructional steps are arranged should not be taken lightly. While the experienced individual may occasionally alter the sequence in which instructions are given, the novice should not take such a liberty. The reason for this is that experienced people see the larger picture, whereas the novice may see only the individual step to be taken.

Sequence refers to whatever order best enables an individual to achieve a particular goal with the least amount of effort. More specifically, sequencing guides learners through a series of statements and restatements of a problem or body of information that are designed to increase their ability to comprehend what they are learning. It also helps them avoid suffering the discouragement that comes with approaching instructions in a hit-or-miss fashion, enables them to proceed at their own speed, and makes complicated instructions easier by breaking them down into smaller units.

To illustrate the importance of sequence, here is an event that actually happened to a friend of mine. About 7:30 one evening, a young man selling the large Webster's dictionary for three dollars a copy rang his doorbell. Naturally, my friend was staggered by the low price and, without hesitation, bought one. Anxious to examine his tremendous bargain, he plunked himself down in his armchair and began thumbing through its pages. In a matter of seconds, he discovered why it was so cheap. *It wasn't in alphabetical order!!*

Time Allotment

We all know that people perform at different speeds and that the longer they have been doing something, the faster they get. Those preparing instructions must be keenly aware of varying performance rates. Beginners must be given more time. Although instructions are field-tested to determine how long an average person should take to get through a particular stage, those selected as being "average" must receive careful consideration. Since any given set of instructions is field-tested before being put on the market, you would think that everyone in the country should be able to follow them. Unfortunately, that is not so. Perhaps the time allotted to each stage is incorrect. For example, instead of saying, "Let it boil for a little while," it should read, "Let it boil for ten minutes." Many people have a distorted sense of time. They tend to over- or underestimate the length of a minute or an hour. Children, in particular, have a curious sense of time. You may say that you will take them to the zoo next week and five minutes later they will ask, "Is it next week yet?"

Manual dexterity can also influence the length of time an individual will need to perform a specific task. Those who design instructions, again, have no way of knowing how dextrous a learner is going to be. They must make an approximation on the basis of what they consider "average." The wise instruction-giver should make an allowance for varying degrees of manual dexterity by clearly stating: "If more time is needed, it should be taken."

Sense Appeal

The more individuals' senses are brought into play, the better they will understand the instructions they are given. Whereas some people are good at following written instructions, others prefer spoken instructions. Then there are those who have still another need: to touch or feel the material or apparatus with which they are dealing. Lastly, there are those who cook and bake. For them to follow instructions faithfully, they must be able to smell and taste the ingredients they use.

The rule of thumb suggested here is that the shortest route to a learner's brain is through the senses. The degree to which such sense experience is denied to a learner may well be the extent to which his or her comprehension of the task will suffer. As stressed throughout this book, understanding something intellectually does not automatically translate into performance.

Feedback

A question commonly asked by those in the process of following instructions is, "How am I doing?" People have a psychological need to know whether they are on the right track; whether what they are doing is OK. Doubt and uncertainty are serious barriers to successful instructional communcation. Feedback that is worked into a set of instructions can act as a signaling device that reassures learners that they are doing the right thing. This nourishes their ego, reinforces their self-image, increases their sense of competence, and encourages them to proceed with confidence.

An example of a feedback device can be found in most amusement parks. It exists in those machines that simulate driving an automobile. You sit behind a wheel and in front of you is a roadway. When you drive and stay in your lane, a green light goes on; if you go out of your lane, a red light goes on. The green and red lights provide the driver with feedback that, at the end of the ride, translates into a score (excellent driver, good driver, average driver, poor driver).

Although instructions that completely lack feedback cause misunderstandings, too much feedback can do similar damage. A few well-placed uses of it are invaluable. Perhaps you recall how helpful travel instructions are that include such hints as "If you see a Shell gas station on the right, you have passed the cutoff." This is a sample of negative feedback—i.e., you have gone past the road you should have taken. Positive feedback would be: "When you see an old covered bridge, you are on the right course." Whether negative or positive, feedback can help simplify any set of instructions.

Proportion

Diagrams are a familiar ingredient of instructions. If they are accompanied by a "key" to explain how they are to be interpreted (one inch equals one foot), they can be extremely helpful. Unfortunately, some diagrams are not that reliable. References to depth and width in a diagram occasionally mislead the reader and prompt the comment "gee, I thought it would be much bigger."

Instructions also employ the use of pictures that may be malproportioned. The wording might instruct the reader to affix a large button (labeled A) to the material (labeled B). This could be slightly confusing if another button is shown that appears to be the same size as the large button but is labeled medium.

The use of pictures or diagrams requires an accurate statement of their relationship to the written text. Proportions must also be preserved, or confusion may easily arise. Unless you are given to believe otherwise, beware of the cliché "a picture is worth a thousand words."

Safety

We have all heard of the youngster who causes an explosion while playing with a chemistry set, or the adult who hurts himself trying out a tool he received as a holiday gift. Many accidents can be avoided if the instructions that acommpany them clearly identify the danger involved. Instructions must responsibly forewarn a user of any inherent danger because the majority of people either fail to read instructions carefully, underestimate their importance, or are convinced that whatever they are being warned against won't happen to them. While warnings should not be exaggerated (Example: *Be extremely careful when mixing these chemicals. Improper mixing can cause explosions capable of resulting in scarring, mutilation, dismemberment, or sudden death by suffocation.*), they should be worded so that they strongly impress upon the reader the importance of adopting the safety measures being recommended. It might also be worthwhile mentioning that picture-warnings are more effective than word-warnings. The absence of any warning at all is downright negligent.

SPOKEN VERSUS WRITTEN INSTRUCTIONS

What is the difference between spoken and written instructions? Since both use words to tell people how to do things, one would think that the difference is insignificant. Not true! There are significant differences, and most outstanding among them is that spoken instructions include paralanguage (vocal qualities) and kinesics (body language). This is particularly evident when instructions are contradicted by how an instructor says them or how an instructor looks while saying them.

Most of the instructions issued on the job are oral: People who know how to do things tell those who do not know. Things would be comparatively simple if all emotionality could be removed from the process. But, because people "feel," it is an entirely different matter. They can invest the oral instructions they are given with all kinds of real or imagined psychological content.

Written instructions, by contrast, are inclined to be much less threatening. Somehow, by not having someone watching you or standing over your shoulder, the tension is lessened considerably. Written instructions have another advantage. You can reread those parts that are unclear several times. With spoken instructions, asking an instructor to repeat something more than once can be embarrassing. Also, if there are words you don't understand, they can be looked up in a dictionary without anyone being the wiser. Lastly, written instructions enable you to proceed at your own pace without being harassed by an impatient instructor.

Whether spoken or written, the successful completion of any task depends upon how efficiently instructions are conceived by an instructor and how well they are delivered to a learner. The learner, in turn, must clearly understand the message received and translate its meaning into an acceptable performance. Thus, to insure the success of such a transaction, here are some general hints to help make instructions clearer:

1. The willingness of the learner to accept instruction must be established.
2. If necessary, instructions must be repeated more than once.
3. To reinforce listening and attention states, good eye contact must be maintained.
4. Where possible, instructors should "show" rather than "tell."
5. Instructions should be couched in language learners can understand.
6. The tone of the instructor's voice should be screened for such qualities as impatience, annoyance, condescension, aloofness, and boredom.
7. Learners should be required to provide instructors with feedback—to repeat a particular instruction to be sure that it was understood.
8. Since they act as distractions, purposeless body movements, gestures, and facial expressions should be eliminated as much as possible.
9. Instructors should be on the alert for non-verbal signs of confusion, resentment, and misunderstanding on the part of the learner.
10. Questions should be encouraged.
11. Instructional steps with multiple parts (Ia, Ib, Ic, etc.) should be avoided whenever feasible.
12. The instructor's patience should be proportional to the learner's ability.
13. The results expected to be derived from following instructions should be stated.
14. For those who seem to require it, explanations should be given as to why something is to be done in a particular way.
15. Instructors should speak clearly, especially when using technical or uncommonly used words.
16. Instructors should provide learners with positive reinforcement by issuing an occasional smile or head nod, a pat on the back or shoulder, a wink, or an acknowledging remark such as "fine, you're doing a fine job!"

174

TESTING YOUR ABILITY TO GIVE AND TAKE SIMPLE INSTRUCTIONS

Here is an opportunity to see what you have learned from this chapter. Below is a series of geometric forms arranged in relation to one another. Attempt to have a friend re-create them by following your spoken instructions. Supply your friend with a blank sheet of paper and a pencil. Then, step by step, provide your instructions. This instructional exercise allows for no feedback from your friend in the way of questions. All you may be asked is to repeat a particular step, not qualify or clarify its meaning. You are also not permitted to use any gestures in the air describing what you mean. Try being as precise as you can in your instructions.

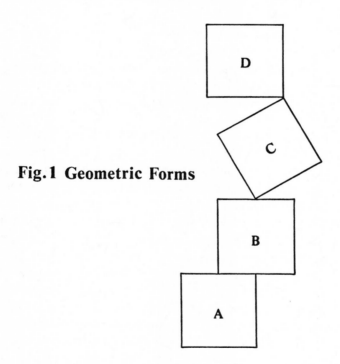

Fig. 1 Geometric Forms

When your friend has finished, see how closely his or her forms correspond with yours. If there were any problems with size, shape, or relationship, ask why he or she went astray. Discuss misleading instructions or their interpretation. When you have thoroughly examined the instructions you have given to your friend, reverse your roles and have your friend dictate instructions to you on how to draw the following form. The same ground rules will apply—that is, no questions or clarifications, only requests to repeat a particular step. Here now is your friend's assignment:

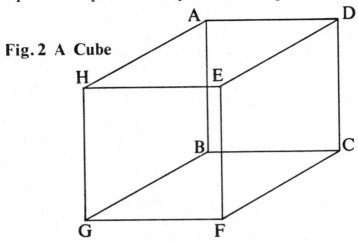

Fig. 2 A Cube

When you have finished, make the same instructional analysis you made on your friend's drawing. Compare how accurately each of you delivered your instructions. Criticize each other freely. Make suggestions for improvement.

The instructions you and your friend have just traded are not very practical on the job. They were used here to get you thinking in instructional terms. There are probably a number of tasks associated with your present job that involve the giving or taking of instructions. Furthermore, you probably have some rather definite ideas on why they would succeed or fail. Perhaps you have enough interest in the subject to write a set of instructions for someone with whom you now work and who might test them out tomorrow. They could include such chores as changing a typewriter ribbon, arranging a conference call, ordering a meal in an elegant restaurant, closing a deal, or setting up a vacation schedule for employees. Choose whatever task is relevant to your work. Attempt to incorporate as many suggestions as you can that were mentioned in this chapter. Clear and concise instructions, regardless of their nature, will ultimately result in a saving to any company, an increase in its productivity, and improved communication among its members.

10
How to Disagree Without Being Disagreeable

Whether you call it arguing, bargaining, bickering, dickering, haggling, or squabbling, they all add up to varying degrees of disagreement. Put another way, you might prefer the more all-inclusive label, "communication breakdown." Under whatever name it masquerades, the truth of the matter is that most of us never learned how to disagree without becoming disagreeable, that is, without getting upset or overheated. Perhaps it is because we were encouraged by our parents to avoid arguments rather than learn how to argue constructively. Take an informal survey among your friends and see how many of them still believe that arguments should be avoided whenever possible.

Since the majority of people currently in the job market were never exposed to the positive side of argument, or taught how to argue without getting emotionally involved, it is high time they were. This chapter has been designed to fill such a need. As long as people are obliged to work together, differences of opinion are certain to crop up from time to time. When they do, it is essential that you know how to handle yourself, how to prevent a difference of opinion from boiling over into an emotionally charged exchange of words lacking both purpose and direction. The ability to do this effectively is a form of self-defense, a mental judo. Actually, it is the art of communication, which requires a great deal of patience, perseverance, and dedication to develop.

The benefits to be derived from making such an effort
are enormous. It transforms that helpless and frustrated feeling, which so often accompanies a breakdown in communication, into a feeling of self-control
and confidence. In other words, you will be able to
disagree without becoming disagreeable.

TYPES OF COMMUNICATION BREAKDOWN

A breakdown in communication can be one- or two-sided. If someone
at work doesn't like you and, on the basis of how that person interprets
your manner of speech or behavior, thinks you are a pompous ass, the communication breakdown can be said to be one-sided. This, of course, only
applies if you bear that person no ill will. But, should both of you share
your dislike for one another, the breakdown would be two-sided. Thus,
whether the disagreement is one-sided or two-sided, it qualifies as a breakdown in communication.

Subjective Communication Breakdown

When a communication breakdown involves how people think, feel, and
behave toward others, it is called a subjective type, that is, a people-oriented
breakdown. To illustrate this, imagine a store manager who doesn't get
along with a particular salesclerk because she is Hispanic. His general
attitude toward her is unfriendly and overly demanding. The salesclerk,
without knowing the real reason for his hostility, is involved in a communication breakdown. Then again, she might know that he is prejudiced
toward her because she is Hispanic and feel equally hostile toward him.
In either case, the basis for the communication breakdown is subjective in
nature—one based upon how these two people think, feel, and behave
toward one another. Without the benefit of a third or fourth party's opinion
to confirm or deny how each of them actually thinks, feels, or behaves, it
amounts to a stalemate—one opinion unmovingly pitted against the other.

Objective Communication Breakdown

This type of breakdown is object-oriented. It involves certain items in
relation to people. For example, if people disagree about shipping or billing
dates, how merchandise is displayed, or the correctness of a work schedule,
they are involved in an objective type of breakdown in communication.
There are material things outside of themselves that can be examined,
evaluated, or manipulated and thereby used as a basis for settling any differences of opinion.

178

Horizontal and Vertical Communication Breakdowns

When a communication breakdown occurs between people of equal status in an organization, such as two section managers of a large department store, it is called a horizontal breakdown. If it occurs between people of different status, such as a vice-president and a supervisor, it is called a vertical breakdown.

Being able to distinguish between a horizontal and a vertical communication breakdown could play a significant role in its resolution. Built into every organization, if its policies have been well thought out and carefully stipulated, is the amount of authority vested in each of its employees and the manner in which it should be exercised. Consequently, a communication breakdown between personnel, if it is vertical in nature, will favor the individual of higher status. If it is between people of equal status, a horizontal communication breakdown, its resolution is usually achieved by calling in someone of higher status.

Regardless of whether one is dealing with a subjective or an objective, a horizontal or a vertical type of communication breakdown, there is something that needs to be remembered. Aside from the position an individual holds in an organization, that person is a human being, capable of experiencing such emotions as depression, anxiety, frustration, embarrassment, alienation, humiliation, and ridicule. While there are certain individuals who have a higher tolerance for the abuse that often comes with a communication breakdown, there are others who are not as thick-skinned and who find themselves much more vulnerable. A seemingly innocent communication breakdown could have far-reaching effects if it involves someone who is not strong enough to cope with it. These effects could influence not only the individual but his or her work and, in turn, the company. Therefore, idealistically speaking, there is no such thing as a "minor" communication breakdown. Each breakdown must be evaluated in terms of the personality and character of people involved and the circumstances surrounding the disagreement.

CAUSES OF A COMMUNICATION BREAKDOWN

Personal Pronouns (I-me-my)

Few things contribute more to the growth and development of a disagreement than the use of the pronouns *I*, *me*, and *my*. Rather than having a calming effect upon the waters of disagreement, they tend to make them more turbulent. They pit people against people, rather than ideas against ideas. The more often they occur in a disagreement, the more aggravated it seems to become. Conversely, the less *I*, *me*, and *my* are used, the more gratifying and tranquilized the exchange of opinion is apt to be.

Most people argue from the heart and gut, not from the head. To do this, they must use ego-centered language—language placing them at the center of their views. Personal pronouns do just that: they give those with whom they are disagreeing the distinct impression that they are assuming full responsibility for the correctness of their remarks. They give the added impression that their opinion or conclusion on a subject is the "last word." While they may not mean to give such an egotistic impression, they nevertheless give it. Instead of using such impersonal phrases as "it would appear from the evidence," "according to the *Wall Street Journal*," or "based upon a study done at the University of Hawaii," they talk as though the only reliable source of information is their own personal opinion. In short, they approach their conclusions from a purely subjective point of view. By so doing, they run a much greater risk of encountering resistance from others than from those who approach their conclusions objectively—using facts, figures, and what other reputable people have to say on the subject.

People and Their Opinions

Wherever you find people, you will find opinions. Wherever you find opinions, you will find clash—that is, opinions in conflict. As indicated in the beginning of the chapter, separating people from their opinions is no easy task. For some poorly understood reason, an enormous number of individuals in the field behave as if their opinions were physical parts of their bodies. As a result, they find it extremely difficult giving up an opinion, especially one they have held for a long time or that represents a significant ego investment. Recognizing this point alone could have a dramatic effect upon the resolution of any conflict. It will insulate you from expecting people to honor your opinions simply because they are logical. As long as people continue to invest their opinions with large doses of feelings and intuitions, logical appeals will have little or no effect upon them. Having someone tell you to buy a particular stock on the basis of a "gut feeling" somehow misses its mark in the logical scheme of things.

Have you noticed how some people make the most outrageous statements and expect to be believed without question? They have a ready comment on subjects ranging from transcendental meditation to transistors, capital gains to capital punishment, and when you have the nerve to challenge them, they are shocked and take offense at your reaction. Their behavior makes you wonder whether they have the foggiest notion of what it means to prove a claim or conclusion.

Confirmation that emotionality in an argument is undesirable comes from the writings of the famous psychoanalyst C. G. Jung: "Rational argument can be conducted with some prospect of success only so long as the emotionality of a given situation does not exceed a certain critical degree. If the affective temperature rises above this level, the possibility of reason's having any effect ceases and its place is taken by slogans and chimerical wish-fantasies." Stretched another way, the more emotional people get when they disagree, the less their chances are of reaching an agreement. If this happens on the job, not only do the individuals involved stand to suffer, but also the company employing them.

Arguing Conclusions

To reach any agreement, you must *not* argue conclusions, only the basis for them. For someone to say, "In less than a year, this company will be bankrupt," is an unsupported conclusion. Without any mention of the reasoning that led to such a conclusion, the statement is meaningless. Experts in the field of argumentation repeatedly stress the importance of arguing *how* people arrive at their conclusions, not the conclusions themselves. Arguing conclusions without a basis for them is a major cause of the average communication breakdown.

Listen carefully for these unsupported conclusions. The next time you hear one, immediately press for its foundation. Make a concerted effort to discover what kind of reasoning led up to it. Constantly bear in mind that an excellent method of shooting down an opponent's argument is to discredit the basis for it.

Faultfinding

On practically every job, you will find self-appointed critics. They criticize the people with whom they work, the work they are paid to do, and the circumstances compelling them to do it. Perhaps these compulsive critics believe that pointing out the faults and shortcomings in others will elevate their own self-worth. Being around such people, you get the feeling that they worship Murphy's Law: If something can go wrong, it will.

Seeing only the negative side of things can create an unhealthy climate for meaningful communication on the job. People like this thrive on negatives instead of positives and, as a result, spark disagreement wherever they go. It is bad enough that so many people are unhappy with their jobs; they certainly don't appreciate having someone ride roughshod over their egos as well as their work. Faultfinding, in the wrong hands, can easily cause a communication breakdown.

Mistaken Perception of Role

In addition to the faultfinders just mentioned, there are individuals who have a distorted sense of the role they are being paid to assume in an organization. Chances are you have run into secretaries who behave as if they owned the company. Or perhaps a switchboard operator whose inflated sense of importance prompts a whole series of decisions regarding who will speak to whom during the course of an average workday.

A basic principle of sound organizational administration is that a job description should correspond with what people actually do. From the outset, new employees should be told what they are to do and be led to expect what will happen before it happens. The probability of a communication breakdown occurring is extremely high when the description, prescription, and expectations related to any job are not standardized. It may well be that the reason so many people have misconceptions about their role in a company is because it is poorly spelled out from the beginning. Countless employees either think or utter the words "I never know what they expect of me" at least once in the course of a typical work week. People need to know what is expected of them. A failure to satisfy this need often leads to unnecessary confusion and ultimate breakdowns in communication.

Predictability

When you set your alarm clock at night, you expect that it will ring in the morning. When you press on the brakes in your car, you expect the car to come to a stop. If your clock and car behave as you expect, there is high predictability. A wide variety of similar expectations exists in every occupation and profession. People at every level of an organization have some rather definite ideas of what they can expect others to say or do. In fact, in a great many ways, they formulate their own conduct as it relates to their expectations of others; i.e., "If he does that, I will do this," etc.

Organizational life flows smoothly as long as people's expectations of one another are satisfactorily met. But what if they operate from conflicting expectations? What if they don't behave in a predictable fashion? What then? Breakdowns in communication are sure to develop. Take a simple case in which an employee is asked to work overtime and, on the basis of being asked by the supervisor, expects to be paid time and a half. On picking up her paycheck, she discovers that she was paid straight time for the extra hours she put in. The employee's expectations were not met. By the same token, if a supervisor expects an employee to stay with a particular job order (work overtime) until it is finished, and discovers that the employee has left for the day, the supervisor's expectations were not met. In both instances, the expectations of another person were not realized. Their respective predictions of what the other would do were intially high but turned out to be much lower than they anticipated. Faulty predictions, in both directions, caused a communication breakdown.

Routinization

Every job, if it is done day in and day out, soon becomes routine. Even those glorified brain surgeons, movie stars, and super sports figures eventually begin to treat what they do for a living as routine. Only a small percentage of the millions who constitute America's work force escape the psychological stigma of routinization.

Like it or not, most of us do essentially the same things over and over again with the same people and at the same place. And, because we do them repeatedly, our communication soon begins to show signs of sameness. Take two different people with different job routines and put them in a room. With little in common, they will share only a limited basis for communication. While it would be unrealistic to say that they couldn't engage in *any* meaningful communication, it would be realistic to suggest that if they had the same job routine, communication between them would flow more easily.

The routine nature of a job usually dictates the type of communication necessary for its performance. Similarly, the way people communicate usually supplies a clue to the kind of work they do. For example, musicians use "musicians' talk"; doctors, "doctors' talk"; and lawyers, "lawyers' talk." The talk and the job are routinized; break the routine and you upset both the job and the talk. Result: a possible breakdown in communication.

Fallacious Reasoning

When you question someone's ability to reason, you are attacking his ability to think clearly. And, since right thinking usually precedes right action, wrong thinking is something to guard against on the job. A frequent consequence of wrong (fallacious) reasoning is a breakdown in communication. People working together must be on the same logical wavelength. The moment one of them commits a fallacy, meaningful communication is threatened. Here is a sample of such a situation:

SALESPERSON: How many dozen can you use this month, Mr. Shaver?
CUSTOMER: I haven't used up the ones you sold me last month.
SALESPERSON: I know, but this season they are expected to sell like crazy.
CUSTOMER: Tell you what. As soon as my brother gets up, we'll send next door for some pizza and watch the ballgame. OK?

183

The reasoning in this dialogue was fine until that last remark about sending out for pizza. It doesn't take an especially trained mind to recognize that a fallacy of reasoning has been committed. It is called a *non sequitur*, which means "it does not follow." Whenever someone wanders off the subject being discussed and brings up something totally unrelated, it is likely to develop into a communication breakdown unless the person who committed it can justify its relevance to the conversation.

Try to identify the fallacy committed in this dialogue:

REGIONAL SALES MANAGER: That gal we took on last month to work the northeast territory isn't working out too well.

NATIONAL SALES MANAGER: Really? She sounded like a real eager beaver when we interviewed her for the position.

REGIONAL SALES MANAGER: I know, but somehow using women in the field always seems to backfire on us.

NATIONAL SALES MANAGER: You said it, ole buddy! Women in the field is downright bad business. It seems like when you've seen one of those gals, you've seen 'em all.

This is a classic case of stereotyping. The national sales manager, clearly recognizable as a sexist, has committed a fallacy called a *sweeping generalization*. This form of wrong reasoning is based on the premise that to know one woman is to know all women. Anyone on the job whose belief system suggests that what is true of a part is true of the whole must be carefully watched—especially if his position involves a great deal of responsibility.

There are several other common examples of wrong reasoning you will encounter in the marketplace. They have been incorporated into the following dialogues. See whether you can identify them.

EXAMPLE A [*Scene: A local department store*]

STORE DETECTIVE: Come here, you kids. What are you up to?

TEEN-AGER: Nothing. We're shopping. Is there any law against it?

STORE DETECTIVE: Do you have any money to buy things?

TEEN-AGER: Excuse me, sir, but if we were adults, would you be questioning us this way?

STORE DETECTIVE: Come on, both of you—out, outside, you look like a couple of troublemakers, anyway. Out!

EXAMPLE B [*Scene: A restaurant*]

PATRON: Waiter, how many pancakes do you get in a full order?

WAITER: Four, ma'm.

184

PATRON: I can't eat four pancakes. Could I get an order of just two pancakes?

WAITER: Sorry, ma'm, we only serve complete orders—no half orders.

PATRON: Why not? Just have the chef make two pancakes, put them on a plate and charge me half the regular price.

WAITER: Sorry, ma'm, I can't do that. I don't make the rules. 1 only work here.

EXAMPLE C [*Scene: A garage*]

CUSTOMER: Hi. My name is Mr. Grey. One of your mechanics gave my car a complete tune-up last Friday.

GARAGE MANAGER: Yes, Mr. Grey, what can we do for you?

CUSTOMER: Well, I'm only getting nine miles to a gallon.

GARAGE MANAGER: That sounds about right for the kind of car you're driving, Mr. Grey.

CUSTOMER: Then how come before I brought it in to be tuned, I used to get between thirteen and fifteen miles per gallon? It was doing fine until you tuned it.

EXAMPLE D [*Scene: A neighborhood clothing store*]

MAILMAN: Good morning. How are you today, Mr. Green?

SHOPKEEPER: Fine, Mr. Mailman, and you?

MAILMAN: OK. Say, did you hear about the head teller down at the bank? They arrested him for shooting heroin.

SHOPKEEPER: You don't mean Mr. Curry? I can't believe it. He's the nicest man over there. As far as I'm concerned, a good person like him just wouldn't do such a terrible thing, especially if it was against the law.

Now compare your impressions of what was wrong with each example to the following explanations. Example A involved a fallacy known as *attacking the person*. Instead of addressing himself to the teen-ager's question as to how they would have been treated if they were adults, the store detective attacked them personally—suggesting that they looked like a couple of troublemakers. From the detective's point of view, the teen-agers were young and didn't look as if they had any money with which to buy merchandise. The fact that the store was open to the general public and the teen-agers had as much right to be in it as any adult didn't seem to concern the detective.

Anytime you observe a situation like this, be on the lookout for an attack upon the individual, rather than his or her ideas. If you happen to be the object of this type of fallacy, insist that the individual respond to what you say, not how you look or where you live.

In Example B, you were exposed to a fallacy called the *excluded middle*. In the dialogue, the waiter has assumed an all-or-nothing position without any middle ground. Either the customer orders four pancakes or no pancakes. Several options were available to both parties. The customer could have: (1) demanded what she wanted; (2) ordered four pancakes and left two on her plate (3) ordered four pancakes, eaten two, and paid for only the two she ate; (4) shared a full order with someone else; or (5) tried to get the restaurant manager to change his policy on pancakes. The waiter could have: (1) served her a full order and charged her half price (which would have been dishonest); (2) tried to get her to order something else from the menu; (3) suggested that she accept four "smaller" pancakes; or (4) let the manager decide the matter. In this case, the waiter's reasoning consisted of only two alternatives—a full order of pancakes or nothing. Middle ground did not exist in his thinking.

Example C is known as the fallacy of *It was all right until.* . . . Wrong reasoning in the mind of Mr. Grey consisted of thinking that because the mechanic was the last person to work on his car, he did something to make it get poorer mileage. The fact that several other possible explanations for getting fewer miles per gallon existed never entered his mind. People who reason this way believe that whatever preceded an event caused it. Making it even more personal, what would you think if you loaned me your car (which was running perfectly) and I called you on the telephone several hours later to tell you that it had broken down? The temptation, while perfectly understandable, would be to think that I had done something to make it break down. The fact that the radiator was ready to go any minute, or a hose was near bursting, probably would not enter your mind. It is more convenient to accuse me, since I was the last person to use it.

In Example D, you were introduced to a *genetic* fallacy. It operates on the premise that good people do good things, bad people bad things. In the case of Mr. Curry, the head bank teller, he was considered to be a good person who was accused of doing a bad thing. Because Mr. Green subscribed to the genetic fallacy of reasoning, he refused to believe that Mr. Curry was guilty of shooting heroin. If it was someone he considered to be a bad person who was accused of shooting heroin, Mr. Green would probably have said, "It figures, he's the kind of person who would do something like that."

There are many other fallacies of reasoning to which people fall prey. It would behoove you to find out what they are and guard against them on the job. Not realizing that one is being used on you could easily cause a breakdown in communication.

CONSEQUENCES OF A COMMUNICATION BREAKDOWN

There are two ways of looking at a communication breakdown. You can concern yourself with what caused it or the nature of the breakdown itself. Whichever method you choose, it will ultimately affect you personally, your job, the firm for which you work, or a combination of all three. Here are some of the more likely consequences you may encounter.

Resolution

The most desirable consequence, of course, is to resolve any differences that might have arisen. Ideally, such a resolution will not leave in its wake any hard feelings or spiteful acts of "getting even." As suggested a few pages ago, the greatest aids to the peaceful settling of any disagreement are to keep emotionality down to a minimum, deal with issues and not personalities, and yield to whatever is in the best interest of the company that pays your salary.

Dismissal, Demotion, or Resignation

These are some of the harsher consequences that could result from a communication breakdown. Any responsible company should consider the dismissal of an employee its last resort. In addition to spelling out, in the clearest terms, the grounds upon which it would consider dismissing someone, it should also make every conceivable effort to avoid taking such a step. One alternative to dismissal is demotion—to reduce someone in rank or responsibility. It informs the employee that he or she is still worth keeping and that the company has enough faith to try to repair any wrongdoing through the process of demotion rather than dismissal.

The act of resignation carries with it more personal dignity. To quit or leave a firm suggests an element of courage and self-respect on the part of the person involved. In a way, it acts as a safeguard against the person who is being terminated going out and bad-mouthing the company. The likelihood of someone who has been fired bad-mouthing an ex-employer is greater than if that person resigned of his own free will. It should also be mentioned that the person who is fired is not the only one who may experience ill feelings. The morale of those left behind may also suffer. They might feel that if they are not careful, they could be next to be dismissed.

Internal Grievances

Aside from those who are dismissed, or who choose to hand in their resignations, there is the problem of dealing with a grieving employee. Few things do more to damage an organization than to have its personnel grieve. Grieving or brooding can pick away at company morale, incite conspiratorial activity, and cut down on production. Aside from bitching to one another, there are a number of ways a grieving worker can express unhappiness. These include: (1) giving co-workers the silent treatment; (2) taking extended coffee breaks; (3) turning out sloppy work; (4) being absent excessively; (5) abusing safety regulations by taking needless risks; and (6) displaying a lack of interest in the job to be done.

Management that is sensitive to these internal grievances can often do something about them. By finding out who is doing the complaining, and what it is about, the problem is halfway solved. Once the grievant is identified, an open flow of communication must be established in which all aspects of the disagreement (real or imagined) are given a thorough airing. The proper handling of an internal grievance entails attending to the grievance promptly, getting all of the related facts, taking the necessary action, and following up on it after a reasonable amount of time has elapsed.

If, indeed, chance does favor the prepared mind, it would be in your own best self-interest to develop a deeper understanding of a communication breakdown and the possible consequences it can produce. The key to such an understanding reverts back to the prevailing theme of this book— there is no such thing as a business or profession, only people who, because of their mutual interests and training, have come together for some common purpose. Hence, consequences on the job, whatever they may be, will *ultimately* lead you back to human behavior, and human behavior back to the art of *communication*.

TYPES OF PEOPLE WHO DISAGREE

There are three types of people with whom you may disagree on the job: aggressors, instigators, and victims. Each will perceive the act of disagreement in a slightly different manner and, as a result, behave differently. To successfully cope with their individual attitudes and behavior, you will find the following insights helpful.

Aggressors

Without the aggressor, you would have very few disagreements on the job. Aggressors are the prime movers when it comes to arguing an issue. In our culture, the reaction to aggressive people is mixed. In certain situations, they are admired; in others, their behavior is frowned upon or deplored. If pressed, most of us would be inclined to admit that our opinion of assertive or aggressive behavior would depend a great deal upon when, where, and how it was used. There are times when an aggressive act, performed with sensitivity and tact, is extremely admirable. International diplomacy, for instance, often requires a diplomat to behave aggressively, to negotiate world affairs with sensitivity and tact, and to disagree without being disagreeable. The aggressor, therefore, should not automatically be taken to be an undesirable member of an organization, but rather one who can move in either direction in a disagreement.

Instigators

Is there a troublemaker on your present job? This is an individual who starts trouble but does not get involved personally. Let us illustrate how certain instigators operate. Imagine yourself witnessing a round-table dispute between city officials and representatives of mass transit. During one of the coffee breaks, you see a man whisper something to one of the principal labor leader negotiators. Returning to the bargaining table, this labor leader makes a statement that thoroughly shocks everyone present. You get the distinct feeling that what the man whispered to the labor leader during the coffee break was responsible for the fireworks that followed. If your observation was correct, you saw an instigator plying his trade.

In a less formal setting, instigators make trouble issuing nasty and uncalled-for remarks, displaying irritable facial expressions, and having a cutting edge to their voices. While seldom doing enough damage to be held fully responsible for an entire breakdown in communication, their contribution to any disagreement rarely goes without notice. Though it is tempting to blame everything on instigators, their efforts would be fruitless if the people with whom they interacted were less susceptible to their influence.

Victims

For some people, arguments on the job take on special meaning. Whenever they become involved in one, they immediately feel victimized. Their stock line is "why is it always me?" Although in every controversy someone's feelings are apt to get hurt, victims are usually convinced that they have been singled out to become the injured party. People who admit having this "victim mentality" could benefit by taking the time to find out why it happens to them and not others. A convenient rationalization for any victim is to blame his or her failure on some inherent trait, circumstances, or just plain bad luck. All these excuses are nonsense. Victims are made, not born. A careful analysis of any communication breakdown should turn up specific instances in which the victim made certain clear-cut mistakes in either judgment or conduct, mistakes that can usually be corrected in the future.

DEALING WITH DISAGREEMENTS

For every disagreement you ever have, there will be someone, somewhere, standing ready to supply you with a foolproof solution. Advice, as you know, has not been hit by recent increases in the cost of living. It is still as cheap as it was two thousand years ago.

Without resorting to a gun, knife, club, or clenched fist, how do you resolve the majority of your own disagreements? The methods to be recommended in the following pages are both rational and nonviolent. While there may be some disagreements that cannot be resolved by any means, the majority can be resolved by the diligent application of civilized methods.

Direct Order

In an efficiently run organization, most disagreements between members of its staff are settled by the direct order of a superior. Those unwilling to obey such an order invite some of the consequences mentioned elsewhere in this section (dismissal, demotion, or solicited resignation). If those involved in the disagreement obey the order outwardly but continue to bear their grievances inwardly, its complete resolution will have to wait until suppressed feelings surface and give way to open discussion.

Compromise

Ideally, every disagreement can be settled through compromise if each faction is willing to give in a little. Most of the efforts to compromise operate on a cost/benefit basis. This means that both sides of a disagreement must carefully weigh the cost they will sustain in relation to the benefits they will derive from whatever compromise they make. Once the compromise is made, those involved must be prepared to deal intelligently with any of the consequences to which it might give rise.

Coercion

The phrase that best captures the spirit of coercion is "I made him an offer he couldn't refuse." There are people everywhere who believe that we all have a price and, if that price is met, we will do their bidding. This is the mentality behind those who settle their differences through coercion. It has existed from time immemorial in the form of money, position, rewards, favors, blackmail, physical abuse, and property damage.

Regardless of what you do for a living, you receive some form of payment for your labors. Most of us do it for a paycheck. If money is not your major source of motivation, perhaps it is satisfaction, recognition, appreciation, or service to others. Once your reward for working has been established, there are those who will attempt to use it as a lever, should you disagree with them. Coercion is such a lever.

Arbitration and Mediation

Arbitration occurs when people agree to let someone else settle their disagreements. The person chosen to settle the disagreement is called an arbitrator. It is someone who listens to both sides of a disagreement and then decides who is right and who is wrong. The decision of an arbitrator is called an "award." Arbitration is often used to settle disputes between labor and management, especially for minor, day-to-day disagreements that neither group feels are worth a major confrontation.

Mediation involves a "third person" (the mediator) who remains attached to a case at the discretion of the two parties involved. It is understood that the disputants reserve judgment until a time of their own choosing on whether to heed or disregard the mediator's counsel. Mediation differs from arbitration in that a mediator cannot make an award, only help the two sides to agree. If, at any point in the proceedings, they come to regard the mediator as a *persona non grata* (unacceptable), they are within their rights to dispense with this person's services.

Collective Bargaining

A labor union or association of employees is said to bargain collectively when a few people representing the union meet with the employers to agree on wages and working conditions for all the members of the union. It is for this purpose that the union is formed.

During collective bargaining, representatives of the union meet with members of the management (representatives of the owners of the company). They agree on how many hours a week the employees will work and how much they will receive per hour's work. Pensions, working conditions, medical benefits, and other issues are also subjects upon which there may be disagreement and over which there may be collective bargaining.

Do-Nothing Approach

This is a method of dealing with disagreements that contends that if nothing is done about a particular problem, it will mysteriously disappear.

On those rare occasions when doing nothing works, it reinforces the confidence of those who use such an approach. To those thinking the technique delays making a decision, let them be reminded that *not* making a decision is a decision; doing nothing is doing something.

Another aspect of this approach deserving your attention is the fact that it often increases the climate of ambiguity among employees. Disagreements beg for resolution. The longer they go unsettled, the more confusion they seem to attract. While things may appear to remain the same, they do not. If the basis of a disagreement is not resolved and is further compounded by new events, the result is apt to be additional confusion. In short, the do-nothing approach is not as innocent as most people might believe.

PROVING YOUR POINT

In any disagreement, there are several points of view. There is what you believe to be true, what you think the other person holds to be true, and what you think the other person thinks you believe to be true. From your opponent's perspective, there are the same three possibilities. This makes for six possible points of view of the same disagreement. Is it any wonder that proving your point is not always a simple matter?

There are people who honestly believe that in any disagreement, the party who is "right" should win. While this is what should happen, it does not always work out that way. What determined who was right in your last argument? Was it because you had better proof, were more intelligent than your opponent, talked louder, or was it because you gave up? Proof, as you may have already gathered, does not remain the same. Yesterday's proof may well be today's folly. Here are some of the more common forms of proof people use to settle their disagreements.

Logical Proof

Logic is artificial, man-made—not a natural phenomenon like rain, lightning, thunder, or earthquakes. It is a method of reasoning that man created, a way for him to manipulate his ideas. And, like so many other man-made methods of doing things, it has its rules. Hence, in settling a disagreement, any proof used that employs logic that breaks those rules must be treated as unacceptable.

Be on your guard when people use logical proof against you. Generals, in wartime, have been known to kill hundreds of the enemy through the use of logic. Courts of law, at this very moment, continue to condemn people to death by hanging, the electric chair, and the gas chamber by using logical reasoning. Just how should logical proof be regarded?

As mentioned in Chapter 8, something can be logically valid but materially untrue. To refresh your memory, consider this logical statement:

Major Premise: All scientists are ethical.

Minor Premise: Dr. Jones is a scientist.

Conclusion: Dr. Jones is ethical.

Although this statement is perfectly valid, according to the rules of logic, it is materially untrue because there are cases on record of unethical behavior by certain scientists. Therefore, beware of any proof whose exclusive claim to acceptance is that it is logical.

Scientific Proof

TV commercials occasionally try to sell their products by claiming that they are "scientifically proven." Too often, they neglect to say *what* they have proven. Does the fact that something was scientifically proven make it better or worse? The bomb dropped on Hiroshima in World War II was scientifically proven, wasn't it? Why must something scientific necessarily be good? Although the use of the scientific method does guarantee a certain amount of reliability and control over whatever is being researched, it can be manipulated to serve any master. Here is an example of one scientific mind at work:

A scientist spent his life studying frogs. One day, he conducted the following experiment. He placed a frog on a table and proceeded (very scientifically) to remove its legs, one by one. After the removal of each leg, he would command the frog to jump. Each time, it jumped, albeit a bit wobbly. After its last leg was removed and it was commanded to jump, the frog remained motionless. This brought the scientist to the following conclusion: Removing a frog's legs renders it deaf.

Authoritative Proof

In every field, you will find experts and would-be experts. These are people who, on the basis of their rank, reputation, and knowledge, are considered superior in their particular line of work. Whether genuine or imposters, for every opinion these experts hold, there are other experts with conflicting opinions.

If allowed to run their course, any disagreements you may have on the job are certain to contain the opinion of some authority as proof. The stock question "says who?" is rarely missing from any respectable communication breakdown. People are more apt to accept what you say an authority says than what you yourself say. This is particularly true when the authority is a well-known individual.

When dealing with this type of proof, be on the alert for the "halo effect." It consists of using the opinion of an authority in one field to prove a point in another field. A famous TV razor blade commercial used this technique. It showed a celebrated baseball star shaving with a certain kind of blade. The audience was expected to believe what he said about the blade because of his knowledge of baseball. When movie stars endorse brand-name automobiles, this same halo effect is brought into play.

The best way to handle someone who tries to win a point by using authoritative proof is to ask these questions:

1. What makes the person you are quoting an authority?
2. What are the authority's credentials?
3. What specific articles or books has the authority written? Where and when were they published?
4. What is this authority's reputation among other authorities?
5. What experience has this authority had in his or her field?

Firing questions like these, while they cannot guarantee that you will win an argument, takes a great deal of wind out of your opponent's sails. In short, your strategy in coping with an authority as proof should hinge heavily upon your line of questioning about that authority.

Journalistic Proof

Do you believe everything you read in newspapers, magazines, and books? A surprising number of people do, without batting an eye. They greet you morning, noon, and night with snippets of information from these various sources and, when you question the reliability of what they have told you, they snap back with, "They wouldn't print it if it weren't true!"

Since the invention of the printing press, the printed word has enjoyed about five hundred years of unchallenged credibility by the general public. It has only been since the turn of this century that its reign has met with organized resistance. Its teachings encourage people to question anything they read, to see that meaning does not exist in words but in people and that words are only symbols people use to represent their thoughts, feelings, and actions.

Frequently, in those disagreements that arise in collective bargaining, arbitration, or mediation, journalistic proof is introduced as evidence. The individual is observed to present an article (or a portion of it) from some newspaper or magazine to support a claim or contention. The opposition then tries to discredit such proof by asking some pointed questions like the ones used in combating authoritative proof: Who wrote the article? When was it written? Is the information being quoted complete or a portion of the article? Was the person who wrote the article biased?

Challenging those who expect you to blindly accept whatever they claim to have read somewhere will not win you any popularity contests. Instead, it will put those with whom you disagree on the alert that they will be made to account for what they say, that having merely read something is not enough to make it true.

Historical Proof

Because humanity uses language, both written and spoken, it enables us to keep the past alive. This ability to pass on information from generation to generation is called "time binding." Not only does it enable us to know what happened in Los Angeles at the turn of this century, but also what happened in Egypt five thousand years ago.

Whether in the field of real estate, dentistry, manufacturing buttons, or building flying machines, what has occurred in the past cannot be separated from the present. The history of any business or profession acts as a blueprint upon which people of the present make improvements upon the efforts of people from the past. This we call progress. There is, however, a flaw. Some people suffer from what is called "frozen evaluation." They cling to some aspect of the past that, in order to move forward, must be either abandoned, modified, or updated. They behave as if nothing has changed and try to defend their beliefs on the basis of such a frozen evaluation.

Watch out for two things when dealing with historical proof. Has its meaning been altered by translation and is the context in which it is being used the same as it was originally? Although there are other considerations to be made, these two are essential. Don't allow those with whom you are arguing to pass off "dead proof" as evidence that no longer fits into the present scheme of things.

Statistical Proof

Numbers, like the printed word, also have a mystical quality. This is especially true today in this Space Age of computer technology. Everything imaginable is numbered, from income tax forms to the tiniest nut or bolt in the parts department at your local car dealer. Those who work with statistics manipulate these numbers and, by so doing, give them meaning. A great deal of our everyday living is governed by how these numbers are interpreted. For example, which of the following statistics sounds more believable: 68 percent, 68.4 percent, 68.72 percent, or 68.001 percent? Would you agree that 68.001 percent would possess the greatest amount of credibility? To many, the more decimal places a number has, the more exacting and the more believable it is taken to be. The more complex a computation, the more readily it is accepted by the untrained mind.

It has been said, perhaps facetiously, that "figures don't lie, but liars figure." It has also been said that any competent statistician can make figures sit up, beg, roll over, or play dead. While the unethical use of statistical proof is largely a matter of conscience, in the hands of those with character and integrity it is one of the more reliable means of determining whether something is true or false.

Here is what you must do to defend yourself from those who try to bully you with statistical proof. Yes, just as you probably expected—ask more questions.

1. Who did the study?
2. Why was the study done?
3. Who paid for the study?
4. Where was the study done?
5. What statistical method was used?
6. How many people were used in the study?
7. Who interpreted the findings of the study?
8. What were the credentials of those who interpreted the study?
9. When was the study done?
10. Was the study continuous or interrupted?

Rest assured, anyone who tries to win an argument with you on the basis of statistical proof will have a devil of a time sidestepping this line of questioning. In addition to creating a "reasonable doubt," being the questioner will put you on the offensive, where you belong.

DIAGNOSING A DISAGREEMENT

Half the trick of settling any disagreement is knowing what caused it. But this is not as easy as it sounds. For every disagreement, there are usually several theories as to its cause. If two people are involved, there are at least two reasons; if four people are involved, four reasons, and so on. In effect, the number of causes is often proportional to the number of people involved. This may be due to the fact that people have selective perception—that is, they see and hear things differently and according to their own bias. This tendency is further complicated by the emotional climate that generally surrounds most disagreements. The question, then, is what to do about it.

Here is a checklist consisting of six checkpoints. Each focuses on one of the more common causes of a disagreement. Using a current disagreement, or one you have had and want to avoid having again, examine it on the basis of each checkpoint.

Checkpoint 1 (Who)

Like certain chemicals, not all people mix well. Consequently, a disagreement can be caused by the fact that two individuals simply clash. The basis for the conflict may be some physical characteristic (type of physique, movement, or taste in clothes) or a psychological trait (introversion, extroversion, or unusual psychoneurotic behavior). Whatever the cause may seem to be on the surface, digging deeper may reveal it to be a matter of two people who are fundamentally incompatible. The concept that all people should be able to get along with one another is more idealistic than practical. Therefore, the way to solve a disagreement between two such people on the job might be simply to separate them.

Checkpoint 2 (What)

Assuming you have ruled out the *who* as the cause of a disagreement, your next step is to determine whether the disagreement was caused by *what* was said. This involves finding out whether the words that were used held the same meaning. Quite possibly, a word or phrase was used that the other person misunderstood and responded to on the basis of that misunderstanding. Then there is the possibility that *what* was said (the word itself) was offensive and caused embarrassment or annoyance. There are people who, for no particular reason, don't like certain words. They appear impervious to whether the word or phrase is relevant to a discussion. Their reaction is based entirely upon the word itself, not the meaning intended by its speaker. They can be overheard saying things like "I don't care what you meant; you said it and that's enough for me" or "if there is anything I can't stand, it is language like that."

A person's body language also falls under the heading of *what*. Without realizing it, there are individuals who will disagree with someone solely because of how they look or behave when they speak. No doubt you have encountered these types who wear a critical, wise-guy, or holier-than-thou expression on their faces. This characteristic alone could act as the cause of a disagreement in a sensitive individual. Because many people don't know how others see them, they become confused by the feedback they get.

The object of this checkpoint is to help you detect people who treat words and actions as separate entities, apart from their meaning. Dealing with them becomes easier once you've discovered their method of communicating. Most of their difficulty can be traced to their lack of awareness of how others perceive them, and the fact that the meanings they assign to words are not necessarily shared by the people with whom they disagree. Evidence of this is that many people have the same argument with the same people, with the same outcome, over and over again. Avoid this happening to you by realizing that words and actions, by themselves, go nowhere—and seldom serve any useful purpose when communicating on the job. Strive, instead, to see the overall relationship among words, actions, meaning, and purpose. Take a holistic approach to shared meaning.

Checkpoint 3 (Where)

Does *where* a disagreement occurs bother you? Does it matter that it occurs in front of your co-workers or would you prefer disagreeing in private? To some, it makes absolutely no difference at all. To others, where a breakdown in communication takes place is extremely important. Executives who are aware of this make every effort to choose where they communicate very carefully. They assign the possibility of being overheard a high priority.

The surroundings in which a disagreement occurs should not be underestimated. People can be influenced by the size of a room, its color, location, furnishings, smell, and temperature. The more comfortable they are in it, the better they may feel about themselves and those with whom they are interacting. Conversely, the more uncomfortable the surroundings, the worse they may feel about themselves and those with whom they are interacting. While this is obviously a sweeping generalization, it is one that both research and experience incline to bear out. An example of this can be seen when a company decides to relocate its home office. While management usually has a number of reasons for relocating (taxes, space, ordinances, etc.), one such reason concerns employee morale. People seem to work more efficiently, argue less among themselves, and exhibit less absenteeism when they are pleased with their surroundings, e.g., plants, carpeting, attractive interior and exterior design.

Since meaning is in people and their communication can be influenced by atmosphere, this checkpoint encourages you to carefully evaluate *where* a disagreement occurs. Its remedy might require little more than discreetly moving people from one place to another.

Checkpoint 4 (When)

Poor timing can also cause a disagreement. A remark made early in the morning could have a significantly different effect upon someone if it is made late in the afternoon. Some people's moods are strongly influenced by the time of day. In Chapter I, we spoke of "larks" (day people) and "owls" (night people). In some disagreements, this distinction could play an important role.

Newcomers to any organization are quick to learn when and when not to talk to certain people in positions of authority. A boss with a stomach ulcer could be extremely irritable before lunch and easily approached after it. People are creatures of habit; i.e., they work, eat, sleep, and play by the clock. They literally have "good times" and "bad times." Sensitive sales representatives know when and when not to call on a particular buyer. They know exactly which ones to see in the morning, which in the afternoon, and which to wine and dine in the evening.

Consider yourself guilty of negligence if you fail to consider the time element in any disagreement. As you already know, most people look for the cause of their disagreement in *who* said something, *what* the person said, and *where* it was said. Only rarely do they think in terms of *when* the disagreement took place.

Checkpoint 5 (How)

In some disagreements, the cause may have less to do with *who* said something, *what* was actually said, *where* it was said, or *when* it was said than with *how* it was said. Certain people have an edge to their voice, which offends others. They can make the most innocent remark sound angry, impatient, bored, or annoying. Although such speech may be tolerated by friends and colleagues, it can be dangerously misunderstood by strangers or newly made acquaintances. At the other end of the spectrum, there are people who can make the nastiest remark sound like a compliment. Thus, how the voice shapes what is said could alter its intended meaning to a listener. In fact, there are experts in communication who believe that *how* you say something carries a greater impact than what you say.

The channel in which a disagreement occurs may also be worth examining. Some job-related disagreements occur on the telephone, others through the mail, and still others face to face. It is erroneous for you to think that any channel would be appropriate to a disagreement as long as the people involved were able to exchange information. The channel used can influence its outcome. Take the case of someone who had been with a company for twenty years and received a pink slip in the mail. Doesn't such long and devoted service deserve the courtesy of something more than a pink slip in the morning mail? Shouldn't such loyalty from an employee warrant a personal meeting with an executive of the firm? Equally inappropriate under the circumstances would have been a telephone call or a telegram informing him of his dismissal. Is it any wonder this emloyee was outraged? The company (or whoever made the decision) had chosen the wrong channel through which to inform him that his services were no longer required.

Although changing one's tone of voice may be more difficult than switching to another channel, the main thing is to find out to what extent the channel being used is affecting the disagreement at hand.

Checkpoint 6 (Why)

If you say something to me with which I disagree, I would like to know *why* you said it. Rational or irrational, we all have reasons for saying what we say. While some reasons may be more acceptable than others, and an occasional Freudian slip might get by our defenses, there are conscious reasons behind most of what we say. Sharing them in a disagreement often helps pave the road to agreement.

The objective of this checkpoint is to illustrate how knowing *why* someone says something can shed light on a disagreement. Unfortunately, this is easier said than done. People often conceal their true feelings beneath layers of psychological armor, which is difficult to penetrate. However, just being sensitive to the fact that such feelings exist can do a great deal to insure a more effective management of communication breakdowns on the job.

DEBRIEFING

The goal of this book was to help you communicate more effectively and, by so doing, better enable you to get a good job, keep it, and advance according to your potential. You were cautioned that learning the art of communication is no easy task; it takes time, patience, and a great deal of self-determination. The key message advanced in these pages is that we all share a common psychobiology. As such, human behavior can be anticipated to a much greater extent than is ordinarily realized. The better we can understand ourselves, the better we can understand other members of our species. This notion is very compatible with the premise upon which *Job Talk* was founded: *There is no such thing as a business or profession, only people who, because of their interests and training, have come together for some common purpose.*

As a communicologist, I have tried to take what I know about the subject of human communication and communicate it to you. Many obstacles had to be overcome. As I began to write and you began to read, an exchange took place. Although we traded having an advantage over one another, at no time was either of us completely without a frame of reference. While I may have occasionally disadvantaged you with a superior knowledge of communication, you may have put me to shame with a superior knowledge of your own field. Regardless of the equation, neither of us came to the other empty-handed.

If those things about which I have spoken jogged your mind into action—*we have communicated.* However the contents of this book made their way from my brain to yours, we shall have both gained something of value from the experience.